WITHDRAWN

D1158225

The Dust of Combat

". . . the dust of the combat is
to him the breath of life . . ."

W. R. Greg

The Dust of Combat

A Life of Charles Kingsley

by

ROBERT BERNARD MARTIN

W. W. NORTON & COMPANY, INC.
NEW YORK

First American Edition 1960

Printed in Great Britain

For
F.K.W.

Preface

Anyone interested in Charles Kingsley must be grateful for the collecting habits of his widow, the first of his biographers. Mrs. Kingsley bequeathed his private papers to her second daughter, Mary, Mrs. William Harrison ('Lucas Malet'), who left them to Kingsley's grand-niece, her own adopted daughter, Miss Gabrielle L. M. Vallings. Miss Vallings, as Kingsley's literary executrix, has allowed me access to manuscripts and pictures, has granted me permission to publish material still in copyright, and has given freely of her constant and friendly encouragement.

I should like to acknowledge the kindness of the other private owners of manuscripts who have put them at my disposal: Mr. C. H. Kingsley; the late C. G. des Graz, who inherited the papers of J. M. Ludlow and left them in turn to the Cambridge University Library; the late E. P. Stapleton, whose family letters from Kingsley are now in the Princeton University Library; Lady Peto, who allowed me to use the family papers which are now the property of her son, Sir Anthony Cope, Bt.; the Rev. R. C. Rudgard, Rector of Eversley; the late Mrs. William Buckler; Miss Marjorie Ackland; Mrs. A. L. Castle; the late Rev. Roger Wodehouse; Mr. R. S. M. Sturges; and Macmillan and Co., who allowed me access to their letter-books.

I am also indebted to the institutions which have allowed me to use material: the British Museum; the Parrish Collection of the Princeton University Library; the Bodleian Library; the Henry E. Huntington Library; the Scott Polar Research Institute; the National Library of Scotland; the Henry W. and

Albert A. Berg Collection of the New York Public Library; the Library of Harvard University; the Brotherton Library, University of Leeds; and the Hampshire Record Office.

I should like to acknowledge the help of Dr. E. R. Ward; the late Guy Kendall; Mr. Neville Masterman; Professor E. D. H. Johnson; the late Humphry House; Mr. A. D. Wainwright; and the others, too numerous to mention individually, who have given me information and assistance. The staffs of the Princeton University Library and the Bodleian Library, in which two places most of this biography has been written, have aided me in more ways than I can acknowledge. Finally, I should like to record my gratitude to Mrs. Margaret Farrand Thorp, author of *Charles Kingsley, 1819–1875*, for her lively interest and unselfish help in the writing of this book, which I hope is a worthy successor to her own excellent work, the first scholarly biography of Kingsley.

Extracts from printed works still in copyright are published with the kind permission of the following: Cassell & Co., the Lewis Carroll executors and R. Lancelyn-Green: *Diaries of Lewis Carroll. Huntington Library Quarterly* and A. A. Adrian: 'Charles Kingsley Visits Boston'. Macmillan & Co.: C. E. Raven, *Christian Socialism, 1848–1854*; C. L. Graves, *Life and Letters of Alexander Macmillan*. Methuen & Co.: L. Masterman, ed., *Mary Gladstone . . . Her Diaries and Letters*. John Murray: S. Chew, *Swinburne*; L. Wolf, *Life of the First Marquess of Ripon*. Oxford University Press: C. C. Abbott, ed., *Correspondence of Gerard Manley Hopkins and Richard Watson Dixon*; H. F. Lowry, ed., *Letters of Matthew Arnold to Arthur Hugh Clough*; W. Ward, ed., *Newman's Apologia*; with Yale University Press: G. S. Haight, ed., *George Eliot Letters*. Mrs. Maisie Ward Sheed: W. Ward, *Life of John Henry Cardinal Newman*.

R.B.M.

Contents

Illustrations

Illustrations

CHAPTER I

A Rectory Childhood

Through one of those useful coincidences on which historians thrive, Charles Kingsley was born in the same year as his Queen. In this case the concurrence of events is perhaps more meaningful than usual, for if there ever lived such a mythical figure as a typical Victorian, that man might be Kingsley. Only the most partisan of observers could mistake him for one of the great seminal intellects of the nineteenth century, but his energy in seizing upon the ideas of men more original than he, in transforming and popularizing those ideas, was tremendous. In his answers to the questions which exercised the Victorians, we hear the tones and see the reactions of a mass of educated upper-middle-class men living a century ago; if his answers no longer all seem satisfactory, they are none the less representative for that. It was clear to many of his contemporaries—more so to us—that his solutions were seldom profound, but the ubiquity of his interests is still surprising. His thought, spread thinly over a dozen fields which attracted him, is frequently a better mirror of his age than that of more brilliant or more intellectual men who were atypical by their very mastery of one area of knowledge.

The mere mention of the occupations he undertook with some success in his half-century of life shows the breadth of his participation in the life of the mind of the period. In his day he was parish priest, Canon of Chester and Westminster, chaplain to the Queen, tutor and friend to the Prince of Wales, Professor of

History at Cambridge, poet, novelist, author of children's books, critic and reviewer, translator, political pamphleteer, sanitary reformer, and popularizer of geology and zoology. What is even more startling than the range of his curiosity is the prominence he achieved in nearly everything he tried, without ever reaching the first rank in any field, except perhaps that of parson. It is fair to say that in all the spheres he explored he remained a gifted amateur, and there are few things which would have pleased him more than the Elizabethan picture of well-rounded, gentlemanly competence which the phrase evokes.

Today his interest for us rests not on any work of genius, but on his own contradictory personality and on the understanding of his age which we find by looking at the impetuous workings of his fitful heart and quick chaotic mind, at once so individual and so representative of his times.

An especially perceptive observer in 1819 might have seen indications of the coming change to Victorianism and of the social reforms which Kingsley was to champion so loudly; the most unobservant could see the need for change. George III lay mad and blind at Windsor while the 'massacre' took place at Peterloo. The Regent, hated by the people and laughed at by the aristocracy, seemed intent on squandering every penny of public funds he could lay hands on. As a royal whim, he reconstructed Buckingham House into a palace and patronized Nash in the extravagant building of the graceful curve of Regent Street to connect Carlton House with the new Regent's Park and its surrounding terraces; he spent hundreds of thousands of pounds on silver and furniture while the hungry grumbled, and tried childishly to rid himself of the unfortunate Princess Caroline as he waited impatiently for the King's death and his own succession. The people, beggared and resentful, scribbled furtive threats on the walls of London and hatched the short-lived Cato Street conspiracy to blow up the Cabinet.

A year before, England and the world had been diverted by the unseemly and hilarious scramble of three royal weddings in little more than a month. Old King George had fathered fifteen children by Queen Charlotte, and seven sons and five daughters still survived; unfortunately, they had not produced another generation of legitimate heirs who would ensure the continuity of the throne, and the dying King was fretful at what might become of the succession at the death of his children. His three unmarried sons, then middle-aged and settled down to *bourgeois* home-life with their respective mistresses, gave up the delights of private domesticity in the summer of 1818, and, one after another, were married in an attempt to secure the succession. In the spring of 1819 the fruits of the hurried unions between the royal dukes and their German princesses began to arrive, and on May 24th Princess Victoria was born in Kensington Palace.

That year Byron published *Mazeppa*, sulked over the reception of the first two cantos of *Don Juan*, and forgot his troubles in the pleasure of Venice and Teresa Guiccioli. For Keats it was the wonderful year of the great Odes, 'The Eve of St. Agnes' and 'La Belle Dame sans Merci'. In Florence Shelley celebrated the birth of a son and wrote 'Ode to the West Wind'. In America Irving's *Sketch Book* appeared, and at home Scott published *Ivanhoe* and *The Bride of Lammermoor*. But just as Victoria was to destroy the conception of the conduct of princes held by her uncles, so the names of some of the writers born in 1819 show the changes which were soon to overtake literature. In America Melville, Whitman, and Lowell were born; in England George Eliot, Ruskin, and Clough. In Holne, Devonshire, three weeks after Princess Victoria had been born in Kensington, Charles Kingsley made his first protesting howl to an unsuspecting world.

Holne is one of the most attractive of Devon villages, set in a pocket of hills high on the shoulder of Dartmoor and surrounded by the woods of Holne Chase. It is a remote handful of houses gathered around a quiet inn, with a parish church dedicated to the Virgin, of which the high, square, embattled tower dominates the village and the valleys diverging from it.

Up the slope of the moor, a few hundred yards west of the church, at the end of a long, curving drive bordered with rhododendrons, lies the thatched Vicarage, of which parts are almost seven hundred years old. The plaster covering its three-foot-thick walls is painted cream colour, and the windows are divided by eighteenth-century leading. In 1819 the house was badly dilapidated, and the Vicar had turned it over as an uncomfortable dwelling to an impecunious curate and his wife, Mr. and Mrs. Charles Kingsley. Here, on June 12th, was born their first child, a son who was named for his father and baptized by him a week later in the village church. Mrs. Kingsley believed that the impressions made on her mind during pregnancy by the beauty of the surrounding country would be transmitted to the child, and her romantic hopes seemed to her in later life to have been fulfilled when Charles Kingsley became famous for his love of the natural beauty of Devonshire and his ability to describe it. The actual bedroom in which he was born is on the corner of the first floor, with the best view of any room in the house, looking over the garden with its three immense copper beeches and its masses of rhododendrons, down past the River Dart hidden in trees, to Holne Chase hundreds of yards away. To the end of his life, Kingsley called himself a Devon man and felt a special affection for the deep woods, the sunken, hedge-lined roads around Holne, and the gaunt grandeur of the part of Dartmoor nearest the village.

The Kingsley family was old, a solid line of gentlemen who occasionally produced a general or an outstanding cleric, but who were more usually soldier country squires, inordinately proud of their ancestry. One part of the family seems to have believed itself descended from Robin Hood, and on that nebulous connection is said to have spent money in an effort to prove its claim to the earldom of Huntingdon. A more probable story is that the family is an old Cheshire one descended from Ranulph de Kingsley, who lived there in the twelfth century. A contemporary record states that 'Ranulph, Earl of Chester, did give and grant the office of Bailiwick and Keeping of the Forest of Delamere to Ranulph de Kingsley his heirs and assigns for ever, with divers other liberties'. Certainly the horn which was the symbol of the forestry rights, 'a bugle strung sable', was proudly borne in its arms by the branch of the family to which Charles Kingsley belonged, and the actual horn was in the possession of the Earl of Harrington a century ago.

Later generations of the family were Puritans, and one of Kingsley's ancestors, Colonel George Fleetwood, who was among the judges of Charles I, was attainted of high treason in 1661 and forfeited his lands to the Crown. Another member of the family, William Kingsley, Archdeacon of Canterbury, married Damaris, niece of Archbishop Abbot, and fathered a backsliding son, who is said to have fought gallantly with the Royalists at Naseby and to have been rewarded by being made Gentleman of the Bedchamber to Charles II. Still another soldier, the best known of the family, was Lieut.-General William Kingsley, whose horse was shot from under him at the battle of Minden. Both Van Dyck's portrait of Archbishop Abbot and the Reynolds portrait of General Kingsley had been handed down in the family and were among the few heirlooms in Holne Vicarage when Charles was born. When he was older, he and his brothers and sister were frequently told of the stirring feats of their ancestors whose painted likenesses hung in heavy frames on the drawing-room walls.

Charles Kingsley, senior, was born in 1781, near Lymington, Hampshire, and left fatherless five years later. His father's considerable fortune, probably deriving from dealings in East and West Indian produce, was to be divided between Kingsley and his sister Lucretia. Unfortunately his widowed mother was unable to look after the estate, and the trustees of the inheritance were negligent or wasteful; by the time he achieved his majority, most of the money had disappeared. He received the education of a gentleman at Harrow and Oxford, where he was matriculated at Brasenose College in December 1800; the college records indicate that he left two months later. Although he was merely following the example of many wealthy young men of his time in leaving the University without a degree, since he expected to live on his inheritance, the duration of his stay was somewhat shorter than was customary.

Mr. Kingsley loved shooting and hunting and, on leaving Oxford, settled down comfortably to a quiet country life in the

New Forest, at Battramsley House, Boldre, near Lymington. Here he managed his estate and combined his love of outdoor sports with painting and a passion for natural history and the literature of several languages. A few years later he met Mary Lucas, a good-looking, high-spirited girl four years his junior, and they were soon married.

Mary had been born in the West Indies, the daughter of Nathaniel Lucas, a judge, of Farley Hall, Barbados. For several generations their family had been planters in Barbados and Demerara, where Judge Lucas owned estates. Among his friends were Lord Rodney, to whom he had seen the Comte de Grasse surrender his sword; Sir Joseph Banks, president of the Royal Society; and the great surgeon, John Hunter. Lucas took care to pass on his own knowledge of natural science to his daughter, and when she was old enough to finish her education, he took her to England and settled at Rushford Lodge, Norfolk. Mary was as lively as she was studious, and she enjoyed society thoroughly. In later years she liked to remember how she had danced with Byron at a Norwich county ball and thought 'he looked like a butcher boy, his face was so red'.

In Kingsley, Mary Lucas found her opposite in nearly every trait of personality. While he was gentle, dreamy, and quite unable to put his intelligence to any practical use, she was alert, impatient of slowness, and had a real flair for management. When their children began to arrive, the differences between the pair became more apparent, and there is some evidence that their later life together was marred by bickering and unhappiness. It is quite possible that Mary's briskness was as irritating to her husband as his procrastination was to her. As a mother she was endeared to her children by her impulsiveness and quick wit, while Mr. Kingsley's aloofness and absent-mindedness became a family joke. After his father's death, Charles Kingsley, junior, wrote: 'My father was a magnificent man in body and mind, and was said to possess every talent except that of using his talents.'

The early years of their marriage were spent at Battramsley, but it soon became apparent to Kingsley that the remnants of his inheritance would no longer keep them without outside assistance. It was a serious problem to face the cheerless prospect of earning a living, for he had neither training nor talent to help him. Commerce was unattractive, difficult, inappropriate for a country gentleman; the cost of an Army commission was prohibitive, and he was, at twenty-six, already too old to begin military life. Since his acquaintance included a number of landowners with benefices which they might bestow when vacant, he decided on reading for holy orders. Mary Kingsley surely encouraged him in the idea, for in his various parishes she handled the administrative work and did most of his visiting with an enthusiasm which suggests that it was only her sex which kept her from being a good parish priest herself. Selling his land and hunters, Kingsley took his bride to Cambridge, where he entered Trinity Hall to study divinity. It is no longer apparent why he did not return to Oxford or what he did in the nine years after 1807, but in 1816 he took the degree of LL.B. at Sidney Sussex College and shortly after, at thirty-five, was licensed to his first curacy, in the Fens. So began the long and wearisome peregrination from curacy to curacy to unsatisfactory living which his late start in clerical life forced upon him.

In August 1819, six weeks after Charles's birth, his father took wife and son to Burton-on-Trent, where he had been offered a position as curate-in-charge. Here he remained for nearly two years and here his second son, Herbert (d. 1834), was born, presumably in 1820. Early in 1821 Kingsley was finally given a living as Vicar at North Clifton, near Newark, and the family moved once more. Two more children were born at North Clifton: Gerald (1821–44)[1] and Louisa Mary, who was baptized on 27th October 1823 and died in infancy.

[1] Because of a mistake in Mary Kingsley's preface to *Notes on Sport and Travel*, his birth year has usually been given as 1816. The parish register at South Clifton records the baptism on 20th October 1821 of Gerald, son of Charles and Mary Kingsley of North Clifton; the father's profession is given as 'Vicar', and the register is signed by 'Charles Kingsley, Vicar' as officiating priest. It seems safe to dismiss the idea that the son of a clergyman might be five years old when baptized. Although not conclusive evidence, the very fact that Charles was given his father's name points to his being an eldest son.

At Cambridge Mr. Kingsley had become acquainted with the Lady Margaret Professor of Divinity, Dr. Herbert Marsh, with whom he shared an interest in German literature and the liberal and scientific method of biblical criticism which Marsh had brought back with him from a long residence in Germany. Despite more than twenty years difference in their ages, the two men became close friends. As charming in private life as he was pugnacious and vitriolic in public, Marsh determined to do what he could for the younger man and kept him in mind after he was consecrated Bishop of Peterborough. In January 1824, he offered Kingsley the vacant living of Barnack, in the Fens near Stamford, to hold until his own sixteen-year-old son, Herbert, could be ordained. The arrangement was not an unusual one in those days of a lax and worldly Church of England, and Mr. Kingsley was glad to accept the Bishop's offer, particularly as it meant that he could leave his curate, John Penrose, in charge of Clifton and retain for himself the main part of the income from that living. With the revenue from his mild pluralism, Mr. Kingsley was able to maintain his family comfortably for the first time since his ordination. At Barnack were born the rest of the Kingsley children, all of whom had the family literary ability. George Henry (1826–92), who was trained as a doctor, spent much of his adult life as an explorer, acted as librarian of Bridgewater House, and was author of travel books, translator and editor. Charlotte (1828–82) married a clergyman and produced both family and several books, including one novel. Henry (1830–76) became a novelist whose popularity rivalled that of his eldest brother.

The Rectory at Barnack was a beautiful fourteenth-century house with plenty of room for an expanding family and an amiable old ghost named Button Cap who haunted the place. Usually the ghost, said to be a former Rector of Barnack condemned to eternal wandering for his avarice, padded comfortably about in flopping slippers, a flowered dressing-gown, and the buttoned cap which gave him his name, but occasionally, when he tired of turning the pages of books quietly in the library, he would slip to the cellar and play poltergeist, angrily rolling barrels about with a thunderous racket, to the consternation of the Kingsleys upstairs. Little Charles, already a highly strung child, was once moved, when ill, into the room where Button Cap most frequently appeared, and his terror at the place haunted his dreams years after.

At four the moral earnestness which was to characterize Charles Kingsley as an adult began to manifest itself. According to his mother, his delight was to play preacher in the nursery, swathed in a pinafore as surplice, haranguing a row of empty chairs on the consequences of sin. Unknown to him she copied down the sermons, as well as the 'poems' which he began to compose with facility before he was five. His earliest effort, which may owe a little in style to the help of his mother's recording hand, already shows the theme on which he was to ring the changes successfully as a popular poet years later:

SONG UPON LIFE

Life is, and soon will pass;
As life is gone, death will come.
We—we rise again—
In Heaven we must abide.
Time passes quickly;
He flies on wings as light as silk.
We must die.
It is not false that we must rise again;
Death has its fatal sting,
It brings us to the grave.
Time and Death is and must be.

As a child he was delicate, subject to severe attacks of croup which kept him much with his mother, whom he adored. His father, towards whom he felt as much awe as love, started his education young, teaching him in his own study. Latin and mathematics were mixed with subjects much nearer the hearts of both, botany and drawing. Mr. Kingsley was an excellent shot, and as soon as Charles was old enough, he was mounted on his father's horse with the keeper, to bring back the game bag.

The Fen country, still undrained, was a wild waste of beauty where Charles learned to love 'the golden reed-beds, the countless water-fowl, the strange and gaudy insects, the wild nature, the mystery, the majesty' of which he later wrote so feelingly. 'Dark green alders, and pale green reeds, stretched for miles round the broad lagoon, where the coot clanked, and the bittern boomed, and the sedge-bird, not content with its own sweet song, mocked the notes of all the birds around; while high overhead hung motionless, hawk beyond hawk, buzzard beyond buzzard, kite beyond kite, as far as eye could see.'

Excursions away from home were frequent for Charles. Mr. Kingsley, who had been appointed examining chaplain to Bishop Marsh, used to take his son to Peterborough, where he sat talking in the gloomy study of the Palace while Charles played in the garden, feeding strawberries to an ancient tortoise. In the summer he was sent to the seaside with a nurse. His laborious letters home, which often took four or five days to complete, sound much more like those of a normal small boy than do the sermons and poems his mother so piously preserved:

June 11

My dear mama

I am very pleased with my book I am going to see A ship launched at 4 oclock with Mrs Barrett my dear mama I hope you and dear Georgey are well I am pleased with the sea we have found plenty of cornelians. I hope you wil my dear mama send away the nasty dog as he eats the ducks and eggs try to find out what made the kitten blind. i have dipt 4 times and begin to like it is my foxglove in flower i am going to tea with Mrs Dade this afternoon Herbert and Gerald are well my love to you and Georgy and Ann.

I am my dearest mama your affectionate son

C Kingsley

Thursday June 16

When he was seven he wrote to a young lady who had been staying at Barnack:

My dear Miss Dade

I hope you are well, is fanny well. The house is completely changed since you went. I think it is nearly 3 months since you went Mama sends her love to you, and sally browne Herbert and Geraled. But I must stop here, because I have more letteres of consequence to write and here I must pause.

Believe me always
Your sincere friend
CK

Miss Dade

To his nurse, Mrs. Knowles, he sent his thanks for a gift in 1828: 'I got both letter and cake quite safe and liked the latter very much. . . . Pray how do the lambs and the little pigs and the old sow do?'

In 1830, after six pleasant years at Barnack, Mr. Kingsley had to keep his part of the bargain with Bishop Marsh by giving up Barnack Rectory to Herbert Marsh, then only twenty-two and recently ordained. Unfortunately for Barnack, young Marsh was not a successful parson, although his father made him Canon of Peterborough in 1833. In 1850 he was declared of unsound mind; the following year he died.

The Fens were magnificent, but life in them had given Mr. Kingsley the ague. At his doctor's advice, he returned to Devon for the mild sea-climate of Ilfracombe, and Charles, then eleven, went back to the country he loved best all his life.

CHAPTER II

The West Country and Chelsea

In taking holy orders, Mr. Kingsley had relied heavily upon the possibility of a good living from one of the landed gentlemen of his acquaintance. But fourteen years had passed, and Kingsley, staying in Ilfracombe lodgings with his wife, six children, and a houseful of servants, seemed no nearer a permanent living than he had been when he left Cambridge. Luckily, one of his friends was Sir James Hamlyn-Williams, who had succeeded his father as third baronet a few months before. Sir James, full of ferocious complaint about the sins of the Tories, gruff but open-hearted, lived at Clovelly Court. In 1831 a curate was needed at Clovelly, and Mr. Kingsley was appointed to the post. The following year the Rector died and Sir James presented the living to his curate.

A whole new life opened for the Kingsleys. At last they were settled, and Mr. Kingsley could remain there the rest of his life if he cared to. The income was not large, but the cost of maintaining a country rectory was equally small. The house itself was pleasant and old-fashioned, across a narrow lane from Clovelly Court on the cliffs above the village. Some distance from the house, at the bottom of a large and tree-filled garden, lay the stables and walled kitchen garden. On a hill rising above the house stood an old oak, still flourishing today, which Charles promptly claimed as his own. There he spent hours on summer days, reading on a comfortable branch or looking out over the crest of the cliff, far into windy Clovelly Bay.

Clovelly Court, once the seat of the Cary family, was largely built in the eighteenth century around a Tudor core. Since Kingsley's day it has been known to countless boys as the home of Will Cary in *Westward Ho!* Next to it is the Norman church in which Mr. Kingsley preached from a fine seventeenth-century pulpit carved with Will Cary's initials and coat of arms. By the preacher's right hand stood an ancient hour-glass which he sometimes turned during the sermon, to the discomfiture of the village apprentices, whose seats were uncomfortable slabs of wood fastened by hinges to the aisle end of the pews.

Down the ravine which split the cliffs below the church lay the tiny village of Clovelly, not yet made famous by the pen of the Rector's son. The whitewashed cottages, roofed with grey slate, sprawled on either side of a single narrow, cobbled stair, dignified by the name of street, so steep that all burdens must be carried up it by hand or on the backs of donkeys. Most of its inhabitants were fishermen, and the normal way of getting to the village was by boat. Mr. Kingsley was at his best with his Clovelly parishioners, for he could handle a boat or a net, hoist and lower a sail as well as they. When the herring fleet put out to sea, he held a short service at the quay; after the not infrequent shipwrecks along the rocky coast, he read the burial service for the comfort of the survivors. When the catch was heavy, he helped unload the boats. It was the happiest period of his clerical life.

As a place to rear five sons and a small daughter, Clovelly was perfect. There were cliffs on which to climb for birds' eggs, a constantly changing shore where the children learned to look for zoological specimens brought in by the tide, ponies tamed from the moor, and, best of all, the restless, endless flux of life in a small fishing port.

There were echoes of history, too. Nearby were the houses, or their remains, of the Carys, the Grevilles, the Drakes, and the Coffins. In the Rectory library were volumes of the voyages of the Elizabethans, glorious accounts of pirates and buccaneers, and the manuscript journals of life in the West Indies and the golden Spanish Main kept by Mrs. Kingsley's ancestors. The village was full of descendants of men who had sailed with Drake, and there were strange stories told up and down the village street, tales of the gipsy's curse at Portledge, and of the maiden who threw herself from the towering cliff of Gallantry Bower in the park of Clovelly Court. As *Hereward the Wake* sprang from Kingsley's knowledge of the Fen country, so *Westward Ho!* was born of his life in Clovelly.

In 1831 their parents decided that Charles, now twelve, and Herbert, a year younger, were old enough to be sent away to school. With the help of a private tutor, Mr. Kingsley had supervised their early learning; as his successor, he chose another clergyman, the Rev. John Knight, who kept a preparatory school in Clifton, Bristol. The boys were accustomed to an out-of-door life and had mingled with their parents' friends, but they were reserved and uneasy with boys of their own age. To add to their difficulties, Charles had a bad stammer which became almost uncontrollable when he was excited.

Mr. Knight found the elder of his new pupils 'affectionate, gentle, and fond of quiet'. Thanks to his father's training, Charles was remarkably capable at turning Latin verse into English and at natural history, but his timidity sometimes led him to flee the schoolroom and his fellows to take refuge with the little daughters of the Knight household and their governess.

A little more than a month after the boys went to Clifton, the Bristol Riots broke out in protest against the rejection of the Reform Bill by the House of Lords. Looking down into the lower depths of Bristol, Charles saw peaks of flame breaking through heavy layers of smoke from the burning prison. The terror of the rioting lasted three days, and much of the city was burned. Fascinated by the tumult and horror, Charles slipped away into the middle of it to watch the savage mob of looters and the patient soldiers sitting quietly on their horses, blood streaming from wounds on their heads and faces, waiting for the order to quiet the mob which the terrified Mayor feared to give. When order was restored, he returned to the ruins and saw the remnants of corpses still in the streets. He said that the sickening sight made him 'for years the veriest aristocrat, full of hatred and contempt of those dangerous classes, whose existence I had for the first time discovered'. One of Kingsley's characteristics as an adult was the ability to interpret a remembered event in whatever way might be necessary to fit a lesson which needed hammering home. There was no dishonesty in his doing so, but excitement and a faulty memory sometimes produced contradictions. At another time he claimed of the horrors of the riots: 'That sight made me a Radical.'

The Kingsleys intended the year spent at Clifton to be an interlude while they decided about their sons' further education. They mentioned Eton, for Dr. Hawtrey, who became Headmaster in 1834, had heard of Charles and would have liked to add him to the promising pupils then under his tuition, but nothing came of the plan. Rugby and Dr. Arnold were rejected because of Mr. Kingsley's 'strong Tory principles and evangelical views'. When he grew up, Kingsley declared that nothing but a public-school education could have conquered his shyness and the resultant stammering. Instead, the boys were sent to Helston Grammar School, and Charles's timidity and speech difficulty continued. Half a century later his widow wrote to a friend:

'He suffered so bitterly as a child from the want of delicate tact on the part of his own Parents (fond as they were of him) with regard to his own stammering. They observed *upon* it, before him, instead of appearing perfectly unconscious as they ought to have done, except where they could help him out of the difficulty, so that he lived in a most painful state of self-consciousness, feeling that it *vexed* his Parents, till from fear & worry, the defect became confirmed, & *almost* irremediable. But then he was a very sensitive child, leading a very solitary spiritual life, & they were very quick exciteable people.'

The Rev. Derwent Coleridge, second son of the poet, was Headmaster at Helston in 1832, when the Kingsley boys, abashed and awkward, arrived in their father's charge: today he is remembered chiefly as biographer of his poet-brother, Hartley, and as editor of some of his father's works. The other master was a young naturalist, C. A. Johns; his love of botany and zoology found a quick response in Charles, who spent much of his free time with him in roaming the moor and shores. When

Coleridge left Helston in 1841 to go to Chelsea as Principal of St. Mark's College, Johns succeeded him as Headmaster, and a few years later started his own school, Winton House, in Winchester, where one of his pupils was Kingsley's son, Grenville. In later years the enthusiasm for natural history which had endeared Johns to Charles made him famous as the author of a series of scientific books, of which the most popular, *Flowers of the Field*, has been reprinted many times since its first appearance in 1856.

Charles was an excellent pupil, strikingly courteous and quick at his studies, but, as at Clifton, less successful with his fellow students than with his masters. He was strong and active, and his courage was unquestioned, but he was awkward at games. The give-and-take of schoolboys never came easily to him, and he found the pain of ridicule almost more than he could bear. As a result, he was much happier with a specimen bucket slung round his neck, climbing the sea-cliffs, than he was with the other boys. His only close friend was Richard Cowley Powles, whom he met in January 1833, after the Christmas vacation. They became intimate almost at sight, for Cowley could easily penetrate the armour of shyness which protected Charles. The two led the school academically, and before they left were so advanced that Mr. Coleridge told them not to consider themselves bound to the school provided their lessons were ready at his hours, but to sit comfortably in Cowley's room out of the bustle of the younger boys. In Charles's last year at Helston, he frequently heard classes when one of the masters was absent. To Cowley he showed his schoolboy efforts at poetry, and 'Psyche: a Rhapsody', written in high-minded praise of love.

Both the brothers had serious illnesses at Helston. Charles had brain fever and a severe attack of English cholera, but recovered quickly. Herbert was less strong, and in the spring of 1834 he had a bad attack of rheumatic fever, which brought on heart disease. He was supposed to be recovering and was nearly convalescent when he died without warning. Charles was summoned from the room where he was working with Cowley Powles, in ignorance of what had happened. Forty years later Cowley could still remember with pain the cry of anguish which Charles gave when he found Herbert. The suddenness of the death made the more gossipy of the Helston townfolk suspect inaccurately that it was being hushed up and that Herbert had actually committed suicide by throwing himself into the Looe Pool.

The summer holidays were full, and Charles had been given his own trawl and dredge with which to work the sea-bottoms around the coast near Clovelly. He attached himself to William Turton ('poor dear old opium-eating Dr. Turton'), a physician living at Bideford, whose knowledge of molluscs and shells was encyclopedic, and the old man and the boy spent day after summer day together, bobbing up and down in a boat. Occasionally Charles had time for drawing and for the poetry for which there was little opportunity at Helston. In the summer of 1835 Johns joined him for a fortnight of tramping around Plymouth. Charles was only eight years younger than his tutor, and they behaved like equals in age, teasing one another about their innocent love affairs and exchanging botany books.

In the spring of 1836 Lord Cadogan presented Mr. Kingsley to one of the best livings in the London area, St. Luke's Church, Chelsea. His father's increased income meant that Charles could be removed from Helston, with which his parents had become dissatisfied. In March Mrs. Kingsley wrote to him from the London house of Lady Louisa Cadogan, with whom she was staying while waiting for her husband's predecessor to vacate the Rectory at Chelsea, to say that the summer term would be Charles's last with Coleridge, and that he would come to Chelsea to study with a private tutor in the autumn. After a year of tuition at home, he was expected to spend a year at King's College, London, polishing up his entrance requirements for Cambridge, where he was to be matriculated in the autumn of 1838. Mrs. Kingsley finished her letter with an injunction to Charles to burn it after reading. Charles answered:

'I received your letter this morning with mingled pleasure & sorrow; for as much as I am pleased with the plan you have in view for me, I cannot but be very sorry at leaving Helleston, where I am already very happy— . . . I hope the tutor you will give me will be a Cambridge man, as I wish to get up as much mathematics as I can, without interfering with my classics, before I go to college—Mr. C. says, "that composition is at present of the greatest importance to me, & that I must principally cultivate that, before I go to college; as one is not *supposed to know any* mathematics before one goes, whereas one is expected to have obtained all requisite classical knowledge at school".'

Chelsea was only beginning to grow out of its village days when the Kingsleys went there. The bow-fronted Georgian shops still opened on to cobbled streets, noisy with the cries of pedlars leading panniered donkeys. Great families still had their mansions there, although the village was reputedly unhealthy, and their equipages, manned by flunkies, rattled through the streets on their way to London. The pollarded trees along the Thames were full of birds, and the breeze brought the wholesome smell of sea-tar. In the cool of summer evenings, white-shirted Cockneys rowed down the river in green boats, Chelsea pensioners in red coats drew pensively on their pipes, across the river in the low-lying Battersea marshes a slow windmill turned above the hummocks, and the calm was disturbed only by the occasional flash of a rocket from Vauxhall Gardens.

In 1834 Thomas Carlyle, newly arrived at Chelsea, had written home to Craigenputtock: 'We lie safe down in a little bend of the river, away from all the great roads; have air and quiet hardly inferior to Craigenputtock, an outlook from the back-windows into mere leafy regions with here and there a red high-peaked old roof looking through; and see nothing of London, except by day the summits of St. Paul's Cathedral and Westminster Abbey, and by night the gleam of the great Babylon affronting the peaceful skies. Yet in *half an hour* (for it is under two miles to Piccadilly) we can be, with a pair of stout legs, in the most crowded part of the whole habitable Earth; and, even without legs, every quarter of an hour, from sun to sun, a Coach will take you for sixpence from your own threshold, and set you down there again for another.'

St. Luke's was a neo-Gothic church, built a dozen years before Mr. Kingsley became its Rector. Its galleries were unsightly and its chancel poor, but it had a fine stone roof, a good ring of ten bells, and an excellent organ. Next to the river, near the Rectory, lay the old church which had served the parish until St. Luke's was built. It was low, dark, crammed with tombs, and crowded with history. Charles was too busy with lessons—perhaps too unresponsive to architecture—to be stirred by it, but Henry Kingsley used the old church and the run-down mansions surrounding it as the centre of one of his best novels, *The Hillyars and the Burtons*.

To the street the Rectory presented a formal, blank face of uninteresting brownish-grey brick, but behind it lay a garden of the size common only to country houses, its tranquillity assured by a high wall. There were gravel paths, pools, limes, the inevitable mulberry under which Queen Elizabeth was supposed to have sat, a great sloping poplar on which George and Henry climbed, and a sweep of drive to the stables. To Charles it all seemed paltry after the pleasures of Clovelly, and his consolation was only to be found in the library or in work in his own room looking over the garden.

The increased size of his parish meant less time for Mr. Kingsley to spend with his children. There were no more sea-side walks, and he seldom had time to draw with them. A bound volume of his sketches in pen-and-ink and wash has survived; they are delicate and imaginative, with an eighteenth-century feeling for a tidy, composed landscape, and are far better than anything that remains of his children's drawings, but almost all of them date from the period before Chelsea.

In the Rectory there was a hum of parochial and clerical gossip, of schools and duties, of vestries and altar-cloths. Writing in loneliness to Cowley Powles, Charles confessed to being sickened by the young women who fell in love with the preacher and his sermon instead of the Bible, and by the eternal talk about the parish. At this time he seems to have had no idea of ever becoming a clergyman himself.

J. M. Ludlow, a friend of Kingsley's fifteen years later, found the elder Kingsley 'a tall, courtly mannered old gentleman, not unlike his son, Charles, but much better looking . . . his mother, an active, clever old dame, from whom her son seemed to have inherited a good deal of his quickness. She did virtually all the work of Chelsea parish, her husband virtually nothing beyond the preaching.' Ludlow remembered 'one quaint axiom of hers, that the only outward test of honesty was the nose; that a man or woman with a good big nose was pretty sure to be honest, but that a small nose was characteristic of a thief'. It is perhaps unnecessary to add that the Kingsleys were conspicuous for the size and prominence of their noses.

Mrs. Kingsley ruled her part of the parish with a just, inflexible hand. It was her firm belief that a first offence punished severely would stop any further misdemeanour. One servant girl, aged fourteen, was caught by the police stealing some cakes. The police inspector called on Mrs. Kingsley, saying that if she so requested, he would let the girl off with a warning. Mrs. Kingsley replied immediately that the girl should be sent to prison, but when she was released, she found a place waiting for her, secured by Mrs. Kingsley, where she was kindly treated. It is pleasant to record that the girl was quite reformed, presumably proving Mrs. Kingsley's theory, and in time married, retaining a high regard all her life for the Kingsleys.

In the Bodleian Library there is a curious MS volume, drawn up in the early days of the Oxford Movement for the private use of John Delane, editor of *The Times*, and called *Principal Clergy of London Classified According to the Great Church Question of the Day*. In it are arranged the names of the clergymen in descending order of Anglo-Catholicism, from Father Bennett of St. Paul's, Knightsbridge ('As near Romanism as possible') to Mr. Garwood of St. Mary's, Spitalfields ('On the verge of Dissent'). Of the eighty-nine so listed, Mr. Kingsley was number forty-five, among the 'Evangelical Moderates', just after Archdeacon Sinclair, Vicar of Kensington ('Moderate: but no doubt decidedly opposed to the High Ch. party'). The entry following Mr. Kingsley's name reads: 'Influential on acct. of family connexions. Related to the Cadogan family. Is a zealous clergyman entertaining views very similar to those of the Archdeacon.'

In the summer of 1837 Charles went with his father to Clovelly to rest from his studies and to recuperate from a congestion of the left lung, before beginning that autumn at King's College, London. He was delighted to be away from Chelsea. Invitations to dinner came in from the neighbourhood, Sir James lent him his boat and a black pony. Charles wrote his mother:

'To prove my remembrance of you, I am reading my Bible, & my Paley—and my mathematics, steadily, & am learning poetry by heart—And moreover, I am keeping a journal, full of thoughts & meditations & *prose poetry*, for I am not alone enough to indite verses—as I have not had any walks by myself—However I hope that the fine weather (which now appears to be returning) will draw out my poetical thoughts again.

'I am exceedingly well here—and have grown fat already—I bathed the other day, & Papa saw me, & said he had no idea I was so fat—my skin has become quite fresh & clear, & my bathe so far from giving me cold, has made me feel quite fresh & strong.'

Then, aware of the high seriousness to be expected of a man of eighteen, he added:

'The dear old place looks quite natural—& yet somehow—it is like a dream when I think of the total revulsion that two day's journey has made in me—& how I seem like some spirit in the metempsychosis, which has suddenly passed back, out of a new life, into one which it bore long ago, & has recovered in one moment, all its old ties, its old feelings—its old friends, & pleasures!'

The next year in London he spent working hard at Greek and Latin in King's College, walking up every day from Chelsea with his nose in a book, oblivious of the passers-by he bumped. Most of his evenings were spent in study, but his free time was made happy by the presence of Cowley Powles, who had finished his work under Mr. Coleridge and followed Charles to King's. As he had been at Helston, Charles was still gentle and diffident to the point of timidity, and he welcomed Cowley doubly. He left King's in 1838 with a good, unspectacular record. Cowley was to enter Exeter College, Oxford, and in the autumn Charles was matriculated at Magdalene College, Cambridge.

CHAPTER III

Cambridge and Courtship

In October 1838 when Charles Kingsley drove into Cambridge, down the Trumpington Road from London, he was unable to see the elegant new façade of the Fitzwilliam Museum, still hidden behind its builders' hoardings. On the occasion of the laying of the cornerstone the previous winter, the Vice-Chancellor, Gilbert Ainslie, had said that the purpose of the new museum was 'to encourage the more elegant and polite arts' in the University. There was room for such encouragement, for Cambridge life was still ruled by the 'fast set'. Those who could afford it, and many who could not, gambled at billiards and whist, played at real tennis, smoked cigars, read *Bell's Life in London and Sporting Chronicle*, and drank too much. Town and gown riots were common, and the most frequent opponents of the undergraduates in fights were bargees from the River Cam. Attendance at chapel was compulsory, but bodily presence was more important than sobriety, and frequently a college was treated to the sight of one of its members, fuddled with wine at four o'clock dinner, stumbling into chapel to sit with his surplice unfastened and his prayer book upside down. Not infrequently the fellows themselves were drunk in chapel. At Barnwell and Castle End were brothels much frequented by undergraduates. Magdalene, the most remote geographically of the colleges, was, if possible, the fastest of them all. One critic of its morals said that it was 'a favourite home for young men who are of the opinion, either from conjecture or experience, that other colleges are too strict for them'.

There is a pleasant reverse side to licence, however, and its name is freedom. There can be few times in a man's life when he is so joyously conscious of his own maturity and independence as the moment when he steps into his first college rooms, closes the door behind him, and realizes that here is his own domain. For Kingsley, heartily sick of the confinement of Chelsea Rectory, it was pure joy.

The set of rooms he occupied is at the top of C staircase in the front quadrangle. The study is beamed, and the roof slants low on both sides—it is really an attic room—and Kingsley, already tall and lanky, must have had to duck his head whenever he came through the doorway. The windows face the front quadrangle on one side, and on the other deep dormers between heavy chimneys overlook the traffic of Magdalene Street. By hanging far out of his window he could just see the river and Magdalene Bridge. Opening out of the study is the bedroom, a narrow and cheerless slip.

In 1838 the Master of Magdalene was the Honourable George Neville-Granville, but Kingsley saw less of him than he did of the Senior Tutor, Samuel Waud, with whom he studied mathematics. Waud was a genial man whose habitual greeting to the undergraduates working with him was: 'Come to my rooms, and we will have a problem or two and an oyster and cigar.' Friendliest of men, he saw at once that Kingsley had few acquaintances and was too shy to make his own way among the cliques of public-school men who dominated the social life of the college. With warm-hearted sympathy he did his best to help Kingsley by asking other undergraduates to call on him, and in a few months Charles had all the friends he could manage to see between the hours of hard study to which he still adhered.

One friend, however, Charles had on coming to the college, Frank Penrose,[1] son of Mr. Kingsley's curate at Clifton. Penrose

[1] Francis Cranmer Penrose (1817–1903), youngest son of John Penrose, theological writer, and Elizabeth his wife, who was well known as the children's author, 'Mrs. Markham'. Francis attended Winchester and studied architecture before coming up to Magdalene, later became famous as painter, architect, and surveyor of St. Paul's Cathedral.

was as gregarious as Waud himself, and between them they soon disposed of the most painful part of Charles's shyness. Before long he joined Penrose in membership in the college boat club. Rowing suited him well, and although he was never so good as Frank, he succeeded by the following spring in earning a place in the second boat. The boat club itself was as much an excuse for conviviality as for exercise; at one supper the members drank fifty-four bottles of champagne from London, twelve of sherry, twelve of hock, and twenty bowls of punch. On another occasion the companionable Mr. Waud presented them with two dozen bottles of claret.

Gradually, as his first year slipped by and the noise of the feet of undergraduate friends sounded frequently on the worn steps outside his room, Kingsley began substituting more worldly pleasures for his intensive studying. The hard drinking of the boat club never became habitual with him, but during his first year he learned to smoke. The nervousness and timidity which had bothered him for years vanished when he held a pipe-stem between his teeth. His mother disapproved, but for once he failed to take her advice, and he was seldom without a pipe the rest of his life. He tried a little harmless gambling, too, but he was still a long way from being one of the wilder members of his college.

Like many other young men at the University, he began to have religious doubts. Unlike most of them, who drifted gradually into a quiet acceptance of disbelief, Kingsley had a characteristically turbulent period of soul-searching. Revolting from his rectory-bred childish faith, he first denied all religious authority, and then conversely felt himself drawn to the most authoritarian of churches, the Roman. The only evidence we have that he ever considered professing Catholicism is his often-repeated statement in later life that he had known the strength of its attraction as well as any convert. It may be that the difficulty of resisting it was exaggerated in his memory, for the period of temptation was certainly short; as early as 1841 the familiar tone of hatred for anything reminiscent of Rome had already begun to be heard. Or perhaps the very sense of danger safely avoided may account in part for the illogical scorn he showed for Catholicism the rest of his life.

Whether it was disbelief which he felt, a yearning for Rome, doubts of the Trinity, or the reassuring moments of faith in the tenets of the Church of England which settled on him occasionally, he could always walk to Clare Hall to talk about the matter with Charles Blachford Mansfield. Penrose had been at Winchester with Mansfield, and during the winter of 1838-9, he introduced him to Kingsley. Just as Tennyson at Cambridge had been dazzled by Hallam's graces, so Kingsley fell completely before the luminous charm of Mansfield. He was born the same year as Kingsley, and he, too, was a son of the parsonage, but the difference between the two men was striking. Mansfield was graceful, handsome, socially poised, easy to know: all qualities which Kingsley admired as completely as he lacked them. Mansfield's social poise came naturally; as a child he had been much in Osborne House, which the Queen was later to make into her retreat on the Isle of Wight, and in the world of the peerage, with which he had several blood connections. When he was a boy, he had been confined to a couch for years by a bad spine, but when he recovered, he was filled with a terrible desire to make up for the lost years by continuous activity. He learned to shoot, to do gymnastic tricks, to run and leap so well that Kingsley said he was more antelope than man. Kingsley became his closest friend. Together they rowed, smoked, and argued over religion and ornithology; when they became interested in mesmerism, each acted as subject for the other's experiments. Mansfield was studying old magic and primitive spells, and he soon interested Kingsley, so that they both spent their odd shillings and free time poking in Cambridge shops for books on the subject. Already Mansfield was developing the eccentricity which both amused and exasperated his friends; his religious faith was intensely individualistic, if strong, and he had come to believe that shooting, fishing, entomologizing, even eating meat, were wrong since they deprived God's creatures of life. But whatever his crankiness, he was just the close companion Kingsley needed. There is some evidence, too, in his mature correspondence, that he and Mansfield conducted research in natural sciences less innocent than ornithology, that they may have gone together on excursions to Barnwell or Castle End. Indeed, the sexual morals of the English upper and middle classes had not changed overnight in 1837 at the accession of Victoria, and the tone of the university was still distinctly Regency; it would be surprising if a healthy and passionate young man had not indulged in a little licence. A passage from *Yeast* may well represent his memory of his feelings as an undergraduate:

'Love had been to him, practically, ground tabooed and "carnal". What was to be expected? Just what happened—if woman's beauty had nothing holy in it, why should his fondness for it? Just what happens every day—that he had to sow his wild oats for himself, and eat the fruit thereof, and the dirt thereof also.'

In spite of some dissipation, he managed to win a scholarship in the May examinations of his first year, and wrote home in jubilation: 'You will be delighted to hear that I am *first* in Classics, and in Mathematics *also*, at the examinations; which has not happened in the College for several years—I shall bring home plenty of prizes, and a very decent portion of honour—the King's college men here are all delighted with me. I am going to stay up here about ten days longer, if you will let me. Mr. Waud has offered to help me with my Second year's subjects, so I shall read the Conic Sections and the Spherical Trigonometry very hard while I am here—I know you and Mama will be glad to hear of my success, so you must pardon the wildness of my letter, for I am so happy I hardly know what to say—You know I am not accustomed to be successful. I am going today to a fishing-party at Sir Charles Wale's at Shelford, where I have been several times already. . . . Give my love to Mama and tell her I have paid a quantity of small bills.'

After his vacation work with Mr. Waud was finished, Charles returned to Chelsea in the middle of June to find his family packing for a summer in the country. Gerald, who had recently gone into the Navy, was home on leave, and George and Henry were back from school when Charles arrived, full of importance as the eldest brother, now a Cambridge man. Mr. Kingsley could scarcely afford to take a country house for his brood, but he had found that his friend, the Rev. R. Twopeny, Vicar of Ipsden, needed a replacement for the summer months. Leaving his own parish in charge of a curate, Mr. Kingsley took the family off to Oxfordshire and settled down in the Vicarage at Ipsden. The village is a quiet one, near Checkendon, in the wooded Chiltern Hills, and it was an ideal summer retreat. To Charles any change from Chelsea was welcome. Thoughts of Cambridge and Mansfield surely buzzed in his head, but he can scarcely have guessed that Ipsden held a future more momentous for him than all that Cambridge had to offer.

Among other visitors at Ipsden that summer was the Grenfell family. Pascoe Grenfell, the father of them all, had died the year before at the age of seventy-six. In the settling of his estate, the family home, Taplow House, a few miles away, had been sold, and those children who had lived at home with him removed temporarily to Braziers Park, a large house in wooded grounds near Ipsden, so that they might at least be in the neighbourhood of their friends at Taplow. Old Mr. Grenfell had gone into the family business in tin and copper ores while a young man, invested in the development of industry in Anglesey and Cornwall, and in 1794, when he had made a large fortune, bought and enlarged Taplow House. In 1802 he became M.P. for Great Marlow, and for eighteen years represented his constituency ably, supporting Wilberforce in the debate on the abolition of slavery, and being called on by the House as a recognized authority on banking and finance. His first wife, by whom he had three children, died young; a few years later he married the Honourable Georgiana St. Leger, daughter of Viscount Doneraile. When she died in 1818, she had produced an even dozen children, of whom the youngest, Frances Eliza, was only four. By the time of his own death Mr. Grenfell had long since consolidated his transition from wealthy merchant to landed aristocrat, by forming ties with several branches of the peerage through the successful marriages of his children.

When the Grenfells came to Braziers, Frances, known to her

family as Fanny, was a gentle and serious-minded young lady of twenty-five. Although her face was too heavy and strong to be pretty, her lustrous black hair, great soft, dark eyes, rather close-set, and the sweetness of her expression made many observers forget the flaws in her beauty. Her movements were slow and graceful, and her whole impression was one of dignity and serenity. She was no longer in the first bloom of youth, at least by Victorian standards, but her troops of elder brothers and sisters still insisted on regarding her as the baby and pet of the family. Fanny thought herself very mature, however, and had taken to the serious study of theology. She knew something of the Higher Criticism from Germany, but her real sympathy lay with the movement begun six years before at Oxford, of which Dr. Pusey and Mr. Newman were the leaders. That her devotion was sincere is unquestionable, but one can scarcely help wondering whether her theological investigations may not have been the result of a ladylike ennui suffered by one who had seen most of her contemporaries married, and who had little more liking for the world of politics and country houses, banking and the London season, in which her family lived, than Kingsley had for the splay-footed pious ladies of Chelsea parish.

On July 6th Charles and his future wife met for the first time. Where they met or how is no longer known, although tradition has it that he rode up to the Rectory at Checkendon, saw Miss Grenfell in the garden, and promptly, irrevocably fell in love. That Fanny felt the same quickening is clear from her testimony forty years later that their first glance ('eye-wedlock', Charles called it) was the beginning of what seemed 'more of a recognition than an acquaintance'. Years after, Charles wrote: 'That was my real wedding-day.' There was little enough that was handsome to attract Miss Grenfell in either Kingsley's hollow-cheeked face or his tall, gawky frame, but there was a burning intensity in both his gaze and his movements which gave him a distinction well beyond conventional good looks. Dark brown hair worn unfashionably long fell in waves over his arched forehead, and side-whiskers grew down his jaws to a clean-shaven chin of remarkable pugnacity. His nose was long and arched, and flared to a generous width. The most prominent features in his face were his blue eyes blazing under overhanging brows. Only an unusually wide and sensitive mouth showed the possibility of the humour within. But at the beginning of their acquaintance it was the lonely quality of his look which drew Miss Grenfell. 'He was then full of religious doubts; and his face, with its unsatisfied hungering look, bore witness to the state of his mind.' Much has been made of the difference in their social position, wealth, and age; what is too frequently overlooked is the loneliness in each which recognized its counterpart in the other.

Fanny found Charles's quick, intuitive intelligence dazzling; he found Fanny's calm, the calm of a woman five years his senior, restful as no other person's companionship had been. As they came to know each other better, they found there were no limits to the subjects they might discuss. Gradually he confessed to her his religious doubts, his confusion about his future—whether he should continue with the law at Lincoln's Inn or not—even the dissipations into which he had fallen at Cambridge. Far from being shocked, Fanny listened with a reassuring warmth, and slowly tried to shake his doubts, to recommend to him the tracts by Mr. Newman. Charles, less shockproof, was horrified at the ascetic view of love between the sexes which he felt must result from Anglo-Catholicism. There were surely lighter moments in their conversation, too, but there is little hint of them in Mrs. Kingsley's biography, for she felt it was hardly dignified to write of them. All the time, however, no word of love seems to have been spoken, although it was implicit and recognized in everything they said. July passed quickly, and August fled. In the middle of September the Kingsleys left for Chelsea (the last mention of Mr. Kingsley's name in the parish register is on September 7th), and Charles prepared to return to Cambridge. The happiness of the summer was little help, for he had not yet recovered his faith, however much he might try, and, for all he knew, he might never see Fanny again. There had been no overt avowal of love and there was certainly no chance of marriage with the wealthy Miss Grenfell; all that remained was the prospect of occasional letters, but no more of those than a stern propriety could countenance. All the same, he did promise her to read his Bible and to pray humbly for guidance and a restoration of his belief. Fanny hardly needed to ask him to pray for her.

And so back to Cambridge he went, in despair over the glimpse he had had of a joyous and unobtainable future. His studies suffered, and he became progressively wilder and more unhappy. Boating, fishing, hunting, shooting, fast horses, boxing with a full-blooded Negro 'professor', climbing out of college for midnight excursions, long hikes (he once walked the fifty-two miles to London in a day): these took up his time, but failed to take his mind from his troubles, for at heart he was as earnest then as he was the rest of his adult life. At last the longed-for change began. Gradually his love of Fanny fused with his love of everything good, and eventually with a love of God. Emotionally his religious difficulties were almost over, but he still had intellectual barriers to pass. His old difficulty about the Trinity came back, and he felt, too, a revulsion from the 'bigotry, cruelty, and quibbling' of the Athanasian Creed. And over and over came his dislike and distrust of the clergy. One can only wonder how much of the last was due to what he considered the incompetence of his father, who had been drawn into holy orders without any real desire to become a clergyman. All this he poured into the infrequent letters to Fanny, and when her answers arrived, her words were as soothing, as reassuring as they had been at Ipsden.

Unfortunately for Fanny, the one thing on which her eleven surviving brothers and sisters agreed about her was that it was foolish to keep up a correspondence with young Kingsley. The Grenfells were on their way up in the world, and there was every possibility that she would marry as well as her sisters had done. It was true that she had been left little by her father's will, but Charles Pascoe, her eldest half-brother, had received instructions to let her have £400 per annum when she married. Obviously she must break with the shy, stammering, awkward undergraduate. What is perhaps not easy to understand more than a hundred years later, when his name has eclipsed theirs, is that the

Grenfells were perfectly right, from what knowledge they had of Kingsley, in thinking him a poor risk for Fanny.

The letters continued all the same, and some time in 1840 Charles seems to have made the declaration of a love which held no promise of a happy future. In November he wrote: 'I have struggled to alter lately, and my alteration has been remarked with pleasure by some, with sneers by others. "Kingsley, they say, is not half as reckless as he used to be." ' Faith was still difficult for him, but a month later he could tell Fanny: 'You cannot conceive the moments of self-abasement and self-shame I have. . . . Still with all my remorse and shame and agitation, I do feel that I am improving.' By the New Year his battle with doubt was nearly won, thanks to Fanny's help, and confidence in the existence and goodness of God flooded over him, bringing a new sense of peace.

With his religious doubts eased, he felt his mind free once more for hard study, and from Cambridge he wrote Fanny: 'I am reading seven to eight hours a day. I have refused hunting and driving, and made a solemn vow against cards. My trial of this new mode of life has been short, but to have begun it is the greatest difficulty.' He hated the rigid, systematic work required and felt himself 'forced to drudge at the acquirement of confessedly obsolete and useless knowledge, of worn-out philosophies, and scientific theories long exploded' and longed to be 'free to follow such a course of education as Socrates, and Bacon, and More, and Milton have sketched out'. The charge most frequently made against him in later life was that his mind was chaotic, unsystematic, for all its perception. The University, where so many Englishmen have learned to give order to their thoughts, failed with him in that respect.

That spring the thought repeatedly came to him that the one profession for which he was really fitted was exactly that against which he had kicked most wildly. It was a shock to find that his own discovery of faith made him want to take on the once-hated yoke of the Church of England. In wonder he wrote to the approving Fanny:

'I feel more and more daily that a clergyman's life is the one for which both my *physique* and *morale* were intended—that the profession will check and guide the faulty parts of my mind, while it gives full room for my energy—that energy which had so nearly ruined me; but will now be devoted utterly, I hope, to the service of God.'

With almost a year left, Kingsley thought he could get a good enough degree to qualify for a Cambridge fellowship, from which he could, in turn, go on to a good parish. He explained in a letter to Miss Grenfell: 'As for my degree, I can yet take high honours in the University, and ought to get my fellowship; but I was very idle—and very sinful—my first year. I attend morning chapel at eight; read from nine to one or two; attend chapel generally again at five. I read for some hours in the evening. As for my studies interesting me, if you knew the system and the subjects of study, you would feel that to be impossible.'

In a curious reversal of companionship, he now found himself spending most of his time with friends who were going into the Church, so that his rooms were 'full of clerical conversation' of exactly the type he had always so disliked at Chelsea. To Miss Grenfell he confessed: 'My only reasons for working for a degree are that I may enter the world with a certain *prestige* which may get me a living sooner.' To Cambridge she sent suitable books—notably Carlyle's works and Coleridge's *Aids to Reflection*—for him to read during the summer.

Luckily, both Fanny and Charles had a confidante in Mrs. Kingsley; when the Grenfells complained of too many letters with Cambridge postmarks, Charles would send his to his mother, who then sent them off to Fanny. What, if anything, the Rector thought of his son's love affair is not recorded; probably he went his bemused way without ever hearing of it.

Charles decided to stay on near Cambridge to study during most of the summer of 1841, living at Shelford in rooms near his family friend, Sir Charles Wale. Sir Charles had led an adventurous life as soldier and as governor of Martinique before retiring with his family to Shelford, where he frequently entertained undergraduates who liked angling. After settling arrangements for tutoring by W. H. Bateson of St. John's and the Rev.

Thomas Drosier, Kingsley wrote his mother that 'the lodgings are very clean, & large, with good furniture, & the people very civil'. Also, he had recovered 'of the missing clothes &c. 2 p. of trowsers, 3 shirts, 3 shirt collars, 2 cravats, & some other minor things'. He then continued:

'I have been reading the [Edinburgh] Review on No. 90 of the Tracts for the Times, & I wish I could transcribe every word & send it to Fanny—Whether wilful or self deceived, these men are Jesuits, taking the oath to the Articles with moral reservations, which allow them to explain them away in senses utterly different from those of their authors—All the worst *doctrinal* features of Popery Mr. Newman professes to believe in—Help me to wean her from this pernicious superstition—I say *me*—because I feel that in *Doctrinal & Polemical* Theology, *I* must hereafter be her guide, while *she* is mine, thank God, *in Christian practice*—Do talk & write to her, & beg her for *my sake* to get that review if possible & read it. . . .

'I saw her picture at the Exhibition yesterday—You cannot think how horribly ugly they have made her—If I meet the artist I think I *must* duck him.'

After he was settled at Shelford, he wrote home once more: 'I wish you would tell me something about Fanny, & if she has got my letter, & whether it will be safe to write to her. . . .

'I have determined to reduce my allowance of beer as you wish it, & my quantity of daily food. I fancy that people often eat too much as well as drink—And I dare say that occasional fasts may be good for a healthy stomach, & influence the mind through the body.

'I hardly find my ten miles a day sufficient exercise to keep me healthy, & very often get a walk in the evening afterwards. . . .

'Does Henry Caddell [Mr. Kingsley's curate] know that I am going into the Church?—both you & he would be surprised if you knew the pleasure with which I looked forward, even to the mere daily routine of business, much more to the life of delightful thought & study, which I can be applying daily as I get it, to the minds of those under my charge—How a good clergyman must understand the human mind.'

As the end of the gruelling summer approached and he prepared to go to Chelsea for a short rest before beginning his last term at Cambridge, he was alarmed to hear that Mrs. Kingsley might have visitors while he was there: 'I have had another letter from Fanny in which she says that she expects to be at home on the 4th of October. Are Lady Louisa & Mr. Marsh coming then? They will not be exactly where I should wish them, in case the Dove should come down to Chelsea as she will. Counsel for your poor children & let them see a little of each other; it will be such a spur to me towards the winter's reading & she says it would make her so happy. I leave it all in your hands. I must shew you some bits of her letters—they are perfect. I wonder who could ever fancy her not clever. If talent be the ability to comprehend exquisitely, & apply surely, every thing that a woman can or *should* know, she has talents.'

Even sympathetic Mrs. Kingsley objected to arranging a clandestine rendezvous, and the meeting fell through. To conceal his hurt, Charles told Fanny in October: 'Do not suppose that I augur ill from our disappointment—rather the contrary—I have always been afraid of being too successful at *first*. I think sorrow at the *beginning* augurs well for the happiness of a connexion that must last for ever—and are we not *eternally* engaged now, Fanny? perhaps not formally in the sight of men—but in our own conscience & hearts—utterly—dare I say irrevocably—that word I fear to write—because my unworthiness will be the only thing which ever can make our plans alter—is it not so?'

The rest of 1841 the degree hung over his thoughts 'like a vast incubus', and he read himself ill, so that between the mathematics and the classics examinations he was under doctor's orders to shut every book. He spent the time fishing the River Cam. Of this period of collapse, as well as the many of his later life, he said: 'My panacea for stupidity and over-"mentation" is a day in a roaring fen wind.' When the examinations were over he had received a second class in mathematics and a first in classics. His degree was not good enough to help him to a fellowship, but he was too exhausted to care, and fled to his birthplace, Holne, first to rest, and then to study for his ordination. Of his lodgings there, he thought, 'washing & all ought to cost a pound a week & no more'. To Cowley Powles at Oxford he extended an invitation to join him:

'I shall be most happy to have you as a temporary sharer in the frugalities of my farm house lodging. Whether you will despise hard beds and dimity curtains, morning bathes and evening trout fishing, mountain mutton and Devonshire cream, I do not know, but you will not despise the calm of a few weeks in which to commune with God in his works.'

At Holne he began to write a prose life of St. Elizabeth of Hungary, intending it, not for publication, but as a gift to Miss Grenfell on their wedding day, if it should ever come. The book, a large folio which he carefully decorated with curiously sensual pen-and-ink drawings, is now in the British Museum. It has a long preface, but little of the main body of the book was ever finished. Instead the story and its theme, the dangers of celibacy and asceticism, were later reworked into *The Saint's Tragedy.*

During the spring he was offered two curacies in Hampshire following his ordination. One was at Kingston, and the other at Eversley. Without realizing how much of the rest of his life would be spent there, he chose Eversley. In July he went to Farnham Castle to be examined by the Bishop of Winchester before being ordained deacon. Although he was nervous, he got through the examination successfully on Thursday and Friday, spent Saturday in prayer and meditation, and was ordained on Sunday. To Fanny he sent the news: 'God's mercies are new every morning. Here I am waiting to be admitted in a few hours to His holy ministry, and take refuge for ever in His Temple! ... Oh! my soul, my body, my intellect, my very love, I dedicate you all to God!'

In more practical vein he wrote his mother the same day: 'Will you send off the Big Box, & in it 3 things. My Frock-Coat which was altered (Cook's coat), a steel pen holder (my ivory one is at Chelsea), & some *free going* steel pens—(*cheap* ones), & a pair of Dumb-bells about 15 pounds weight each. *Pray* get them they are about 5d a pound properly if they are Lead, but second hand you may get them for a song, I do not care whether they be lead or iron, but I would not mind waiting a few days for the box, if they came with it. . . . Write & tell me when I can have the £100.'

As his widow wrote: 'And now Charles Kingsley settled down at the age of twenty-three, in Eversley; little thinking it would be his home for thirty-three years.'

CHAPTER IV

The Young Priest

When Kingsley arrived at Eversley the day after his ordination, the Rector was preparing for a six-week holiday, during which he would leave the parish in the charge of his very new young curate. In Mr. Hawley's absence Kingsley was to live in the Rectory while he looked for rooms to occupy when the Rector returned. The Rectory was built in the seventeenth century, and additions were stuck on as the years passed. The numerous rooms are large and light, there are pleasant bow windows, and it is but a step from the main rooms of the house into the garden. Although it became a neat and fairly comfortable house after Kingsley was presented to the living, during Mr. Hawley's tenancy it had fallen into disrepair, there were sagging chimneys, loose windows, and broken grates. The lawn was taken up by a series of dank ponds which overflowed into the low-lying house when it rained, and even in dry weather kept the rooms damp.

For his own use in the Rectory, the curate had a 'large, low, front room, with a light paper and drab curtains, and a large bow window', probably the room which later became his own bed-room. From it he could look across the front lawn with three huge Scotch firs, past a sunken lane which led to Bramshill, to the glebe beyond, which swept up to a low wooded eminence known as the Mount.

Through a gap in the hedge bordering the side garden leads the Rector's path to Eversley Church. There is an old tradition that a small church, on the site of the present one, was a sanctuary for the deer-slayers, of which the parish, once largely populated by smugglers and poachers, had more than its share. There was almost certainly a church on the same spot in the eleventh century. The present building, into which parts of a sixteenth-century structure were incorporated, dates from 1724. John James, a pupil of Wren, designed the red-brick church, which is an attractive but fairly commonplace example of the early eighteenth century. The churchyard is now neatly planted with trees, but when Kingsley first saw it, it was full of the sheep of neighbouring farmers and badly neglected. The interior of the church was in little better shape; a cracked kitchen-basin held baptismal water, alms were collected in an ancient wooden saucer, and a broken chair leaned crazily against the altar, which was covered by a disgraceful cloth full of moth holes.

Kingsley took his first service the Sunday after he arrived, July 17th. There was only a small congregation, for the parish had drifted away from regular attendance; when Mr. Hawley felt so inclined, he was in the habit of sending the clerk to the church door at eleven, to tell anyone who might have arrived that there would be no service that day. The responsibility of his first service weighed heavily on Kingsley, even though he had prayed earnestly for help before mounting the old three-decker pulpit.

He was lonely, rattling around in the big Rectory, and his schoolboy brother Henry came down from Chelsea to keep him company. Part of the day Charles taught in the parish school, an evil-smelling room ten feet square. The rest of the time he spent in parish visiting, walking around the three scattered hamlets which comprised the village. He liked the wild look of the country, on the edge of Old Windsor Forest, and was particularly pleased by the lonely moors and the fir forests, of which he wrote to Fanny: 'Every step I wander they whisper to me of you.'

One of the curate's first visits was to the lord of the manor and patron of the living, Sir John Cope, who lived in the great Jacobean house at Bramshill Park, which had been built as a royal palace. Sir John, who had been a companion of the Prince Regent, was seventy-four, a five-bottle man, and a strict and choleric game preserver. The excesses of his youth would have killed another man, but although his mind had begun to fail, he still served as M.F.H. to the Bramshill Hunt, and when he could not ride, he followed the Hunt by carriage. The pleasures of this life were all that interested him; for curates and their business he had little care. As a young man he had been a solicitor before inheriting his title from his elder brother. The story is told that he was examining a deed when he received a black-edged note announcing Sir Denzil's death and his own succession. Hastily reading the contents of the letter, he threw the deed to his partner, shouting: 'Hang the law; now for fox-hunting!' Today there is still a reminder of him at Bramshill Park: 'Sir John's Gate', which is not the entrance to a garden which one might expect, but a swinging barricade at the foot of the stairway, designed to keep the foxhounds running loose on the ground floor of the house from mounting to the bedrooms. He is said to have been married at one time, but he was now a widower with no children, and the baronetcy, which was an old one, seemed destined to become extinct for lack of an heir. One of Kingsley's friends, John Malcom Ludlow, left one published account of Sir John and a less kindly one in an unpublished autobiography. In the latter he says frankly that Bramshill Park had become the centre of demoralization in the parish. From Kingsley's correspondence it is clear that Sir John's conduct of business had been allowed to slip into the unscrupulous hands of an overseer and his wife.

But if Sir John was a bad influence on the parishioners, there was another influence much worse, about whom Kingsley began to find out when the Rector returned. John Toovey-Hawley had been presented to the living by Sir John ten years before. Ludlow tells us that he was a well-to-do and cultivated man, most knowledgeable about painting. He was well travelled and spent much of his time abroad, leaving the parish in charge of a succession of curates. Beyond preaching two or three times a year a well-written, scholarly sermon, far above the heads of most of the simple congregation, he did no parish work, save to send an occasional cup of broth to an old woman. What work did get done was carried on by the curates. He was courteous and kind to Kingsley, but the latter's suggestions for parish improvements brought forth only a polite and non-committal smile. What was worse was that Mr. Hawley had a wandering eye and a persuasive tongue for his female parishioners. Not until Hawley's misconduct became public knowledge did Kingsley find out that all the labourers in the parish had known of it for years, but with the close mouths of their kind had said nothing to him. Small wonder that the church was almost empty and dissent increasing rapidly.

When Hawley returned, Kingsley found comfortable rooms in a thatched cottage called the Brewery on the corner of the village green at Eversley Cross. With Fanny's books around him, he was almost happy, although at first he was lonely for educated company, until he met one of the churchwardens, Augustus Granville Stapleton, who lived in Warbrook, a fine house built by the architect of Eversley Church. Mr. Stapleton, who was a natural son of the first Lord Morley, was a Cambridge man who had been Canning's private secretary and later his biographer. For hours Kingsley and Stapleton would talk politics until the curate forgot his loneliness; Mrs. Stapleton took care, too, to invite him frequently to dinner to meet the county families who visited Warbrook.

In his long walks through the parish, Kingsley got to know every farmer and labourer within miles, and soon they began joining the women at the newly regular church services. For they knew he was as good a man as they; he could swing a flail with the threshers, turn a swathe with the mowers, or pitch with the hay-makers, and they respected him for it.

At the same time that he was getting accustomed to Eversley, the Grenfells made one last effort, a cruel one, to cause a break between him and Fanny. She was twenty-nine by now, but still a baby to her family. In August a complete prohibition was laid on their correspondence, and Fanny was packed off to Germany with Lady Gainsborough, in the hope that a year among the wonders of the Rhine would make her forget the two months in Oxfordshire. Long letters of farewell were exchanged, full of exhortations to be strong until their eventual triumph, and complete with instructions to each other how to fill the time until they might be together. Sadly Charles wrote:

'If you died, I would never marry, but live on, a quiet old bachelor, working hard, and praying much, and fasting, and wearing sackcloth to my dying day, and loving other people's little children, and widows, and orphans, and so labour on with a gentle melancholy, and humble repentance for the sinfulness which had taken you from me, till I joined my one blessed only wife in heaven, and there waited with her to take possession of the new heaven and new earth, in the train of my blessed Lord and Master.'

Of course, as any reader of Victorian novels could guess, the separation only made the lovers more resolute; Fanny's correspondence, instead of being neglected, was written into a carefully kept volume. Mrs. Kingsley once more took pity on the pair, and kept them informed about each other. Her kindness was well repaid in later years by receiving from Fanny the kind of devotion few mothers-in-law are given.

Charles had written special prayers for use during their separation, to be inserted into morning prayers: 'That it may please thee to turn the hearts of our families *& to teach them thy truth!* . . . That it may please thee to preserve us through the miseries & dangers of celibacy. . . . And here & forever accept, Oh Lord, our solemn devotion to thee of our love, our souls & bodies—so that if it be thy will that we should die apart, we will still apart labour for thy glory, & if thou art pleased to have mercy on us & restore us to each other's bosom, we will by thy help shew forth thy glory as a pattern to all married persons. . . .'

A year passed in this fashion. It is no longer possible to know whether or not this was a stipulated period, after which Fanny was to be free to do as she liked. In any case, at its conclusion she began active agitation for help in finding a living for Charles. When they were married she would have £400 a year, besides whatever Kingsley would earn. The living at Eversley was worth £600; if his own payment of curates when he became Rector is any guide, Kingsley probably received about £100 from Hawley. When Kingsley was ordained priest in July 1843, a year after becoming a deacon, his father arranged for him to hold a sinecure clerkship in holy orders at St. Luke's, Chelsea; all that it involved for £200 was an occasional sermon. In 1850, when he could afford to have a conscience about such things, Kingsley resigned the post. In 1843 he was also appointed domestic chaplain to Viscount Sydney, a position which he held until his death; for this the remuneration, if any, was surely negligible. In all, his income by the end of the summer of 1843 must have been little more than £300, a respectable amount for a curate in those days, but hardly enough to impress the Grenfells.

One of Miss Grenfell's sisters, Emily, had married the Honourable Sidney Godolphin Osborne, Rector of Durweston, Dorset. To him Fanny turned, for he was devoted to her, and, as a country parson, he understood Kingsley's position. Durweston was in the gift of Lord Portman, who had several other livings to bestow, and Osborne prompted him to help Kingsley. In September Charles gave notice to Mr. Hawley that he would leave his curacy at Eversley at Christmas because Lord Portman had given him a similar post, including a good house, at Pimperne, Dorset, and had promised him the first vacant living in his gift. At this the four-year opposition of the Grenfells collapsed, and Fanny and Charles resumed their correspondence. One October morning a military friend from Sandhurst walked into the cottage at Eversley Cross to find Kingsley madly stamping his clothes into a portmanteau and shouting: 'I am engaged. I am going to see her *now—today*!' Outside the cottage the Stapletons' gig and horse waited, ready to whirl him off to a train.

Plans were made at once for a marriage immediately after Kingsley left Eversley. The remaining time as a bachelor limped along slowly, but he worked at his life of St. Elizabeth and wrote frequently to Fanny, planning with her their establishment at Pimperne:

'We must have a regular rule of life, not so as to become a

law, but a custom. . . . Family prayers before breakfast; 8.30 to 10, household matters; 10 to 1, studying divinity, or settling parish accounts and business—our doors open for poor parish visitants; between 1 and 5, go out in all weathers, to visit sick and poor, and to teach in the school; in the evening we will draw and feed the intellect and the fancy. . . . We must devote from 9 to 12 on Monday mornings to casting up our weekly bills and accounts, and make a rule never to mention them, if possible, at any other time; and never to talk of household matters, unless urgent, but between 9 and 10 in the morning; nor of parish business in the evening. I have seen the *gêne* and misery which not following some such rule brings down!'

During the autumn he worked hard to while away the months of waiting: 'I am getting very strong, and have been threshing wheat a good deal these last two wet days, which is splendid exercise. I look forward to working in the garden at Pimperne. What a place for summer nights! We will go and sit in the church sometimes on summer nights, too . . . but I am not fond, you know, of going into churches for private prayer. We must go up into the chase in the evenings, and pray there with nothing but God's cloud temple between us and His heaven!'

Trying to steer a middle course between Tractarianism and the dullness he had seen in so many churches, he told Fanny: 'We will have no innovations in ceremony. But we will not let public worship become "dead bones".'

Meanwhile Fanny was preparing for the wedding itself, she informed her friend Mrs. Kennaway: 'I expect in January to be united to a Clergyman who has long been attached to me, & with whom I have the most entire union of *soul & heart*. Mr. C. Kingsley, a disciple of Maurice's, if he may be said to be a disciple in any school but that of Christ! At some future time I trust you will allow me to introduce him to you.'

'Shall I bring down *all* your letters to Cheddar?' Charles wrote from Chelsea, and then answered himself with the quiet satisfaction of his anticipation. 'I think so. My darling—we will classify them, & put the answers with them, & keep a box on purpose for them, & often look at them in after years—and at last leave them as an heirloom to our children—to be studied often. . . . How much they may learn from our struggles! How it may "attendrir" the heart of a son or a daughter, just struggling impatiently with opening life, to call him apart, and open that sacred box, & read him one of those letters, & say, My Son see how *I* felt, when in thy place and age!'

The wedding was held at last in Trinity Church, Bath, on 10th January 1844. Once the Grenfells knew the marriage for a certainty, they gave in with a good grace, however much they might disapprove of Kingsley. There is no detailed account of the wedding left, but it seems to have been a large one with several bridesmaids, of whom Charlotte Kingsley was one. Mr. Kingsley had been invited to perform the ceremony, but he suggested gracefully that the honour should go to Sidney Osborne, who had done so much to help make the marriage possible.

When the ceremony was finished, Fanny and Charles drove to Cheddar, and in the days that followed, they walked at Cheddar Cliffs, admiring the romantic chasms and exploring the caves in the rock. From there they went to Chelsea, to live at the Rectory until March, when Kingsley was to report to Pimperne.

Fanny stayed on in London with her sister Mrs. Warre when Charles left for Dorset. For a few weeks he lived at Blandford, and then accepted the invitation of the Osbornes to stay with them; from Durweston he walked through three miles of forest to Pimperne for his duties. Mr. Osborne (who became Lord Sidney in 1859 when his brother inherited the dukedom of Leeds) was nine years older than Kingsley. His real interests were medicine, surgery, and microscopic investigation, rather than religion or theology. Like Swift and Sydney Smith he was in the Church of England rather than of it. He had entered the clergy with neither inclination nor distaste, but simply to fulfil the duty of a younger son of a good family. Lord Godolphin's decision about his son's career had been communicated to young Osborne while out shooting, and he quietly and unenthusiastically accepted his lot without being put off his aim. As a Dorset parson he threw himself into a campaign against the stinking

Mrs. Kingsley, 1856

Kingsley, c. 1851

Mrs. Kingsley in middle age

Kingsley, c. 1860

hovels in which agricultural labourers were housed, and, of course, he irritated both the suspicious labourers themselves and the county families whose pocketbooks were threatened with costly repairs. He wrote a half-dozen books and a spate of pamphlets, but his most enduring fame came from a long series of letters in *The Times*, written over the course of forty years and signed with the familiar initials, S.G.O. In them he spoke his pugnacious mind on everything from Free Trade to cattle plague and cholera.

To Kingsley, fresh from the abuses of Eversley, it was meat and drink to find his own ideas spoken so vehemently by Osborne. Both knew a good horse, and they rode together, talking over the possibility of decent housing for the labourers, and their hatred of Tractarians and Tories. What was perhaps the most important thing was to find that a man could attack the privileged and still retain his place in the rigid Victorian social hierarchy. To Kingsley, worried about the good opinion of the Grenfells, it was heartening to hear Osborne talk, for he found him 'very clever and instructive. I am learning so much from him, and he seems to be doing great good. God grant I may be half as useful in my generation as he is!' A few weeks later he wrote Fanny that 'S.G.O. is deep in statistics and abuses. Heaven knows, when there are so many abuses, we ought to thank a man who will hunt them out. I will never believe that a man has a real love for the good and beautiful, except he attacks the evil and the disgusting the moment he sees it! . . . It is very easy to turn our eyes away from ugly sights, and so consider ourselves refined. The refined man to me is he who cannot rest in peace with a coal mine, or a factory, or a Dorsetshire peasant's house near him, in the state in which they are.'

The pluralist Rector of Pimperne, Dr. Wyndham, lived permanently away from the parish, for he held three other livings as well, and farmed all of them out to curates. He had asked Kingsley to take over Pimperne in April, when the present curate, Mr. Austen, was scheduled to leave, but before then trouble had arisen at Eversley, and Kingsley never did move into Pimperne Rectory.

Mr. Hawley had long been unsatisfactory, and one of the parishioners who disliked his activities most was Mr. Stapleton, his churchwarden. On 15th March 1844, Stapleton received a letter from the Bishop of Winchester, which said that 'a formal charge of a most revolting nature has been laid before me by the husband of the female whom you saw in the parish of Eversley, against the Rector of the Parish'. Meanwhile Hawley had fled the country with parish funds; whether he also took 'the female' is not clear. Bishop Sumner continued: 'It will be my duty to issue a monition at the proper time, calling him into residence, & in default of his appearing within the period prescribed by law, his benefice will be declared void.'

Sir John Cope's appearances in church had been few, so he had better reason to remember the long-legged Kingsley, whom he had often seen running after the hounds, than he had to think of the curate, Charles Smith, who had succeeded him. If Sir John could get a hunting parson, who would perhaps soak with him after dinner, so much the better. Mr. Stapleton expressed to Sir John the hope of the parishioners that Kingsley might receive the living. On May 7th, Sir John went to call in the neighbouring parish of Heckfield at the summer home of Sir Henry Dukinfield. Sir Henry's word carried some weight with Sir John, for he was not only a baronet, but also a prebend of Salisbury Cathedral and Vicar of the fashionable St. Martin's-in-the-Fields. After a long conversation, Sir John went to London to see the Bishop of Winchester to ask for Kingsley as Rector. Sumner had liked what he saw of Kingsley, and it was easy to get his consent.

Meanwhile Kingsley was in an agony of suspense and sent daily bulletins to Fanny. On May 11th he preached at Chelsea and at St. George's Hospital. The next day Sir John called him to Arthur's Club in St. James's Square, where he said that he could do no better for himself and the parish than to take Kingsley as Rector. The two agreed that Smith should have compensation for the extra work which he had been doing as priest-in-charge. When Kingsley was gone, Sir John wrote to Stapleton:

'When he was a Curate of the Parish I was most pleased with

his Doctrine as a Clergyman & his attendance to the poor. I can assure you that my sole object has been to appoint a really good and efficient person to do the duties of the Parish—and from the Character that you & Sir Henry Duckingfield give him I place great Confidence that I have appointed a Gentleman that will give Satisfaction to both the rich & poor of the Parish —He is willing to take part of the furniture &c. in the rectory . . . and for the present he wishes Mr Smith to continue as Curate.'

That week Kingsley was instituted into the living in London, and the following week-end a van moved the household possessions into the Rectory which he was to call home the rest of his life. There was much to do before it could be lived in comfortably, and there was little cash for the repairs because Hawley's disappearance deprived the new incumbent of the dilapidation money to which he was entitled. 'The commonest decencies of civilization' were lacking, and Kingsley was forced to replace 'by necessary conveniences the disgusting nuisances within the house itself'; a tumbling stack of chimneys had to be levelled and rebuilt, and all the rooms but one in the house had to have new grates and chimney-pieces. No structural repairs had been made within the memory of the oldest parishioner, and dry rot was everywhere in the supporting timbers. Even worse was the terrible dampness from the ponds surrounding the house. Plants were cut off by the cold of the fog from them a month earlier than in the rest of the parish. Water froze in the pitcher in the bedrooms with the lightest of frosts, books and clothes mildewed, and prints were spoiled on the wall; all this in spite of constant fires and stoves upstairs and down.

Worst of all, Fanny's health was too delicate for the constant damp, and when she moved into the Rectory she was already expecting her first child. Kingsley set to work with the help of the gardener to drain the ponds and divert the stream which fed them. Even so, heavy floods would break down the yard wall to stand a foot deep in the kitchen.

Inside the house Mrs. Kingsley did the best she could with the worthless furniture Hawley had left. When the worst of it was repaired, and when their wedding gifts were set out, the Rectory began to look habitable. It took a great deal of money, however, and they had far too little. Before he could touch a penny of the tithes for himself, Kingsley had to pay Hawley's bills, £60 in bishop's fees, the salary of the curate, Smith, and the unpaid Poors' Rates. Old Mr. Kingsley was unable to help, and Charles was forced at last to borrow £300 from his bankers. It was nearly ten years before the living became remunerative, although £600 a year was actually a handsome sum to Kingsley.

Parish conditions were dreadful after a decade of Hawley as Rector. The ale-houses were full on Sunday, drunkenness common, and immorality the general rule. The parish registers of the period show that almost all the marriages recorded for the labourers of the district were followed shortly by an entry in the registry of births. None of the labourers could read, and they had had no religious instruction.

The parish clerk was the local cobbler as well as schoolmaster, and he heard the lessons of the children in his shop, hammering away as the pupils shouted to make their recitations audible. As soon as possible Kingsley replaced him with a quick-witted local boy, Frederick Marshall, whom he sent to Winchester Training College to become a teacher. Kingsley himself held a night school for adults in the Rectory three times a week, and Sunday School met there every Sunday morning and afternoon. For the old and the feeble in outlying districts he established weekly cottage lectures. It was hard work, for Kingsley was finally forced to let Smith go and to manage his parish without the help of a curate, in a desperate attempt to cut expenses. Gradually he began a lending library, a mothers' club, and a loan fund. Of the last Mrs. Kingsley wrote years later to Sir John's successor:

'We were our own Disbursal Fund—& when we first settled at Eversley wages were very low, & our loans were principally to enable the Cottagers to buy the poor man's great friend, *a Pig*. We advanced the money for buying many a pig—simply asking for an I.O.U. in return till the pig was killed, & then we got our guinea or 15/ or whatever the small pig cost, back again with many thanks. We never lost any pig money except in one case where the wife of the owner of the pig was a drinking woman, who was very well able to pay. We seldom or never advanced money for *Rents*. The rents as you know are very low in Eversley & Bramshill, & my husband felt that if a man cd. not pay 1 s. or 1/6 a week, he certainly could not repay a loan. We sometimes lent for fitting out girls & boys for service, which was returned at the end of the 1st. years wages. But of course we were obliged to be particular as if people dont intend to pay, the loan system is only a fresh source of demoralization.'

Slowly the parishioners came to know and respect Kingsley, but his relations with his patron were less easy. Sir John had expected his Rector to get drunk with him, and he was furious when Kingsley, instead, asked for improvements in the cottages of the parish; finally Sir John drove him from Bramshill Park with a request never to return. We learn from Ludlow that Sir John's health was bad, and when he was more than usually ill, he would repent of having sent Kingsley away and, in abject fear of death, would call him back, making maudlin promises of amendment which he broke as soon as he recovered. To Mr. Stapleton Kingsley confessed sadly: 'I do hope that I may live to see things bettered in this parish: but it is most painful to feel certain that the only event which can bring about a decided change, must be the death of so kind a friend as Sir John is.' Increasingly the invalid Sir John became dependent upon his overseer, George Clacy, and Clacy's wife Sophia. To Kingsley the Clacys seemed the evil geniuses of Bramshill, hiding the true state of affairs from their employer: 'I am certain that Sir John would be furious at *some* things which go on—but the great evil—the Laissez-faire on his part, the complete serfage of half the inhabitants to Clacy's will & pleasure, no interference could prevent— & Madame alas! is a worse thief & tyrant, I am afraid, than Monsieur.'[1]

Some of Sir John's other employees were more to the Rector's liking. The stablemen admired him for his way with a horse or

[1] After Clacy's death in 1849, Mrs. Clacy moved to Bramshill to nurse Sir John; for her care she was rewarded in his will with the tenancy of a large house in the neighbourhood and £200 a year until her death in 1853.

a dog, and when Kingsley began instructions for the first confirmation after his induction, the stud groom from Bramshill brought a message from the whips and stablemen to say that they had all been confirmed once but would be happy to repeat the ceremony if it would please the Rector.

Kingsley's ear for music was receptive if untrained, and he soon set about reforming the liturgical music of the parish, replacing 'three or four poor men, with a trombone and two clarionets' by a choir trained in an adult evening class. (Eventually, years later, the church acquired a good small organ, and its first organist, at a salary of £20 per annum, was a young man who subsequently became Principal of the Royal College of Music, Sir Hugh Allen.) Repairs to the church building followed, and a new gallery was built to accommodate the growing congregations. Reluctantly, Sir John agreed to its construction if its cost would not exceed £100. The chancel was redecorated, the screen painted with Kingsley's own design of lilies, and a large neo-Perpendicular window installed over the altar.

On the little land attached to the Rectory he began small-scale farming with his gardener, experimenting with more scientific methods of crop-growing than were common. While he was at Pimperne, through Sidney Osborne he had met a neighbouring clergyman, Anthony Huxtable, Rector of Sutton Waldron, who practised and wrote of the use of chemical fertilizers. Kingsley followed him in dressing his land 'with lime and salt, and various other "chemico agricultural" applications', although the expense was so great that he found himself a 'Huxtable-without-profits'. Once the ponds around the house were drained, the garden bloomed under his hands. As the parish flourished Kingsley found scraps of time for his own outdoor amusement, hunting on borrowed horses or fishing in a roaring wind, but never shooting, for fear it would involve him in unpleasant relations with his poaching parishioners. He loved the life of the country and in inviting Cowley Powles for a week-end he wrote: 'We can keep you comfortably enough after the fashion of George Herbertian parsonages, and though alas! not quite as holy as Bemerton, are at least trying to be busy. . . .

You will find your old friend a little humanized, I hope, but still with a strong predilection for the *gaudia ruris*, thick shoes, and a wood axe.'

The first year at the Rectory was one of deep content for the Kingsleys; they were at last married, the parish work went well, and if they were worried by a shortage of money, at least they had the happiness of looking forward to Mrs. Kingsley's approaching confinement. Kingsley wrote Stapleton that Fanny assured everyone 'that I am the best of husbands, & that she attributes her present health & comfort entirely to the daily blessing of my fostering care. Joking apart, & thanking *God* for our happiness, she is very well indeed, & all anxiety seems to have settled down in both of us into calm expectation.' On 7th November 1844, only ten months after their marriage, she was safely delivered of Rose Georgiana. It was Mrs. Kingsley's last uneventful pregnancy; although three more children were born alive, she had several miscarriages, and for the rest of their lives together her husband's letters were full of concern over her health. She was never again strong, and the cost of nursing her, of sending her away for rest, and of taking her to London gynaecologists constantly depleted the Kingsleys' purse.

Rose (1845–1925) was the first of four children; the others were Maurice (1847–1910), Mary St. Leger (1852–1931), and Grenville Arthur (1858–98).

Rose was educated at home and trained as a nurse at Chester when her father was Canon there. She was as fond of travelling as her father was, and she went with him on his trip to the West Indies in the winter of 1869–70. A year later she returned to America, to visit her brother Maurice in Colorado and Mexico. When Kingsley went to the United States and Canada in 1874, she acted as his companion and secretary. Rose never married, but settled at Eversley, where she built the cottage known as The Keys. She had her share of the family writing ability and contributed to magazines in England and the United States, and published books on her travels in France, the history of the Order of St. John of Jerusalem, French art, and rose gardening.

The elder son, Maurice, was born in February 1847, and baptized by his father in April. He received the name of his godfather but resembled him only slightly in intellectual powers. He attended a school in Blackheath run by Cowley Powles and then went to Wellington College and on to his grandfather's college, Trinity Hall, Cambridge; he left Cambridge without his degree in order to study at the Royal Agricultural College in Cirencester. For some years he lived in South America, where he failed to find the fortune he expected; after a visit to England, he returned to the Americas as a railroad engineer and surveyor. In 1874 he married an American girl, Marie Yorke, daughter of a Philadelphia banker, at the American legation in Mexico City. He had two sons, Kingsley's only direct descendants.

Mary, the third of the children, had the family flair for drawing, but after studying at the Slade School she abandoned art as a career in 1876 when she married William Harrison, a former curate of her father, who became Rector of Clovelly. After some years of marriage with no children the Harrisons were separated in what seems to have been an amicable parting. In 1902 she became a Roman Catholic. Meanwhile she had begun a successful career as a novelist under the pseudonym of 'Lucas Malet', a combination of two family names which she assumed because she did not want to be accepted on the merits of her father and uncles. *The Wages of Sin* and *The History of Sir Richard Calmady* are best remembered of her novels, which in their day were thought to be shockingly outspoken. She adopted a cousin, Miss Gabrielle Vallings, also a novelist as well as an opera singer, and lived chiefly on the Continent. Her handsome face and figure and lively conversation made her well known in literary circles, where she counted Henry James and Romain Rolland as close friends. She died on a visit to England, a year after receiving a Civil List pension.

Grenville was a sickly child much spoiled by his parents. Neither of the sons had the drive and character of their sisters, but Maurice had a feckless charm which Grenville seems to have lacked. He was educated at Winton House, Winchester, where the headmaster was C. A. Johns, Kingsley's own tutor at Helston. After leaving Winton House, Grenville continued his studies at

Harrow for a little over a year. He went to Queensland to become a sheep farmer and died there when he was only forty.

Three months after Rose's birth Kingsley suffered the hardest blow death had yet dealt him. *The Times* of 24th February 1845 carried under its 'Naval Intelligence' heading the brief news that H.M.S. *Royalist* had been brought into Singapore the previous November by Second Master Parkinson, who had taken command of the mast-sprung, rotten-geared ship after her three officers had died. Gerald Kingsley had been second in command when she sailed; when the commander of the fever-ridden ship died in May the previous year, Gerald had commanded her until his own death in September in the Torres Straits, and by then half the crew had perished. Old Mr. Kingsley received the news by overhearing a gentleman say in the library where he was reading: 'Dreadful bad business this about the *Royalist*—every single officer on board her dead—those who did not die of fever were eaten by cannibals.' At the news the old man fainted dead away. For Charles the loss of his seafaring brother was an almost insupportable shock.

It was with relief that Kingsley turned to his first visit to Yorkshire on the occasion of being installed as Honorary Canon of the Collegiate Church of Middleham. Dean Wood, having two vacant stalls, offered them to Kingsley and to his own son, Peter Wood, a Magdalene friend of Kingsley's. There were no duties connected with the canonries, but the induction was excuse for a reunion and trip for the two friends. They were entertained with real Yorkshire hospitality and spent their spare time sightseeing and fishing, resolving to bring their wives there the following year. Kingsley kept his stall at Middleham until 1856, when Dean Wood died and the deanery was abolished.

In spite of his growing family and the constant demands of his parish, Kingsley felt isolated at Eversley, particularly after Mr. Stapleton moved his family to London and rented Warbrook. Kingsley was a born talker, despite his stammer, and, although the posts between Eversley and the Stapletons' London house constantly carried long chatty letters on politics and religion, he needed closer contact than the post provided. More and more he came to lean on his intimacy with two friends, Frederick Denison Maurice, whom he met in 1844, and his old companion Charles Mansfield. Instead of coming between them, as wives sometimes do with college friends, Fanny was soon as intimate as her husband with Mansfield. The same gentle tolerance and lack of shock which had first charmed Kingsley at Checkendon made her the complete confidante of Mansfield. And he had a great deal to tell her of what had happened to him since leaving Cambridge. The exact facts of his life can probably never be reconstructed, for aside from Mansfield himself, there were not more than three or four persons who knew his whole history, and out of love for him and sorrow at his early death they destroyed nearly all the records of what J. M. Ludlow called 'a strange, sad life, involved as it was in almost incredible moral complications, out of which he had only just shaken himself when death . . . overtook him'. However, in the mass of letters which Ludlow preserved, many of them from Kingsley, there are enough hints to piece together the general pattern.

After taking his Cambridge degree late because of illness, Mansfield had tried a medical career, but after 'walking' the hospitals for some time he began to feel that there was no certainty in medicine and so gave it up for chemistry, at which he showed great skill. But his Bohemian ways, his vegetarianism, his cloth shoes were too much for his family, who had long been shocked at his lack of social conformity. When he made it clear that he had lost his religious faith as well, they cut him off. There was worse to come. For some time he had been in love with a Miss Gardiner. Why he did not marry her is not clear; probably it was because she refused him. In hurt he turned to another woman, married her in haste and then discovered that she could never be faithful to him. At last she eloped to Australia with one of her lovers. Mansfield never divorced her, probably because of the cost and difficulty involved in such proceedings, and after a time he began keeping mistresses. One of them, a poorly educated woman whom he always referred to as 'the Magdalen' in his letters, seems to have been his mistress intermittently for several years. Another 'female person', his mistress about 1853, was a Mrs. Meredith, whom he described as 'the *step*mother of a volume of poems you may have met with'. It is fascinating to speculate whether she may have been Mary Ellen, daughter of Thomas Love Peacock and wife of George Meredith, whose *Poems* of 1851 received a critical boost from Kingsley. Mary Ellen left George Meredith in 1858 to elope with an artist, but whether Mansfield was one of her earlier infidelities will probably remain nothing but conjecture.

All this confusion Mansfield poured out to his friends at Eversley, as yet the only people whom he could trust with his troubles, telling them of his sense of guilt over the course of life which he could not break off, and his remorse at his loss of faith. Kingsley would call on him in London, and there, he wrote Fanny, he found Mansfield 'undergoing all the horrors of a deep, and as I do think, healthy baptism of fire—not only a conversion, but a discovery that God and the devil are living realities, fighting for his body and soul'.

Mansfield could be heart-breaking, but not so Frederick Denison Maurice, for to him, a man fourteen years his senior, Kingsley turned for comfort in the same way that Mansfield looked to Kingsley. Maurice had been a Unitarian, but while at Cambridge, where he was one of the 'Apostles', he had slowly been moving towards the orthodoxy of the Anglican Church, and after leaving Cambridge he had been baptized in the Church of England and eventually ordained. He was a man of frightening sensitivity to the criticism of others, but behind the shy mask of his delicately modelled face lay one of the most daring minds of the century. It is perhaps difficult a hundred years later to see how alien to most of his ecclesiastical contemporaries was his notion that the Church must minister to the social as well as the spiritual brotherhood of man, and that this might mean a concern with both the body and the soul. Probably easier to comprehend is the consternation caused by his refusal to believe in a literal hell where souls were damned for an eternity that was mere unending earthly time. To his contemporaries (except the simple of heart or those who troubled to pay close attention) he seemed more obscure than even Coleridge, from whom he had learned so much, but historical perspective makes it clear today that his was one of the greatest intellects of his day, and that a Church of England torn into factions by Darwinism and the Oxford Movement owes much of its continuing vitality to his mind.

In the summer of 1844 Maurice had rented Chelsea Rectory from Mr. Kingsley, and Charles first wrote to him there, asking advice on a 'philosophical method of reading the Scriptures' and on the very practical problem of 'the great prevalence of the Baptist form of dissent' in his parish. Maurice's reply was prompt, friendly, helpful to Kingsley, and characteristically long. A meeting followed, and from then on their intimacy grew rapidly. Maurice's brother-in-law, John Sterling, who had been the friend of Coleridge, John Stuart Mill, Wordsworth, and his biographer Carlyle, died that autumn, and Kingsley took his place in Maurice's affections. The relationship was always one of father-and-son or of master-and-pupil (Kingsley addressed Maurice as 'Master'), but it was a genuinely intimate one for all that. Ludlow, who probably knew their friendship better than anyone else, wrote that 'Mr. Maurice's affection for him was unspeakable; in fact, with all his kindness and friendly benevolence, I have often doubted whether he ever really loved anyone except Kingsley of all the young men who from this period began to gather around him'. Kingsley learned much of his theology from Maurice, and to the end of his life Maurice remained the one man who could control the headstrong younger man. When they met, Maurice was Professor of English Literature and History at King's College, London, and chaplain of Guy's Hospital; within two years he became Professor of Theology at King's and chaplain of Lincoln's Inn, where he attracted the admiration of a group of devout young lawyers who were to become the core of the Christian Socialist movement. When he became one of the founders of Queen's College, London, in 1848, he secured the appointment of Kingsley as Professor of English Literature, and later recommended him for a lectureship at King's College. Kingsley's love for his mentor was demonstrated when he named his first son after Maurice.

Since 1842, Kingsley had been working in a desultory fashion at his prose life of St. Elizabeth of Hungary ('the only healthy Popish saint'). Fanny's Puseyism had been the reason for his decision to write, for he intended to show the fatal 'Manichean' tendencies implicit in the Romish practice of celibacy. Originally the book was meant as a wedding present, but it was never finished, and nearly all that remains is a long, rambling preface, addressing Fanny on the dangers of celibacy and monasticism, and a series of pen-and-ink illustrations. It was into these drawings that Kingsley poured his real energy; they are not particularly skilful, but the passionate, perhaps overwrought, interest he displayed in the nude female figure is a clear example of the inextricable tangle which sex and religion formed in his mind. Certainly they are successful illustrations in one sense, for no one could be in doubt after seeing them what Kingsley's views on celibacy would be. A student of Freud would be interested in the significance of much of the detail surrounding the figures. Although the folio was never finished, the story and the ideas begun there lingered in Kingsley's mind.

To a friend who contemplated vows of celibacy he wrote: 'The highest state I define as that state through and in which man can know most of God, and work most for God: and this I assert to be the married state. He can know most of God, because it is through those family ties, and by those family names that God reveals Himself to man, and reveals man's relations to Him. Fully to understand the meaning of "a Father in Heaven" we must be fathers ourselves; to know how Christ loved the Church, we must have wives to love, and love them; else why has God used those relations as symbols of the highest mysteries which we (on the Romish theory) are the more saintly the less we experience of them?'

The contempt he felt for Roman Catholic converts found a convenient outlet in 1845. To Mr. Stapleton he wrote (in terms which explain part of his attitude nearly twenty years later when he became involved with the most famous convert of the century): 'How silently Newman has glided over *to his own place*! No doubt more will follow—which will do them little harm—& us much good.'

In 1846 he began reworking his history of St. Elizabeth, this time in blank-verse dramatic form, which bothered him considerably, for he confessed to a friend: 'I never wrote five hundred lines in my life before the "Saint's Tragedy" . . . I do not know half enough to be a poet in the nineteenth century.' By May 1847 the play was completed and dispatched to Maurice, whom Kingsley consulted about publication as well as asking the opinion of his Helston friends, Derwent Coleridge and Cowley Powles, and that of the neighbouring Rector of Strathfieldsaye, Gerald Wellesley. All four men agreed that it should be published. Maurice suggested several changes and finally, with some misgiving, fearing that his name would do the book's reputation no good, wrote a Preface to be printed with the play. Finding a publisher was not easy, although Maurice tried to help by circulating the play among his friends, including Tennyson. At last Kingsley could write home: 'St. Elizabeth is in the press, having been taken off my hands by the heroic magnanimity of Mr. J. Parker, West Strand, who, though a burnt child, does not dread the fire. No one else would have it.'

So began a long association between Kingsley and the Parkers; young John Parker, the partner of his father—also named John—had been at King's College with Kingsley. A tiny man of deceptively explosive temperament, he was fundamentally of a deeply kind nature. As he got to know Fanny and Charles better, he told them, like Mansfield before him, of his disappointment in love, of how he had been forced to give up marriage to the girl he loved so that he might provide for his destitute widowed sister and her small children. Besides publishing *The Saint's Tragedy*, the Parkers offered to buy articles from Kingsley for *Fraser's Magazine*, of which they were the publishers.

The Saint's Tragedy appeared in January 1848. Maurice's Preface ascribed to Kingsley the solid anti-didactic artistic doctrine that drama 'should not aim at the inculcation of any definite maxim; the moral of it lies in the action and the character. It must be drawn out of them by the heart and experience of the reader, not forced upon him by the author.' For most readers the failure of the play would lie in the inability of Kingsley to keep the creative distance implied in Maurice's words. In his Introduction Kingsley set forth his own more didactic purpose:

'If, however, this book shall cause one Englishman honestly to ask himself, "I, as a Protestant, have been accustomed to assert the purity and dignity of the offices of husband, wife, and parent. Have I ever examined the grounds of my own assertion?" ... If, again, it shall deter one young man from the example of those miserable dilettanti, who in books and sermons are whimpering meagre second-hand praises of celibacy. ... If, lastly, it shall awaken one pious Protestant to recognize, in some, at least, of the Saints of the Middle Age ... *Protestants*, not the less deep ... because utterly unconscious ... then also will my little book indeed have done its work.' As one could guess from this Introduction, the characters too often speak with the voice of Kingsley.

St. Elizabeth undergoes a change from the familiar miraculous figure with a basket of roses to a somewhat Victorian young wife, 'a type of two great mental struggles of the Middle Age; first, of that between Scriptural or unconscious, and Popish or conscious, purity: in a word, between innocence and prudery; next, of the struggle between healthy human affection, and the Manichean contempt with which a celibate clergy would have all men regard the names of husband, wife, and parent'. Her struggles are worked out in the conflict which she feels to be present between her love of God and her love of husband, children, and fellow-men. One by one, by death and renunciation, the normal human outlets of her affection are cut away from her until at last she dies a pauper's death, worn out by self-denial and self-chastisement. Unfortunately, Elizabeth's mind and its conflicts are scarcely interesting enough to hold the reader; like Browning with Pompilia or Thackeray with Amelia Sedley, Kingsley found that a passive, suffering, innocent woman is difficult to make dramatic or even credible. Instead, the centre of the narrative and psychological interest shifts to the monk Conrad of Morpurg, the Pope's commissioner for the suppression of heresy, who has determined to make a martyr and saint of the Landgravine Elizabeth, whose spiritual director he is. Kingsley gives Conrad just enough touches of human conflict, of lust, of faint remorse to make him a more fully three-dimensional figure than the saint herself; perhaps our sympathy for him is even stirred by the obvious distaste which Kingsley shows for his own creation, and certainly Conrad is the only character who betrays the presence of a real mind. Lewis, Elizabeth's mild husband, is a conventional young lover who dies in the Crusades; Elizabeth's protector from Conrad, the priest-baiter Walter, representing the 'healthy animalism' of the Teutonic mind, has his bluff beginnings in Kent, Enobarbus, and Mercutio. Indeed, the blank verse, rustic clowns, the coarse nurse and other half-familiar characters, a mad scene, self-conscious archaisms, and even the direct quotations from Shakespeare, all show the associations which made John Ludlow think the play contained 'the promise of a Christian Shakespeare' and why Baron Bunsen, the Prussian ambassador, advised Kingsley to continue Shakespeare's historical plays, 'to place by the side of that sublime dramatic series from King John to Henry VIII, another series from Edward VI to the landing of William of Orange'. As a first attempt the drama is surprisingly successful, but the Shakespearian comparison is, of course, nonsensical.

It is apparent that Kingsley had some trouble finding a consistent tone for the language in the play; there is a neo-Shakespearian alternation between verse and prose, and a more disturbing shift between standard Victorian English and the standard Victorian version of medieval English, an uneasy flirting with 'anon' and 'opine'. The five hundred lines of poetry he claimed as his preparation for the play were hardly enough; the accent of the verse is uncertain, the language frequently flat. Yet there are metaphorical flashes that show his real poetic promise:

Our life's floor
Is laid upon eternity; no crack in it
But shows the underlying heaven. (III, ii)

or

Is that angel-world
A gaudy window, which we paint ourselves
To hide the dead void night beyond? (IV, i)

Not surprisingly, the reviews were fairly well divided in their opinion of the drama, according to how well they agreed with its theology, but it could hardly be claimed as a sensation anywhere save in Oxford, where Kingsley found himself lionized in March when he went to visit Cowley Powles at Exeter College. His admirers were chiefly those grouped around Jowett, Stanley, and Clough, in opposition to the high church movement. The very roughnesses of writing recommended themselves to the undergraduates for their manliness, a quality of Kingsley's writing which later was mockingly called 'Muscular Christianity'.

One of the opinions of the play which was ultimately to be most important to Kingsley was that of a young Scot named Daniel Macmillan, who first heard of him through *The Saint's Tragedy*. Macmillan, with whose publishing firm Kingsley was later to become closely associated, wrote a friend:

'I know very few books of note lately published. There is a small book called *The Saint's Tragedy*, by a Mr. Kingsley, which gives a most living picture of the Middle Ages. You would be greatly pleased with it. He has also advertised a volume of Sermons, which I have no doubt will be good. He seems to me a man of great mark, and worth your notice.'

The Saint's Tragedy was the only drama that Kingsley ever completed, although Tom Taylor asked him in 1852 to collaborate on a comedy, with Kingsley contributing dialogue and Taylor helping with practical knowledge of the theatre. Nothing came of that scheme, nor does Kingsley seem ever to have finished the drama of which he wrote Mansfield in South America, several months after Taylor's offer:

'Please find out for *me* whether any remains are to be seen of Sebastian Cabot's fort or tower, about 30 leagues up from Buenos Ayres, at the mouth of the Rio Terceiro which comes out of the Mountains of Tucuman into the Paraguay, & please let me know what you can about the scenery, vegetation, animals, river-beasts, fishes, &c. of that lower part of the *Paraguay*: for I have in *petto* a tragedy about "Cabot's Tower" which I may make a fine thing of, if I can only get a clear sight of the Entourage, so as to make a grand semi-tropic back-ground and atmosphere, to glorify the whole. . . . I feel more and more that if we wish to put new blood into the exhausted veins of English poetry, it is to foreign countries we must go; not I mean to foreign schools of poetry, like the Germanizers but to foreign lands—because strictly speaking, no land is foreign to the world-searching Englishman, & Paraguay is as near and homelike to him now, as Italy was to Chaucer, even to Shakespeare.'

By the time the play was in proof, Kingsley was already working on his first article for *Fraser's*, following the same direction as *The Saint's Tragedy* but casting off the difficulties of verse and character. 'Why Should We Fear the Romish Priests?' helped work off some of his hatred of Rome. His tone is contemptuous, his misunderstanding of the position of the Pope and hierarchy great. At some points the Roman clergy seems diabolically clever, elsewhere contemptibly stupid, whichever suits Kingsley better at the moment. His faith, he says, is in the common-sense of the Roman laity, although even they may 'be really, as some say, inferior in intellectual development to the average Protestants of the same rank'. The chief interest in the article is its attitude to Newman, an attitude Kingsley accepted as so patently true as to need no examination; his attack on Newman in 1864 showed that he had never thought deeply about the matter but had merely been busy reinforcing the prejudices already fully formed in 1848:

'Among [the German] converts it cannot name a single first-rate man. . . . So it is with our own late conversions. Have we lost a single *second*-rate man even? One, indeed, we have lost, *first*-rate in *talents*, at least; but has not he by his later writings given the very strongest proof, that to become a Romish priest is to lose, *ipso facto*, whatever moral or intellectual life he might previously have had? . . . Above all, in all their authors, converts or indigenous, is there not the same fearful *want of straightforward truth*, that "*Jesuitry*", which the mob may dread as a subtle poison, but which the philosopher considers as the deepest and surest system of moribund weakness?'

The article probably convinced no one who was not already on Kingsley's side, but it gave him an agreeable sense of accomplishment. Here was an opportunity to speak to a much wider audience than his own parish flock, to become a part of the literary world of London, to be liberated from the narrow confines of strict theology in his preaching, and even to add to his inadequate income. One of the most energetic propagandists of the century came into being.

CHAPTER V

Christian Socialism

The sun rose on London on the morning of Monday, 10th April 1848, in all the brightness of an English spring, and, for once, most of the Queen's subjects were sorry to see the fine weather, for they had been hoping that the soaking rain of the day before would continue and drown out the giant meeting of Chartists set for that morning at Kennington Common. Feargus O'Connor, a fire-breathing Irish radical M.P., was to preside over the gathering, and England was afraid of what might result. O'Connor's associate, Bronterre O'Brien, had withdrawn from the movement the day before, fearing that O'Connor, who was already showing signs of incipient insanity, might so stir up his followers that some of them would carry out their threats to use gun and torch to enforce their demands.

The People's Charter, with its famous 'six points' of electoral reform, seems tame enough today when five of the points have long since become law, but to England in 1848 it looked like the thin edge of the revolution which was spreading over the Continent. It was difficult for an Englishman to believe that peaceful London might become the scene of an armed revolution, as the government feared, but occasionally in the past, meetings of rural Chartists had left the burning hay-ricks of prosperous farmers as blazing symbols of their determination, and only the month before, a small gathering at Kennington had been followed by the smashing and looting of a Camberwell shop by a crew of Chartist rowdies. To be sure, fifteen of the hoodlums had received prompt prison sentences, but 150,000 demonstrators were expected on this sunny April morning, and after the meeting they intended to march in force to Westminster to present the Charter to Parliament. What would happen if they were turned back was not clear.

The government had already done what it could to forestall trouble. The Home Secretary, Sir George Grey, announced in the House of Commons the government's policy of considering the procession illegal and dangerous to the public peace, and he called on all 'well-disposed persons' to help keep that peace. The aged Duke of Wellington was put in charge of the military forces in the city, which included regiments brought from all over the country as well as a large number of sailors and marines. The merchant marines, however, were to be kept under close watch by the Thames police, for they were suspected of sympathy with the Chartists. The entire police force was mustered, and 150,000 of the 'well-disposed' volunteered their services as special constables; this was approximately equal to the number of demonstrators expected. All in all, there were nearly 200,000 defenders of the peace ready that morning. The mounted police were armed with broadswords and pistols and there was at least one order for 30,000 staves to arm the volunteers.

Heavy gun-batteries had been brought up from Woolwich and set up to guard strategic points in the city. The public buildings were fortified with material that varied all the way from the cannons poked through the loopholes in the logs and sandbags barricading the Bank of England to the bound copies of *The Times* with which clerks blocked the windows of the Foreign Office. Several hundred police guarded each of the bridges across the Thames, and beneath them stood boats with steam up, ready to transport police and troops to trouble spots. The Queen had already been taken to safety on the Isle of Wight and her valuables removed from the Palace; even her stables were cleared of horses and the royal carriages.

One of the few calm men in London was a young barrister named John Malcolm Ludlow, a friend of Maurice's, who had lived for many years in France. As a nine-year-old boy, he had been through the revolution of 1830 in Paris, and only a few weeks before he had been back there on the eve of another revolution. Ludlow refused to be alarmed, for the streets of London seemed to him to show no signs of revolution, and he could not feel that insurrections came off so precisely by the calendar. That morning in suburban Chelsea he had been amused at the sight of the special constable sent to guard the quiet street before his house, a tiny, lame, earnest man whom one revolutionary of normal size could easily have held in the air to let dangle. Ludlow and his mother, who lived with him, laughed at the constable, but he continued to limp up and down the pavement with an air of intense and comic patriotic self-importance. Positive that there would be no trouble, Ludlow walked to work as usual, intending to keep normal hours in his chambers in Chancery Lane. The streets through which he went were abnormally quiet, there were almost no vehicles, all public conveyance had been stopped. Many of the shops were closed, their shutters reinforced, and silent, well-behaved knots of people gathered in the streets, most of them merely curious, although here and there a Chartist working man hurried off to one of the numerous meeting-places in the city from which the demonstrators were to march to Kennington.

If Ludlow was interested in continuing the normal routine of life that Monday, his clients were not, for none came to see him. But in the middle of the morning his clerk announced Mr. Kingsley, a country clergyman from Hampshire. As Ludlow's tall young visitor came in, he stuttered out something about 'M-M-Maurice' and presented a note to the barrister.

John Parker had been spending the week-end at Eversley, and he was nervous about his office in the Strand. As he left, he said, half in joke, to Mrs. Kingsley that she might expect to hear of his shop being broken into and himself taken around the corner and thrown into the fountains of Trafalgar Square. Although he knew that his cloth disqualified him as a constable, Kingsley accompanied Parker to London, both to keep the peace in any way he could and to see that his parents in Chelsea were safe. He and Parker went to be sure that the publishing shop was undisturbed and then walked to Queen's Square to consult Maurice, who was kept indoors by a cold. Parker went back to the shop, but Kingsley went off to Ludlow with a note from Maurice:

'Meantime (as I am confined to the house by a cough myself) will you let me introduce you to my friend Mr. Kingsley. He is deeply in earnest & seems to be possessed with the idea of doing something by handbills. I think there is hope in this: will you talk with him about it.'

Years later Ludlow wrote of his initial impression of Kingsley as 'thin and gaunt, lanthorn-jawed, I might say; the large mouth indicative of great resolution, but at the same time singularly mobile. A single glance at him showed that you had no ordinary man before you'. In his turn, Kingsley saw before him a small and delicately built man two years his junior. Ludlow's finely shaped head had a noble breadth of brow, and his intelligent brown eyes were singularly bright, but the set of his mouth showed a certain lack of humour; it was the mouth of a man who does his duty however much it may hurt others.

Kingsley waited until Ludlow had finished the note, then told him that he had come to London to help in any way possible to prevent a collision between the Chartists and the troops. The poor fellows meant well, however misguided they were; it would be horrible if there were bloodshed. He was going to Kennington Common to see what one man could do; would Ludlow go too? Ludlow replied that he would go, of course, but he did not think anything would happen, and if it did, he was afraid they would be too late to stop it. He turned his chambers over to the clerk for the rest of the day and the pair set out for Kennington in the rain which had finally begun. By the time they came to Waterloo Bridge, they saw the Chartists streaming back from the disbanded meeting. On questioning one of them, Kingsley found that O'Connor had made a wildly emotional speech, blessing the demonstrators, calling them his children, saying that he had been without sleep for six days, that his breast was like a coal of fire, that his physician had forbidden him to speak, but that he was willing to neglect his own health, even willing to die, for the cause. Rather anti-climactically he had urged that there be no procession, no violence, and that he be allowed to take the Charter peacefully to the Houses of Parliament with the other members of the executive committee. Then he and the rest of the committee got into three hired hacks, had the Charter strapped to the carriage-tops in three ponderous bales, and set calmly off to deliver it as the crowd disbanded in the slow rain.

When the House's Committee on Petitions had the Charter weighed and counted by thirteen law-stationers' clerks, who worked ceaselessly for seventeen hours, it was found that instead of weighing five tons and being signed by six million petitioners, the Charter actually weighed only a little over five hundredweight and had fewer than two million signatures, among which the committee found such unlikely names as 'Pug Nose', 'No Cheese', 'Duke of Wellington', 'Prince Consort', and even 'Victoria Rex'. These last three eminent signers had been so enthusiastic as to repeat their signatures several times. And there were 'others included, which [the Committee would] not hazard offending the House and the dignity and decency of their own proceedings by reporting. . . . Language the most disgusting pervaded the whole petition; there were words in it which the vilest strumpet in the street would blush to name.' On one page the committee found the words: 'We could not get paid for any more today.'

As Kingsley and Ludlow turned away from Waterloo Bridge, they met Charles Mansfield and his brother Robert, who had volunteered as 'specials' with no results save getting hot, dusty and tired. After dropping a note to Fanny to let her know that London was safe and that he would be with his parents in Chelsea that night, Kingsley set off with Ludlow to tell Maurice the good news.

As they went through the streets to Bloomsbury, they saw the shopkeepers taking down their shutters and the life of the city slowly returning to normal, and as they walked, they talked of what lay behind the day's happenings. Kingsley was delighted to find his views confirmed by a man of such obvious intelligence, and Ludlow found Kingsley's 'conversation fascinating by its originality; keen observation, strong sense, imaginative power, deep feeling, righteous indignation, broad humour, succeeding each other without giving the least sense of incongruity or jar to one's feelings. His stutter, which he felt most painfully himself as a "thorn in the flesh" in fact only added a raciness to his talk as one waited for what quaint saying was going to pour out, as it always did at full speed, the stutter once conquered.'

On one thing the two men found themselves in particularly strong agreement: admiration for the wisdom of the Chartists in banding together to present their views. True, the meeting had been a failure, but the state of England that day was proof that thousands of men, even common labourers, could make themselves heard as a group when individuals went unheeded. The Charter was a political matter, but the method was applicable to social and religious problems, if only the fruits of working together might be mutual help rather than an upset of organized society. Ludlow talked of how he had watched the rise in France of the new creed of socialism; of working together, instead of working against one another, of possessing together instead of possessing exclusively for one's self. It was worth notice, too, said Ludlow, that French socialism was not necessarily atheistic; from Fourier, child of the first French Revolution through St. Simon, Proudhon, Louis Blanc, and Leroux, however unorthodox might be their belief, the leaders had held to the necessity of faith in God. As the people became more powerful there was more respect for things religious. When Ludlow was a boy in Paris in the revolution of 1830, there was great hostility to the Church; during the past month or two when he had been once more in Paris at the beginning of the revolution which had unthroned Louis Philippe, he had seen priests, instead of putting on lay dress, pass in their clerical costumes unmolested through the streets, and Sisters of Charity met with nothing but affectionate sympathy. French tolerance of Roman Catholic priests, to be sure, had little to do with the respect honest Englishmen felt for their Church, Kingsley thought, but it was clear that socialism needed to be entirely

Christianized or it might become an alternative to Christianity and shake the Church to its foundations. The Church needed to work with socialism, not against it, for no man could serve two antagonistic masters; if one had to go, it might prove to be Christianity.

The two concurred in wholehearted delight; on this, their first meeting, they were in complete agreement for perhaps the last time in their lives. Years later Ludlow wrote: 'Kingsley, I must own, was very prompt in flinging himself into intimacy with anyone whom he found congenial to his many-sided nature. He was essentially an artist, and was fascinated for the time by any new type that struck him. He was thus apt to overvalue a newly made friend, as I am afraid for a time he overvalued me.'

The friendship was made in haste and repented at leisure; another fifteen years of slowly dissolving mutual regard were to pass before the break was complete. The seeds of the eventual split were sown early; only three days after their meeting, Maurice had to write to Ludlow explaining away a misunderstanding with Kingsley, which Maurice assured him came from Kingsley's 'sense of inferiority'.

That afternoon Maurice and Ludlow agreed with Kingsley that the time for action had come. Their first step would be to make placards, and once that was done they could make further plans.

Events moved swiftly for the next few days. Kingsley's return to Eversley was postponed, and the following day, Tuesday, he and Ludlow sat up until four in the morning writing out placards, which were posted on Wednesday. Kingsley's placard was addressed to 'Workmen of England!' and signed 'A Working Parson'; in it he assured the workmen that the clergy were aware of the miserable conditions in which the poor lived, but that no Charter could free one if he were the slave of 'one's own stomach, one's own pocket, one's own temper'. He concluded with the prophecy that a nobler day was dawning for English workmen, a day of freedom, science and industry.

For three years Kingsley had been chafing for a magazine which would express the liberal ideas of young men in the

Church and government, one which would not be under the domination of his conservative elders. As early as 1845 he and Cowley Powles had been working on the idea, but James Anthony Froude and Maurice, who were asked for help, could not join them, and the idea had flickered out.

On Tuesday afternoon Kingsley went to a meeting at Parkers' and took the lead in planning a penny weekly addressed to the working classes. Maurice and Ludlow were to be joint editors. Maurice's own plan for a series of tracts, modelled on Newman's *Tracts for the Times*, was temporarily shelved, but the group were to continue writing independently, as well as for the weekly, the name of which was changed from *The People's Friend* to *Politics for the People*. It was easy to find a publisher, for the elder Parker was much taken with their ideas (he had been moved to tears by Kingsley's placard); besides that, one of his former assistants, Charles Knight, was now publishing a journal called *Voice of the People*, and the Parkers, who resented Knight's defection from their firm, were anxious to offer him competition.

After a hurried visit to the Principal of King's College, Dr. Jelf, who said that he was anxious for Kingsley to get the lectureship for which Maurice had recommended him, Kingsley went back to Eversley, much exhausted, to prepare a sermon on Chartism for his parish the following Sunday. The week after Easter Ludlow came to spend three days at Eversley to talk over plans for the paper and to get to know Mansfield, who was interested in helping with their work. Mrs. Kingsley was at first frightened by Ludlow's austere manner, but when she saw how much interested he was in Mansfield, she took him aside to tell him all she knew of Charles's story. By the end of their stay Ludlow and Mansfield were friends, and Mansfield was committed to help with the periodical as soon as Ludlow had introduced him to Maurice. There was probably a little flicker of jealousy on Kingsley's part as he saw how easily his two friends got on together; perhaps he would have understood more easily if he had known that part of Ludlow's interest in Mansfield grew out of his own affairs of the heart. For Ludlow was another of the Kingsleys' friends who was hopelessly in love and could not afford to marry, but his own reticence kept him from talking of his cousin, Miss Maria Forbes (whom, after a long and silent courtship, he eventually did marry). Ludlow also saw the periodical and the work connected with it as an opportunity to consolidate the belief in Christianity which was slowly returning to Mansfield.

There were sixteen pages in the first number of *Politics for the People*, which appeared on May 6th. The name was intended to convey the founders' idea of a paper addressed to no particular class or people. In reality, they were somewhat embarrassed that, as yet, they knew almost none of the working classes for whose help they had banded together, and to whom *Politics* was really directed, in spite of its attempted catholicity. All the founders were distinctly middle or upper class, and for a time most of those who joined them were of the same sort. Kingsley brought Frank Penrose into the group, and Cuthbert Ellison, the 'swell' of the movement, had been at Cambridge with them for a time. He was the companion of dukes, a magnificently fastidious dresser, and was said by Ludlow to have been the original of Thackeray's Arthur Pendennis, but he plunged into the work and even interested Thackeray, with whom he shared barristers' chambers in the Temple. Although the original members were inclined to sniff a bit at his plum-coloured cravats, Ellison's eagerness and his lovable nature soon made them forget that they thought him too fine a gentleman.

Another helper for whose interest Kingsley was responsible was his wife's brother-in-law, the formidable 'S.G.O.', who contributed a pair of articles on politics written from the countryman's viewpoint, and who gave them frequent advice on lively journalism.

Mansfield brought with him Charles Walsh, the cheerful doctor with whom he shared apartments in Half Moon Street. Ludlow thought Walsh the sweetest-tempered man he had ever come across, and his conciliatory powers were frequently needed in the curious group of strong-minded individualists among whom he found himself. Walsh's interest in sanitation and preventive medicine endeared him to Kingsley. Another of Mansfield's 'finds' was his own cousin Archie Campbell, a native Scot who, like Mansfield, was a vegetarian, and, unlike him, was a strong advocate of 'fonetic' spelling.

Still another who joined them early was Ludlow's friend, Frederick J. Furnivall, whose orthodox Christianity had not yet been exchanged for the bad-mannered agnosticism of his later life.

Others attached themselves to the group, usually out of regard for Maurice; among them were the Parkers, Archdeacon Hare, Viscount Goderich (later Marquess of Ripon), A. H. Clough, the Macmillan brothers Daniel and Alexander, Arthur P. Stanley, Archbishop Whately, and John Conington, to mention only a few of the most prominent. Not all of them contributed to *Politics*, but they gave freely of their time in planning and supporting the movement.

But the backbone of the whole group was made up of the four friends, Maurice, Kingsley, Ludlow, and Mansfield. Gradually, as they worked together, their relative positions were clarified. Maurice, always referred to as 'The Prophet' or 'The Master' by the younger men, was undisputed head of the group but hardly their leader. His almost morbid fear of publicity and notoriety made him cautious, slow in his decisions, but when they were once made, they were unquestioningly obeyed by his headstrong but worshipping friends. In later years, as they wrote of the history of the Christian Socialist movement, the worst the younger men could say of such people as Ruskin or Furnivall was that they had questioned Maurice's authority.

The real 'brains' of the group was Ludlow. He was as shy of being known as Maurice himself and always hated public lecturing, but he had less of 'The Prophet's' caution. Of the whole group he was the only one who had actually seen socialism at work, and he was probably the only one who had a clear idea of what the term meant. Furnivall called him 'the true mainspring of our Christian Socialist movement', but his genius was for behind-the-scenes work, and his talent for polemical writing was usually concealed by the *nom-de-plume* of 'John Townsend'. He had a breadth of knowledge greater than that of any of his friends except Maurice, and he was modest about his intelligence, but tact never came easily to him.

Mansfield wrote comparatively little for *Politics* and its successors, and then usually on his favourite subjects, vegetarianism and ornithology (his *nom-de-plume* was 'Will Willow-Wren'), but he was invaluable in drawing new recruits to the group and in lubricating the difficulties which arose among his fellows.

From Eversley Kingsley bombarded his friends with letters filled with comfort and advice, suggestions and contributions for *Politics*. When he came to London he charged in on Ludlow and Maurice, exploding with all the enthusiasms which he had been unable to express by letter. The fire he breathed was exhilarating, but it seemed a bit scorching to more level-headed, perhaps less open-hearted, friends like Ludlow. To one of his reprimands Kingsley answered more meekly than was customary: 'I quite feel what you say about the difference between [Maurice] & me being the difference between bold thoughts & bold words. But how is one to get bold thoughts unless God gives us them? & how can I expect him to give them, till I can use them?'

Although none of the contributors was paid and Parker took on part of the risk of publication, *Politics for the People* never had a circulation of more than two thousand, and that was not enough to pay its limited costs; Parker had begun worrying, too, about the damage to his business which association with the journal caused, and after three months it had to cease publication. Kingsley had contributed three pieces on the National Gallery and the British Museum, two sets of letters addressed to the Chartists and to the landlords, and four poems. Something of his fire came through the writings, so that they were easily recognizable over the signature of 'Parson Lot', and his contributions were soon singled out for notice as particularly inflammatory or heart-warming, according to the sympathies of the reader. Because of his flamboyant style and the notoriety he attracted, he was generally regarded as the centre of the Christian Socialist movement, to the neglect of the real leaders, Maurice and Ludlow. Maurice's brother-in-law, Julius Hare, found Kingsley's contributions 'conceited'; more serious was the attitude of Dr. Jelf and the authorities of King's College in deliberately rejecting him for the lectureship for which he had been recommended, not preferring another but simply saying that Kingsley would not do. Maurice correctly interpreted their action as an admonition to himself to watch his company and to avoid such revolutionaries as his young friend.

Ludlow, who heard the news of the rejection first, commiserated with Kingsley: 'Never you mind. They only reject you because you are too good for them. The day will come when you will see two-thirds of those same dons at your feet.'

Kingsley consoled himself with the reflection that even Jelf's action was some indication that *Politics* had been read, and turned to other writing to forget his troubles. When *Politics* finally stopped, he wrote Ludlow: 'I am afraid my utterances have had a great deal to do with the Politics' unpopularity—I have got worse-handled than any of you, by both poor & rich. There is one comfort, that length of ears is in the donkey species always compensated by toughness of hide. . . . This is a puling quill-driving soft-handed age. . . . The world . . . would have gelded Apollo before it let him attack the Python— & put him on a pinafore & goloshes, & kept him waiting a year to get his *warrant* made out.'

The last of those most closely connected with Christian Socialism to join the group was Thomas Hughes, who in the late summer of 1848 volunteered his services to Maurice, whom he had heard preach at Lincoln's Inn, where Hughes kept his chambers as a barrister. At the time Hughes was only twenty-five, a former Rugbeian and a graduate of Oxford, where, as a member of Oriel, he had been a close friend of Arnold and Clough, and where he had a great cricketing reputation. His athletic frame, his frank blue eyes, his open and friendly air, and his gay sense of humour all seemed to belong more to his background as son of a country squire than to the man of 'genuine though unobtrusive seriousness' which he actually was. The story is well known of how Maurice brought Hughes to meet Mansfield and Ludlow at the latter's dinner-table. The project occupying their minds at the time was the establishment of a night school in Little Ormond Yard, Bloomsbury, a yard so rough that the parish clergyman could not enter without being insulted; no policeman would venture in at night alone. When his name was suggested, Furnivall, who knew Hughes slightly, said: 'Oh, he won't do. A very good man for a cricket match, or as umpire at football, but no good for teaching.' By the end of the dinner, Mansfield and Ludlow looked at each other and agreed: 'He'll do.' Hughes taught well and was invaluable in getting the confidence of the working men by his athletic ability, particularly by the dexterity of his fists, which could be used either for sport or for thoroughly convincing the rougher men of the virtues of peace. He was intelligent but entirely unintellectual, and his common sense frequently served as a leavening agent when Ludlow or Kingsley embarked on a hare-brained scheme. His nature was so completely lovable that each of the Christian Socialists was sure that he was Hughes's best friend. His intimacy with Kingsley was slow in growing because of the distance between London and Eversley, but their deep love of fishing and hunting drew them together. Some of the most delightful pieces Kingsley ever wrote are the letters on fishing he sent Hughes. Probably Kingsley found him a relief from Ludlow, who sometimes seemed overly intellectual and serious, and prickly in discussion. Not unnaturally, Fanny Kingsley loved both Hughes and his own wife, Fanny. Many of the Christian Socialists were considerably less presentable than Hughes: Ludlow had a number of disturbingly un-English mannerisms, and even Fanny's dear Charles Mansfield was apt to show up in cloth shoes and the beard which he wanted the other Christian Socialists to adopt as their distinguishing mark (he wrote in exasperation to Ludlow that 'Walsh, Penrose, & Hughes are anti-beard men, and think shaving a divine ordinance—second only to circumcision'). Hughes, however, was well educated and the son of a 'county' family; Fanny was no snob, but she knew that her family looked askance at some of her husband's queer friends.

Sir Norman Moore, who knew all of them, wrote of the four

F. D. Maurice

Thomas Hughes

Charles Mansfield

J. M. Ludlow

most closely connected in the popular mind with Christian Socialism: 'Of the three Ludlow seemed to me the gravest, Maurice equally serious but less clear, Kingsley the least profound. Ludlow left me with a clear impression of the whole group; Maurice seemed fit to be his colleague; they seemed to have mysteries and arcana which Kingsley held less seriously. In the Christian world I would have compared Ludlow and Maurice to holy abbots, Kingsley to an itinerant preaching friar, and Hughes to a lay-brother of some attainments.'

The foremost religious ancestor of Christian Socialism was Samuel Taylor Coleridge, whose work *On the Constitution of Church and State*, 1830, with its assumption of the social ethic implicit in Christianity, had influenced Maurice's thinking when he was studying at Oxford, where he had gone after leaving Cambridge. To Maurice, Ludlow, and Kingsley, their own theological position, roughly that of what came to be known as the Broad Church movement, seemed the only one capable of carrying out Coleridge's ideas. On one side of them were the Evangelicals, both Anglican and non-conformist, who looked forward to a future state of grace which made unimportant the social abuses of this world; on the other side were the Tractarians, who were so absorbed in re-establishing their Patristic inheritance that they seemed to have little time for the condition of their fellow men.

In their social thinking the Christian Socialists were descended from the French socialists and from Robert Owen, the free-thinking Northern manufacturer who schemed for communistic 'villages of unity and co-operation'.

Obviously, the two strains, religious and social, had to be adapted if they were to be contained in one ethic. The problem was to socialize Christianity and to Christianize socialism. As a clergyman Kingsley felt the major part of his own duty was to promote the social consciousness of the Church.

By the time the King's College authorities rejected him, Kingsley already had a big undertaking begun, his first novel, drawn from his experiences in Eversley. Sir John Cope's laxity as a landlord had been a nagging worry to him. As Sir John became older and more infirm, his estates were increasingly mismanaged. All around him the Rector saw scenes of country misery nearly as acute as those he knew from the city. The heir to the baronetcy was William Cope, a Minor Canon at Westminster Abbey and a distant cousin of Sir John, descended from the first baronet; there is a family story that neither was aware of the relationship until Kingsley commented on their name and set them to tracing their common ancestry. There was little love between the cousins, and Sir John seems to have regretted ever finding a successor to keep the title from lapsing. William Cope was well educated, musical, and devout; although he was an extreme high churchman, Kingsley looked forward to his eventual tenancy of Bramshill with the hope of a new life for the poor labourers of the parish.

All over England in 1848 the condition of the country poor was appalling. The crop failures which helped produce the great Irish famine of 1846–7 left many of the underprivileged dangerously near the starvation point. The fault, Kingsley saw, lay with the employers rather than the labourers.

On May 22nd, he sent Ludlow the outline of 'a tale of the country' which he thought might be suitable for *Politics*: 'A young squire getting into a miserable neglected (*really*, not externally) chalk estate, brought to a sense of his duties, & setting to work . . . I shall be very hard on the landlords—because they deserve it: but I will promise *to invent nothing*.'

By the beginning of July *Politics* was forced to announce that its publication would be suspended by the end of the month. Kingsley lamented its early death, but he had already arranged with Parker to print his new novel in *Fraser's*. The last six numbers of 1848 carried instalments of 'Yeast; or, The Thoughts, Sayings and Doings of Lancelot Smith, Gentleman'. Ludlow, who read the first part in manuscript, wrote his friend:

'There is a little awkwardness now & then in the putting together, but for depth, & breadth, & wit, & fun, & thought, & feeling, & interest, it holds as much of all this as a first-rate three-volume novel of the day. It is easy for you to become the greatest novelist of the age. . . . It will be expedient for you to continue it, & to try to make it if possible, ten times pleasanter, thoughtfuller, truer than before, & to shew to all the world what a great Xtian work a novel can be, written by a great Xtian man. But there, I am afraid, I must say, stop. Write never tale more till you are 60.'

In spite of his cautious praise, Ludlow did not like the story, but the real reason he advised Kingsley to leave novel-writing was his feeling that Kingsley was a poet, one who might 'have stood forth in his age as Tennyson's true successor', and that his writing of prose was a mere crotchet. Kingsley had even gone so far at Queen's College as to insist that prose was a higher thing than poetry, 'for no reason', said Ludlow, 'than that he found prose more difficult to write, it not being his native language—and so neglected and kept down his special gift instead of cultivating it'.

John Parker liked the later instalments less and less, and they show both his pushing of Kingsley to finish the story and the author's own fatigue, worn as he was by parish work, his lectures at Queen's College, and the necessity to complete the novel in six instalments. The novel, published anonymously in *Fraser's*, did not appear as a book until 1851, and then only because of Kingsley's insistence on its republication, for Parker claimed that it had already ruined his reputation as a publisher.

In explaining the name of his novel, Kingsley wrote: 'These papers have been, from beginning to end, as in name, so in nature, Yeast—an honest sample of the questions, which, good or bad, are fermenting in the minds of the young of this day, and are rapidly leavening the minds of the rising generation.' The deliberately loose title reflects the portmanteau quality of the novel into which he thrust everything of which he had been thinking, frequently without any attempt at artistic ordering. It is, of course, concerned with the country poor and their plight, but also with Roman Catholicism and high Anglicanism, non-conformity, degenerate celibacy, healthy animal passions in marriage, distorted Pre-Raphaelitism, historic art (the highest form of painting), banking practices, game preservation, sanitary reform, the Poor Law, and the contemptible Irish.

The central character is Lancelot Smith, a wealthy young squire who comes from the University with an education of the intellect but none of the heart or of the moral senses. This part of his training is provided in his love for Argemone, the daughter of Squire Lavington, and in his friendship with Tregarva, the philosophical Cornishman who is Lavington's gamekeeper. Smith loses his money in a bank crash, goes to London as a labourer and apprentice artist, and finally meets the enigmatic Carlylean figure, Barnakill, called 'The Prophet', who straightens out Smith's thinking. At the end of the novel, in fulfilment of an ancient curse, Argemone dies of typhus contracted in nursing the poor on her father's estate, who are ill because of the inadequate sanitation provided by her father.

Just as the major ideas of the book are immediately recognizable as those which had been filling Kingsley's letters and conversation, so the characters are clearly modelled on people he knew well. Lancelot, as one might expect, is recognizable as Kingsley's idea of himself at the time he met Fanny, and even has Kingsley's own stammer in moments of stress. His meeting with Argemone is an idealization of the meeting between Charles and Fanny. The more amiable aspects of Sir John's character and his lack of interest in the labourers' condition undoubtedly provided Kingsley with Squire Lavington. One unnamed character, 'a certain remarkable man' recently converted to Roman Catholicism and ordained in that faith, is Kingsley's distorted version of Newman, and to 'the "Father" ' Kingsley attributes all the slippery grace and feminine charm which he thought characteristic of 'the great pervert'. But character detection is more complicated when one comes to Argemone and her sister Honoria, 'the two poles of beauty: the *milieu* of which would be Venus with us Pagans, or the Virgin Mary with the Catholics. Look at them! Honoria the dark—symbolic of passionate depth; Argemone the fair, type of intellectual light!' Argemone's physical description is not too far off that of Mrs. Kingsley, except for her colouring, and in her love affair with Lancelot-Charles, Argemone clearly has much in common with Fanny, who indicated in her own copy of the novel that Argemone's meeting with her lover was parallel to her own. Argemone's gentleness was characteristic, we know, of Mrs. Kingsley. But, on the other hand, Argemone is much more like Charlotte Grenfell in her violent (and, to Kingsley, vacuous) Tractarianism. John Martineau and Max Müller, both close friends of the Kingsleys, were sure that Argemone was Charlotte and Honoria Fanny. Still another identification was offered by John Ludlow, writing of Charles Mansfield's elder sister Caulia and of his younger sister Anna (Mrs. Gifford): 'Kingsley told me once that in *Yeast*, Caulia Mansfield had been his type for Argemone and Anna Gifford for Honoria, but the latter by no means does justice to her model. I have been much amused lately (3 Nov. 1894) in reading a *Times* obituary notice of J. A. Froude (probably by Dr. Max Müller) to see a quite different identification of the two characters laid down *ex cathedra*, the identification of Mrs. Kingsley with Honoria being simply ludicrous.' Although Kingsley habitually drew on the characteristics of people whom he knew for his characters, it is impossible to make a one-to-one identification of either Argemone or Honoria; both as artist and as gentleman Kingsley would hardly have transcribed literally the characteristics of anyone so dear to him as his wife. Probably the best comment was offered by Martineau, who concluded his identification with the warning that 'investigating the circumstances makes a confusion between the two ladies' characters, and there is not much identity'.

Carlyle, whom Kingsley had known ever since coming to Chelsea, and whose books he knew thoroughly, is Kingsley's literary model in the book; he is quoted as Lancelot's guide, and such names as 'Doctor Autotheus Maresnest, the celebrated mesmeriser', and 'Lord Peu de Cervelle' are obviously fathered by him.

Kingsley had agreed to Ludlow's suggestion in July 1848 that he write no more novels. 'Why should I?' he asked. 'I have no more to say.' But by November, when he turned in the last instalment of *Yeast* to Parker, he was ready to write two more novels to complete a trilogy. He intended to show Lancelot's struggles as a London artist, and Argemone, by means no longer clear, was to be raised from the dead as heiress of her father's estate. Once more Ludlow threw cold water on his plans: 'All your friends agree in thinking that with the exception of a few pages it is spurious, written by a treacherous . . . devil that had taken your shape & forged your hand. . . . It is completely mendacious.' Perhaps because of Ludlow's discouragement, more probably because he became interested in other plans, Kingsley never attempted the ambitious scheme.

CHAPTER VI

The Growth of Reputation

The strain of writing *Yeast*, added to the worry over his finances, was too much for Kingsley. In the spring of 1848 he took a flying trip to Devon, and in the summer, after the first chapters were written, he took a vacation with Maurice and Ludlow in the Fen country and returned considerably refreshed. But by October his strength had run out once more, and he and his family sought the sea air of Bournemouth for a month. In writing serially, Kingsley could never bring himself to get far ahead of the demands of the month, so that like other Victorian novelists he sometimes found himself publishing the middle section of a novel when he still had little idea of how he was going to end the story. As a result, he found himself having to work hard at Bournemouth instead of taking the rest he needed, and it was obvious when he returned to Eversley that he was still ill.

There was another check on his recovery at Bournemouth, for his young brother Henry, who had just left King's College School, joined them there. The brothers were devoted, but Henry's button-bright wit and schoolboy enthusiasm were trying to Charles in his run-down state. Why Henry was in neither school nor university from 1848 to 1850 is no longer known, but it seems probable that the reason was connected with what Ludlow wrote of him at this time: 'His family were at one time in great trouble about him, he having got into bad courses while at King's College. It was then I first knew him, and I liked the lad notwithstanding his misdoings. There was a good deal of resemblance in character between Charles and Henry, but Henry was much weaker, and with lower aims, though a really good fellow at bottom.'

Henry's later life exhibited an embarrassing wealth of 'bad courses' which may have begun then: his 'misdoings' certainly included overindulgence in drink, tobacco, and gambling, heavy debts, and possibly sexual abnormality as well. Since so much has been written trying to determine the exact relationships between the two gifted brothers, and between Fanny and Henry, it is illuminating to see what Mansfield wrote Ludlow at this time:

'Whether or not it be good for him that his brother should be removed, I cannot decide; but it seems certain that his brother's presence causes him continual anxiety, and he is not fit to bear care-wearing. I think Mrs. K. rather exaggerates the *positive* effect which his annoyance about his brother had in causing his present state; because she does not see that he was undermined before, and that this occurrence was only the weight laid on which broke in the shell of the hollow: but still I do not think she is altogether wrong in thinking Henry an unsuitable companion for him now. I think Mrs. K. is scarcely aware of the terrible effect which overwork has had on his intellect; as a woman she naturally looks more to the feelings and affections as the source of disturbance; and this helps to remove the accusation from his *pen* to his kindred.'

Two years later Henry matriculated at Worcester College, Oxford, where he spent three delightful years working at sculling and dissipation, leaving in the end without a degree to spend several years prospecting for gold in Australia.

On his return to Eversley Kingsley worked in a state bordering on hysteria to finish *Yeast* and to keep up his Queen's College lectures. At last it was apparent that he must give up his chair at Queen's, and Mansfield came to Eversley to act as companion and nurse until the story was completed. By the end of November he had packed the whole family off to Ilfracombe, where he reported from 'Runnamede Villa':

'The Kingsleys had taken a house on trial in the town here, but it did not meet approval altogether, so Mrs. K. went out *nesting*, and discovered this place, which they have taken for a term:—and it really is a most perfect bijou of a place; having every thing that could be wished for except a view of the sea.'

In 1848 Ilfracombe was still a quiet seaside village, uninvaded by tourists, and the smell of frying in fish-and-chip shops had not replaced that of the freshly landed catch on the fishing-boats. For Kingsley it was ideally restful to walk among the long, finger-like combes leading down to the sea, the great rocks and shallow pools, and he was exhilarated by the strong winter winds whistling up the narrow passages from the water to the main street. Old Mr. Kingsley wrote from Chelsea, blaming the Fen trip of the previous summer for his son's illness, deciding from his own experience that Charles must have the ague. Mansfield wisely insisted that his friend do almost nothing save stare at the sea and pick up an occasional shell, and that he should spend as much time as possible in the soothing company of Fanny, from whom too much time had been taken by the writing of *Yeast*. With less success he tried to persuade Kingsley to cut down on his excessive smoking and to give up meat, citing as a horrid example of the eating of flesh the illness of his own sister, who suffered from 'a cursed cold-veal attachment'. Then twice a day he 'magnetized' Kingsley, putting him into a child-like sleep, the effects of which were unfortunately usually lost when Kingsley awoke and excited himself with talking or reading.

Mansfield and Kingsley had both been interested in the work of Mesmer, the Austrian mystic, since their college days. Although Mesmer had largely been discredited before his death, there was a resurgence of interest in England when the reputable Dr. James Braid began his investigation of what he called hypnosis. For a time there was a vogue for mesmerism among intellectual circles; the devotion of Harriet Martineau is well known. Mansfield, a confirmed 'materialist', had begun believing once more in spiritual values when he had seen an innocent-minded young girl resist lascivious suggestions made to her when she was in a hypnotic trance; naturally enough, the scientific and the religious tended to merge in his mind. He told Ludlow:

'I have no faith in magnetism as a thing—for the cure of disease. It is in the effectual fervent prayer of a righteous man, acting thro' this physical means, that I have the most absolute faith. I believe that diseases may or may not be cured by "mesmeric manipulation". The devil is, doubtless, often expelled by this means, which God has given us for that end; but we do not know enough of the matter *scientifically* to make sure of the result, or to be certain in any case that it will fail.'

The so-called mesmeric passes of the hands were usually at the head, although they might pass an inch or two from the body, and, when making these passes, an experienced therapist like Mansfield claimed to feel the illness and infection manifesting themselves in increased body-heat at the sore points. It was an exhausting business for the mesmerizer, and Mansfield once developed a toothache and swollen face after a long session with Kingsley. When he left Ilfracombe at the beginning of 1849, Kingsley chided him by letter for his vegetarianism:

'[If] C. B. Mansfield had the share of beef-&-beer magnetism in him which God intended, he need not fear putting his hand on a fever patient's head, or *eating* one either si bon lui semblait. . . .

'I am being bedrugged. It is humiliating—but it is the fashion. One shaves one's beard—one wears a hat—one goes to the university—because Englishmen do—why not take medicine for the same reason?'

Mansfield believed that the passes built up in the body a supply of 'animal magnetism' which wore off gradually. Kingsley's belief in mesmerism was qualified, but he did occasionally feel 'de-magnetized'. One of his biographers has made heavy and repetitious fun of his use of the term, but it is obvious that she did not understand what he meant by it.

Without success Mansfield tried to talk Kingsley out of writing novels. To Ludlow he wrote: 'In receiving Maurice's mantle, or even the skirt of it, for *that* vocation, it seems to me that our dear friend here would be much more fulfilling his mission than in writing novels, or by whatever other name decorated lies may be called.' Although Mansfield could rail against novels with impunity, he knew that Ludlow's criticisms only irritated Kingsley, and eventually he asked Ludlow if he would not tell Fanny his criticisms of Kingsley's work and 'let her give it out by allowances to Charles'.

By this time Mansfield had not only completely recovered his faith in Christianity but was determined to take holy orders, although his tangled domestic affairs would prevent him from holding more than a humble clerical position. Ludlow rejoiced for him, and Maurice suggested that the ideal place for him would be as Kingsley's curate: 'It would be such a delightful arrangement so far as our weak intellects can go, on subjects of the kind, for both parties. I say this with a salutary & deeply rooted dread of match making; but it seems as if Kingsley's weakness might be providentially appointed for that very purpose.'

Mansfield eventually decided that a man who had been deserted by his wife scarcely had the requisite reputation for a clergyman, and he was never ordained, but he did help his friends in another fashion. Kingsley's precarious finances were completely disrupted by his long illness. He had to pay a curate to take his duty at Eversley in his absence, and the loss of both what he had actually been paid by Queen's College and what he had hoped for from King's made the picture blacker. The £500 which he had borrowed from an insurance company had melted away, and at last he appealed in real desperation to Ludlow: 'Can you, as a Lawyer, as well as a Friend, tell me of any means of borrowing £500 for, say, five years at reasonable interest?' By that time, he hoped, 'my books may be selling well, or my house may have stopped falling about my ears, or—or God may think that we have suffered enough from the crushing weight of unavoidable debt, & open up a deliverance for us in His own good way'. He sent Ludlow a careful estimate of his expected income and expenditure, concluding: 'My father would, but cannot help me, & therefore I dare not ask him: & as for certain rich *connexions* of mine, I would die sooner than ask them, who tried to prevent my marriage because forsooth I was poor.'

Mansfield, to whom Ludlow showed the letter, reacted characteristically by taking £140, all he could immediately lay hands on, and stuffing it in an envelope, which he proposed to send anonymously to Kingsley, so that he would be unable to pay anything back. At last Ludlow convinced him that a more regular method would be preferable to Kingsley, but Mansfield stipulated that no security should be posted and that Kingsley should not know from whom the money came, so that no embarrassing feelings of gratitude might come between them. Ludlow drew up a sham paper which looked to Kingsley's unpractised eye like a legal document, naming as creditor 'H. B. Turnstiles'. When Kingsley received the document and a letter promising the balance of £500, he dictated and Fanny wrote an ecstatic thanks to Ludlow. Fanny added as her own postscript:

'Dear Friend I believe you have saved my husband fm. going out of his mind & me from a broken heart! Yet we have no claim upon you! It is truly unspeakable—but I am not *surprised* —for my *daring* to propose to Charles to tell *you* our troubles came from a sudden inspiration in Church where I was praying (in quite an agony at the early daily service) for deliverance & suddenly you came before me & I took courage.'

'Eventually, however,' wrote Ludlow, 'when Kingsley was able to repay, Mrs. Kingsley twigged the trick, & there was a grand scene—tho' I am not sure that Kingsley quite relished my having been the means of humbugging him.'

At the beginning of March 1849 another guest arrived at Ilfracombe for an indefinite stay. James Anthony Froude, whom Kingsley had met at Oxford with Cowley Powles and who was a friend of Clough, took his degree in 1842 at Oriel, where his elder brother had been a friend of Newman and a leader of the Oxford Movement, and in due time he was elected a fellow of Exeter. In 1844 he became a deacon, but he never continued the usual career in holy orders by being ordained priest. Some of his fellows at Exeter viewed his laxity in this matter as a possible indication of heterodoxy, an impression which seemed confirmed in 1847 by the appearance of his semi-autobiographical work, *Shadows of the Clouds.* The full wrath of a narrow Oxford broke over him in January 1849, on his publication of *The Nemesis of Faith*, a piece of fiction, hardly a novel, about the dissolution of belief in a young clergyman. Froude protested that the voice of the central character was not his own, but on February 27th, William Sewell, Senior Tutor of Exeter, denounced the book in a vehement lecture in the college hall, took a copy from a pupil, tore it to bits and threw them on the hall fire. Froude had been on the point of giving up his fellowship before he published the book, but on the day of Sewell's high-handed action he resigned, to leave Oxford. One result of Mr. Sewell's book-burning was a great stimulus to the sales of an otherwise rather dull book; a less pleasant consequence was that Froude's father, the autocratic Archdeacon of Totnes, withdrew his financial support of Anthony and forbade him to come home. Froude was to return to Oxford more than forty years later as a professor, but at the moment he had nowhere to go. Kingsley had found Froude glacial in his manner and antipathetic in temperament, but the moment he heard of the Exeter incident, he sent off a generous invitation, offering his house at Ilfracombe as a refuge to Froude, who accepted with alacrity. Kingsley's reputation, already a little suspect, suffered from Froude's visit, but he never allowed Froude to know how much abuse he had to bear for harbouring him. He told Ludlow that longer acquaintance made him like Froude much better:

'I have staying with me now poor persecuted Froude, the author of the Nemesis of Faith. He is certainly an extraordinary man, & *much improved* you may tell Maurice, in every way since I saw him last. But his intensely sensitive mind is utterly abattu by the misconception & persecution to which his book has given rise, & the cruelty of his own family. I do hope & believe that his visit here will do us *both* good.'

There are dozens of records of the charm, the intelligent conversation, the beautiful manners of Froude, but in most of them there is a hint of his slight condescension, his great reserve; Ludlow, who reviewed *Nemesis* for *Fraser's*, and Mansfield were anxious to know him, and Kingsley gladly arranged the meetings, but both sides were disappointed. The gentle Mansfield wrangled with Froude over the writing of fiction, a literary form which Mansfield disliked. Ludlow found his new acquaintance immature, womanish, feline, but he was pleased to see that 'he speaks of Sewell with the most perfect fairness & composure'. Kingsley told Ludlow:

'I do not think that you would be afraid of Froude if you knew him. There is an under-current of deep earnest reverence & tenderness, now coming more & more to the surface daily, in him, which shews that all is right at bottom. He is no Mephistopheles no one less. . . . You, like myself, & every one else, have fallen into the mistake of supposing his book to be an autobiography; & the *total* of his belief. It is, he assures me, only the *negative* side thereof—& he wanted to shew what had been & might have been, not what is. . . . He will make a man yet, depend on it. The best trees take longest growing, & the noblest animals lie longest in the womb.'

Years later Ludlow wrote of Froude's visit to his house at this time: 'He stayed a few days, and I suppose our disappointment was mutual, for though always on friendly terms neither of us afterwards ever sought out the other, and we scarcely ever met. The "Nemesis of Faith" had, I must say, led me to expect in him a man deeply in earnest as to spiritual questions. It seemed to me that there was no depth at all in him. A very charming man, no doubt, but usually charming men have never been much in my line.

'To express my whole feeling as to Froude—he appears to me like Ruskin—to have had a woman's soul in a man's body. That is, I take it, the main explanation of the extraordinary fascination for both of that essentially male genius, Carlyle. . . . Kingsley was greatly taken with him, but his influence upon Kingsley was not, I think, a good one.'

Kingsley was kept busy justifying Froude, who moved with them to Lynmouth in April. When even the elder Mrs. Kingsley joined in the attack, he wrote a long defence but concluded in filial humility:

'But now, having said all this, I must say, that whatever may seem to me to be my duty to Froude there can be no doubt of my duty to *you*. "Honour thy father & mother." There is no mistake about *that* at all events. And therefore *I solemnly promise you, either to get rid of Froude, or leave Lynmouth immediately and not to remain in his company one day longer than the common courtesies of life require. Can I say more?*'

Whatever Ludlow's faults might be, he was at least sufficiently un-English by breeding to worry little about Victorian conventionality, and it was a relief for Kingsley to tell him his troubles:

'I have been dreadfully worried lately. People seem to think that my companionship with Froude is dangerous to my orthodoxy. On the contrary I must say, that while on all subjects of *positive* belief, I find to my delight that we thoroughly agree, no man could be more careful not to intrude a single doubt or negative argument. So much so, that I blame myself for not having forced on his attention many points on which we painfully differ. . . .

'He tells me that I have done him good—that I have perhaps saved him from suicide. His father has disinherited him & there is no malicious slander which "the world"—true to its master has not set on foot anonymously against him. He goes in a few days. I have learnt much from his visit, & thank God for it: but its accessories have been sore work—& most humiliating. I will tell *you* all some day.'

Ludlow hated the intolerance of acquaintances who criticized Kingsley for sheltering Froude; he could 'imagine the disagreeable accessories of Froude's stay . . . hortatory letters of friends, hints from neighbouring clergymen, interruption of acquaintances' visits, perhaps a cut or two', but his sense of fair play did not prevent him from disliking Froude personally, and by the time he reviewed the *Nemesis* he felt it was a really harmful book. At last he could no longer restrain himself from telling Kingsley his opinion of the troublesome guest:

'I can perceive no sign or token about him of his feeling any conviction of sin, any sense that he has been a soul-murderer . . . that horribly false laugh, which chills the blood in one's veins to hear; that foul sensual mouth & eyes, that horrid made up voice of common talk. . . . Not that, even taking into account both laugh & voice, I should call him at all a false man; I am quite persuaded that he states his opinion, or says nothing.'

Fanny Kingsley, who dreaded the opinion of society, was terribly worried by the shocked letters which her husband received, and she was shocked herself by Froude's views. But her feelings were complicated by his presence during the visit of her sister Charlotte, who was about to enter a convent. She wrote to Ludlow that she was desperately unhappy that Charlotte should take the veil, in spite of her own leanings in that direction before marriage:

'It is a hopeless case though, for it is not the fancy of leading a conventual life that is leading her to Rome, but her devotion to Rome that has enabled her to conquer her dislike to a life of retirement & self-denial. She has been now 2 years & more an avowed Romanist, & had been one in heart for some time previously. . . . She considers that she "has a vocation" & so does her Jesuit confessor Father Brownbill of Hill St. London who confesses all the ladies of the world & nearly all the London priests & Romish dignitaries. . . . She is to have a year's novitiate at New Hall Essex where the nuns the St. Sepulchrens bring up & Educate young Ladies of the World. . . . The anguish of her Sisters has decided her on giving us 6 months more; but I have no hope. Strange strange to say Mr. Froude has taken the matter in hand. . . . She is charmed with him as I suppose Most people wd. be, & deeply *attracted* by him, but I fear the only result will be to Make her feel how dull the nuns are when she has to depend upon them for Society. I *hope* I wd. rather see her in a convent even, clinging to any positive faith in our Blessed Saviour however much error was tacked on to such a faith, than belonging to me again with poor dr. Mr. F's views.'

As Fanny guessed, the attractions of the cloister paled for Charlotte when a handsome, outcast young man stood before her. Furthermore, his fiancée had just broken their engagement. Obviously he needed consoling. Six months later, at the time she had intended to enter the convent, Charlotte was married to Froude at St. Peter's, Belgrave Square, and there is no record that she ever entered a Roman Catholic church again. When she died, Kingsley officiated at the funeral, and she was buried in Eversley churchyard. The whole affair, thought Kingsley, was further proof that Roman Catholicism was really satisfactory for no one except a sex-starved woman.

To a young clergyman 'on the point of becoming a Romanist' Kingsley wrote that same spring: 'If by holiness you mean "saintliness", I quite agree that Rome is the place to get *that*—& a poor pitiful thing it is when it is got—not God's ideal of a man, but an effeminate shaveling's ideal. Look at St Francis de Sale's [*sic*] or St Vincent Paul's face—& then say, does not your English spirit loathe to be such a prayer-mongering eunuch as *that*? God made man in His image, not in a imaginary Virgin Mary's image.'

No one can doubt that the motivation of Kingsley's hatred of Rome was at least partially sexual. The security he felt in his own marriage made him contemptuous of the celibate life; but beyond this is a hysterical, frightened note in his constant attribution of effeminacy and abnormality to Roman Catholicism. If there is any validity in the conjectures which S. M. Ellis made about the essential homosexuality of Henry Kingsley, observation of sexual abnormality in his brother may partially account for Kingsley's own abnormal hatred of the unmarried state.

The cost of maintaining his family in Devon and a curate in Eversley kept Kingsley in constant anxiety over money. To add to his income, he offered to review for *Fraser's*. In January 1849 he praised Clough's *Bothie of Toper-na-Fuosich* for its health and vigour which he had not expected from an Oxford graduate; instead he had supposed the poem would be 'some pale and sickly bantling of the *Lyra Apostolica* school', the last refuge of 'Wertherism'. In a later review he congratulated Mrs. Jameson on *Sacred and Legendary Art*, with its honest English and Protestant attitudes ('For the time, we think, for calling Popery ill names is past; though to abstain is certainly sometimes a sore restraint for English spirits . . .'). It was evident to him that *The Strayed Reveller and Other Poems, by A* was 'the work of a scholar, a gentleman, and a true poet'; 'The Forsaken Merman' was 'the gem of the book', but 'Resignation, to Fausta' was a 'yawn thirteen pages long', and the poems in general were lacking in rhythm. In chastising the anonymous Matthew Arnold for his sadness, Kingsley recommended that he 'rejoice in his youth, as the great Arnold told his Rugby scholars to do'.

In his review of *The Tenant of Wildfell Hall*, Kingsley guessed the sex of 'Acton Bell', for the 'vulgarity is just such as a woman, trying to write like a man, would invent', and it was so coarse that the novel was 'utterly unfit to be put into the hands of girls'.

'I confess that the book has made me ashamed of myself,' he admitted to Mrs. Gaskell after reading her biography of Charlotte Brontë: ' "Jane Eyre" I hardly looked into, very seldom reading a work of fiction—yours, indeed, and Thackeray's are the only ones I care to open. "Shirley" disgusted me at the opening: and I gave up the writer and her books with the notion that she was a person who liked coarseness. How I misjudged her! and how thankful I am that I never put a word of my misconceptions into print, or recorded my misjudgements of one who is a whole heaven above me.'

His highest praise he kept for Mrs. Gaskell's *Mary Barton*, with its facts about 'why working men turn Chartist and Communists' and its descriptions of 'life-in-death—worse than many deaths, which now besets thousands, and tens of thousands of our own countrymen'.

Mary Barton hit a sympathetic chord in Kingsley, for at the time he read the novel he was already meditating a work which he described to Ludlow as 'the Autobiography of a Cockney Poet, which has revealed itself to me so rapidly & methodically that I feel it comes down from above—& that only my folly can spoil it—which I pray against daily'. Later he called it his 'Autobiography of a Chartist poet'. All during the spring he wrote easily on it, asking his town friends occasionally for 'any matter elucidating the struggles of poor geniuses'. The book finally appeared anonymously the following year as *Alton Locke, Tailor and Poet. An Autobiography*.

By the beginning of June Kingsley felt up to leaving his West Country retreat. On the way back to Eversley, he stopped to see his London friends and was just in time to attend a large meeting of working men called by the Christian Socialists. The idea behind the meeting was to get the two classes to know each other better. Mutual trust was not easy; for all their good will, some of the Christian Socialists were unused to the ways of people in other walks of life. It was presumably for this meeting that Hughes, acting as treasurer, put down two half-crowns as the rent of the room in which the meeting was to be held. When the tavern keeper rang them on the table to be sure they were genuine, Hughes flushed red to the ears. The working men were suspicious, too, of their new friends and several of them spoke heatedly against the clergy and what seemed to them a do-nothing Church. At the meeting Ludlow sat beside Archie Campbell, next to whom was David Masson, later well-known as biographer and editor, but at this time a raw young journalist from Aberdeen making his way in London by writing for *Fraser's*. Two or three seats away sat Kingsley, who came into the meeting late. When the invective against the Church became warm and the meeting seemed about to collapse in quarrelling, Kingsley quietly rose in his place, folded his arms across his chest, and stammered out: 'My f-friends, I am a p-p-parson and a Ch-ch-chartist,' adding almost *sotto voce*, 'Ch-church of England, I mean.' From there he went on to explain earnestly how much he sympathized with the Chartists' sense of injustice, but how mistaken he thought their methods were. Perhaps it was the only speech which could have held the meeting together; the working men listened respectfully, won over to readiness to co-operate with the parsons. To his horror, however, Ludlow saw Campbell stuffing his handkerchief in his mouth, writhing with almost uncontrollable laughter. Ludlow looked threateningly at him, but his furious glances only seemed to excite Campbell's risibilities. After the meeting, he managed to explain to Ludlow between roars of laughter that Masson, who had never seen Kingsley before and was unprepared for his stammer, had leaned over when he began speaking and whispered in broad and concerned Aberdonian: 'The man is drunk!'

Besides going to the meeting, Kingsley had breakfast with the

Prussian ambassador, Baron Bunsen; visited Froude and Francis Newman, brother of the man whom Kingsley so despised; went to Cheyne Row to call on Carlyle; and attended Lincoln's Inn Chapel to hear Maurice, whose 'head looked like some great, awful Giorgione portrait in the pulpit'.

After his quiet life in Devon, the rattle of London tired him out, but he had little time to rest when he returned to Eversley, where an epidemic of fever had broken out. Nurses were difficult to find, and the Rector himself sat up with the sick. The predictable result was that within two months he had broken down again and returned to Devonshire for another month of rest. It was proposed that he and Mansfield should go to America, but he felt that he could not separate himself for so long from Fanny, so he set out instead for Clovelly, where he visited boyhood friends, fished at Torridge, read Rabelais in his first-floor room at Mrs. Whitfield's, took a day's trip to Lundy and saved a woman from drowning on the trip home. But frequently, as he told Ludlow, he spent his time thinking of Fanny:

'Blessed be God for the rest—though I never before felt the loneliness of being without the beloved being, whose every look & word & motion are the keynotes of my life. People talk of love ending at the altar. People are an ass. I am ten times more *in love* in love, in every sense of the word, animal, intellectual, & spiritual, than when I married—& I glory in it. . . . I already long for the return *to bliss*.'

To Kingsley Clovelly seemed to have been served badly by the clergy since his father's departure. The curate, Dalton, one of 'these priest-cattle', he found 'shallow, cunning, good natured, slippery—in a word Irish'.

At the time Henry was staying at Colebrook, where he and two other young men were studying with Thomas Drosier, the Rector of the village and Charles's former tutor at Cambridge. Henry was preparing for his entrance into Worcester College, Oxford, that year. On a flying visit to see him, Kingsley was 'delighted & satisfied' with Henry's progress and was overjoyed to see Drosier again, with whom the three young men were 'playfellows rather than his pupils'.

Then, after a month, back he went to Eversley, where his daughter Rose was ill, but where he found himself 'as well as ever I was in my life in health & spirits, quite strong, & able to walk stoutly 20 miles & more a day'.

Less than two weeks after his return to Eversley, Kingsley read in the *Morning Chronicle* an account of 'A Visit to the Cholera Districts of Bermondsey', describing in particular the disgusting state of the section known as Jacob's Island. To the tidal ditch which surrounded it, serving both as water-supply and sewer, the locality owed its name and the cholera which was ravaging it in the autumn of 1849. The area was already infamous from its description in *Oliver Twist*, but little had been done to clear it out. The inhabitants themselves were too ignorant to realize the danger of drinking the water into which all the human waste of the neighbourhood was thrown.

Characteristically, Kingsley and his friends decided to help the unfortunate tenants of Jacob's Island. Their first aim was to make enough agitation to cause either the landlords or the local authorities to supply drinking water and decent drainage; while their speeches and pamphlets were getting attention, they took the more immediate steps of driving carts around the district to dole out drinking water, and of building water-butts to hold a reserve supply. The young clergymen and their friends were as innocent as they were idealistic, and the butts they brought were large, built of seasoned oak, and fitted with brass cocks to which the tenants were given keys. The reformers expected to blow up the butts at the end of ten months, by which time they felt that the tenants would refuse to return to using ditch-water. Almost immediately after the butts were installed, the inhabitants of the locality began stealing the brass cocks, and they steadfastly refused to believe that the ditch-water was unhealthy; at last even the heavy butts themselves disappeared. Still more discouraging was the knowledge that the healthiest of the thieving locality were the heaviest drinkers, for gin was less poisonous than the water which they had been drinking.

It was disheartening work, but as usual Kingsley threw himself into it. It meant frequent trips to London for consultation, even to drive the water-wagon to Jacob's Island, it meant jaunts to Oxford to see Bishop Wilberforce, visits with all the important men whom he knew or to whom he had introductions. With Mansfield and Ludlow he cooked up a scheme for a Health League, he besought help of Tom Taylor in *Punch*, and he wrote 'to S.G.O. for a Times letter—but entre nous he is so conceited & contrary that he will perhaps not do it, just because the dirt is not of his own finding'. For the simple fact was that Kingsley became bored with Eversley when he stayed there too long, and he loved to throw himself into schemes which demanded his presence elsewhere. Not that he neglected his parochial duties or thrust them on to his curates; he worked hard at Eversley, was loved by his parishioners, but he needed the excitement of a good fight, and in the larger world of social reform there were more combats than in a peaceful Hampshire village. His letters are full of his sense of isolation from the great world of London.

The first of the co-operative associations which the Christian Socialists sponsored rose out of a meeting on 8th January 1850. With a capital of nearly £300, which they finally succeeded in raising, they set up a round dozen tailors in a rented house in Castle Street, under the managership of Walter Cooper, a Scotsman and former Chartist and lecturer on Strauss. When he was in London Kingsley made a point of spending as much time as possible with Cooper, in whom Kingsley was particularly interested because he was a working tailor. Kingsley was still at work on *Alton Locke* and also on an inflammatory little pamphlet to be called *Cheap Clothes and Nasty*. Late in January 1850 it appeared as one in a series of 'Tracts by Christian Socialists'. At first Kingsley preferred to incorporate his facts into *Alton Locke*; he wrote to Ludlow to complain: 'I am embodying all this, & Jacob's Island, too, in the Chartist Novel—so you are cutting open the goose prematurely to get at the golden egg.'

Even today it is difficult not to be moved by the descriptions in *Cheap Clothes and Nasty* of the living conditions endured by the tailors who were virtual slaves of the 'sweater'. Cooper had known the horrors of such a life, and he wanted to help Kingsley do something about them. Walter Cooper was pulling himself up by his intellectual bootstraps; he had made himself known to Ludlow, who became interested in his quick mind and took him to hear Maurice preach. It was several years before Cooper became converted to orthodox Christianity, but he was in complete sympathy with the social aims of the Christian Socialists.[1]

Another Cooper, this one Thomas, was also helpful to Kingsley in the writing of *Alton Locke*. Indeed, Locke himself is probably an amalgam of the two Coopers. Thomas Cooper had led a various life before Kingsley met him: the son of poor parents, he had tried the life of the sea, had been a shoemaker, schoolmaster, preacher, newspaperman, and bookseller. During the early 'forties he was a radical Chartist and served two years in prison for 'sedition and conspiracy' in connection with strikes. While he was in prison he wrote a long political poem, 'The Purgatory of Suicides', which won the admiration of Kingsley. In 1848 Kingsley deliberately sought out Cooper, then lecturing on Strauss, like Walter Cooper, and made his acquaintance. It was the beginning of a long friendship, and until Kingsley's death the two corresponded frequently; eight years after their meeting Cooper was reconverted to Christian orthodoxy, largely through the influence of Kingsley, and spent the rest of his life as a lecturer on the proofs of Christianity.

With the aid of the two Coopers and by reading Mayhew's articles on the London poor in the *Morning Chronicle*, Kingsley filled in his background for *Cheap Clothes* and for *Alton Locke*. At times he felt he was unequal to the task of writing the book, and when Ludlow wrote an article on 'Labour and the Poor' for *Fraser's*, Kingsley confessed himself 'not great enough for such times, alas!' and suggested that Ludlow might better undertake the task. Probably this suggestion should not be taken too seriously, for in their correspondence there is a curious note of self-deprecation in Kingsley's letters which does not ring true,

[1] Unfortunately, Christianity was not a complete bulwark to Cooper's morality. Early in his association with the Christian Socialists he was charged with mismanagement of funds of the Working Tailors, but was able to clear himself. In 1860, when he had risen to the social status of Vicar's Warden at the Church of All Saints, Margaret Street, he was convicted of misappropriation of profits of the Tailors and was subsequently sentenced to prison.

a trace of arrogance in Ludlow's, and furious complaint to third parties when either of them was criticized by the other.

When he was working on *Yeast*, Kingsley was forced to write late at night when the house was still, and the overexertion was partially responsible for his breakdown. He had hoped to write *Alton Locke* at a more reasonable hour of the day, but the continuous worry over money drove him to take two pupils in 1850, and in order to give them their lessons, he had to rise at five in the morning, heat his coffee, and write until breakfast. Part of his money troubles came about because he had resigned his sinecure clerkship in his father's Chelsea church; he felt he could no longer hold with good conscience a post which he had to fill with a deputy; going to Chelsea for the duty was out of the question. He was further cramped because he returned ten per cent on tithe payments to the Eversley tenant farmers, who were feeling the economic slump that year.

Alton Locke is one of the most effective pieces of writing which Kingsley ever produced, but it bears all the marks of being written in haste and in fatigue, which is perhaps part of the reason he had trouble getting it published. John Parker and his father, who were probably at heart never very radical, had become less and less so in the two years since the Chartist meeting at Kennington Common, and they wanted to avoid a reputation as publishers of radical literature. To them it seemed that the publication of *Politics for the People* and the appearance of 'Yeast' in *Fraser's* had lost them prestige, so they refused Kingsley's second novel when he offered it to them. Thomas Carlyle, to whom Kingsley turned for help, wrote that he was delighted with the 'new explosion, or salvo of red-hot shot against the Devil's Dung-heap', and he recommended the book to Chapman and Hall, who agreed to publish it. Contracts were signed in May and Kingsley immediately and thankfully asked for an advance. To Edward Chapman he complained that ' "an exposition of sleep" has fallen on the printers, who have sent me no proof since Sunday last; a rate of progress which will make the publication of Alton Locke coincident with the repayment of the Greek loan, & the vindication of Lord Palmerston's honesty. Pray consider this, for I quite agree with you, that the sooner the book is out the better'. Meantime he was delighted to find that *Cheap Clothes and Nasty* was attracting a good deal of attention, that even in the Guards' Club three copies lay on the reading table; still more exciting was the news that several members had actually gone to order clothes from the Tailors' Association in Castle Street. Two other surprising patrons of the Tailors were Bishop Wilberforce of Oxford and Cardinal Wiseman, both of whom gave orders for liveries for their servants, although they presumably bought their own clothes elsewhere.

Alton Locke finally appeared in August 1850. The narrator and central figure is a Cockney, the son of a widow who is unable to support her children, but who tries to instil into them her own fierce and unlovable Calvinistic Baptist belief. All Kingsley's scorn for the worst of nonconformity is poured into the scene in which she entertains a missionary, 'a squat, red-faced, pig-eyed, low-browed man, with great soft lips that opened back to his very ears; sensuality, conceit, and cunning marked on every feature. . . . How he filled his teacup half full of the white sugar to buy which my mother had curtailed her yesterday's dinner—how he drained the few remaining drops of the three-pennyworth of cream, with which Susan was stealing off to keep it as an unexpected treat for my mother at breakfast the next morning—how he talked of the natives, not as St. Paul might of his converts, but as a planter might of his slaves.'

Young Locke is appenticed by a wealthy uncle to a tailor and so learns the horrible life of the workmen who starve and freeze as they sew in the garrets over the smart Mayfair shop. This section of the novel is *Cheap Clothes and Nasty* cast in narrative form. From the tailors he learns coarseness, but from one of them, Crossthwaite, he also learns of the aims of Chartism, which he adopts as a creed. In his few leisure hours he lurks around a bookshop to read stealthily, until he is finally befriended by the old Scottish bookseller, Sandy Mackaye. To the ends of physical violence advocated by Crossthwaite, Mackaye opposes the ideal of self-development as the answer to the working man's plight. Both in speech and in thought Mackaye is clearly modelled on

Carlyle, whom Kingsley had known ever since living in Chelsea. Presumably with tongue in cheek, Carlyle wrote to Kingsley of the old bookseller, the most fully developed of all the characters in the book: ' "Saunders MacKaye", my invaluable countryman in this book, is nearly perfect; indeed I greatly wonder how you did contrive to manage him—his very dialect is as if a native had done it, and the whole existence of the rugged old hero is a wonderfully splendid and coherent piece of Scotch bravura.'

At Mackaye's suggestion Locke's growing literary powers are turned toward becoming a 'People's Poet', toward showing the poetry implicit in the lives of the poor: 'All around ye, in every gin-shop and costermonger's cellar, are God and Satan at death grips; every garret is a . . . Paradise Lost or Paradise Regained.'

Locke meets the aristocracy by an introduction into the home of Dean Winnstay, with whose daughter Lillian he promptly falls in love. The pretty and empty-headed Lillian and her quiet, thoughtful cousin Eleanor Staunton, are partial re-creations of Argemone and Honoria in *Yeast*. Because of his love for Lillian, Locke is persuaded to emasculate his poems of the elements Mackaye had admired, to make them into mere polite verse.

Against the aristocratic world of the Dean's household and the Young England landlord, Lord Lynedale, whom Eleanor marries, Kingsley sets the vulgar, pushing middle-class represented by Locke's wealthy cousin George, the son of the uncle who makes Locke a tailor's apprentice. George attends Cambridge and is then ordained to advance himself socially. By slandering Locke, George replaces him in Lillian's affections and becomes engaged to her. George's death comes from typhus contracted of a coat which he buys of a cheap tailor who sweats his workmen, one of whom has been covered in death by the coat.

In attempting to stop a Chartist riot Locke is taken as one of the conspirators and is thrown into prison for three years. He is released in time to see the debacle of Chartism at Kennington Common. That night he contracts fever; his nurse is Eleanor, now widowed and engaged in social work. In conversation with her, Locke gives his ultimate view of Chartism, one which is clearly that of Kingsley:

'If by a Chartist you mean one who fancies that a change in mere political circumstances will bring about a millennium, I am no longer one. That dream is gone—with others. But if to be a Chartist is to love my brothers with every faculty of my soul—to wish to live and die struggling for their rights, endeavouring to make them, not electors merely, but fit to be electors, senators, kings, and priests to God and to His Christ—if that be the Chartism of the future, then am I sevenfold a Chartist, and ready to confess it before men, though I were thrust forth from every door in England.' On a voyage to the New World, Locke dies, disappointed in all his worldly hopes but secure at last in his knowledge of the true relation between men being a shadow of their relation to God.

Kingsley's view of the proper social structure of England is clear in the book. Like Disraeli in *Sybil*, he distrusts mobility between the classes, but stresses the mutual responsibility between them. The upper classes are to rule, but to rule with compassion; the lower classes must improve their moral status but accept their inferior station. In answer to some criticism of the book, Kingsley spelled out the point:

'The moral of my book is that the working man who tries to get on, to desert his class and rise above it, enters into a lie, and leaves God's path for his own—with consequences. . . . I think the cry, "Rise in Life", has been excited by the very increasing impossibility of being anything but brutes while they struggle below.'

Much of the book is lacking in form; the characters, with the exception of Mackaye, are unbelievable; the plot is sometimes unmotivated and melodramatic; many of Kingsley's ideas are poorly assimilated into the action. But for all its literary flaws, the book remains one of the great social documents of the century, largely because of Kingsley's ability at dramatic scenes of the life of the poor. Locke's first view of the sweater's den (probably a transcription of what Kingsley had heard of the working conditions in the shops of the wholesale tailors, Elias Moses and

Son), the Chartist riot, the description of Jacob's Island: these still command the reader's sympathy, although the conditions which inspired them are long gone. One of the vivid scenes is the revolting market in St. Giles, where Locke is taken by Mackaye:

'It was a foul, chilly, foggy Saturday night. From the butchers' and greengrocers' shops the gas lights flared and flickered, wild and ghastly, over haggard groups of slip-shod dirty women, bargaining for scraps of stale meat and frost-bitten vegetables, wrangling about short weight and bad quality. Fish-stalls and fruit-stalls lined the edge of the greasy pavement, sending up odours as foul as the language of sellers and buyers. Blood and sewer-water crawled from under doors and out of spouts, and reeked down the gutters among offal, animal and vegetable, in every stage of putrefaction. Foul vapours rose from cow-sheds and slaughter-houses, and the door-ways of undrained alleys, where the inhabitants carried the filth out on their shoes from the back-yard into the court, and from the court up into the main street; while above, hanging like cliffs over the streets—those narrow, brawling torrents of filth, and poverty, and sin,—the houses with their teeming load of life were piled up into the dingy, choking night.'

To Kingsley's contemporaries such scenes might be the cause of deep shame or merely disgusting, but it was difficult to ignore the book. Almost all the influential journals carried notices of the novel; depending on the complexion of their social and political views, their reviews were more or less scathing, for few of them were favourable, although today it is usually referred to as his most influential, if not his most finished, work. The *Edinburgh* was severe with it, the *Quarterly* vitriolic; *Blackwood's* found it 'so preposterously absurd as rather to excite ridicule than to move sympathy'. Even though Kingsley was a regular contributor to *Fraser's* (edited by the Parkers, who were perhaps jealous of the success of the book which they had refused), that magazine followed the lead of the others. One shrewd, although hostile, review was that of *The Times*:

'*Alton Locke* is the composition of any one but a Chartist. The favourite author of the writer, whoever he be, is Thomas Carlyle, and his production is precisely what Thomas Carlyle would call a "wind-bag" and "a sham". We are free to confess that great power, strong feeling, and masculine language are visible throughout the work, but in allowing so much we have stated all that can be admitted in the way of commendation. *Alton Locke* is not the labour of a working man with a smattering of learning, but of a scholar with an inkling of Chartism. Not another word need be said to prove its utter worthlessness as a handbook for our guidance.' Needless to remark, the reviewer did say a good bit more; the review filled three and one-half columns. The *Edinburgh* took thirty-three pages for its condemnation, and *Blackwood's* devoted thirty-six columns to the book.

Strong approval of the book was expressed by Shirley Brooks, who is best known to modern readers as the editor of *Punch*, when he wrote Chapman and Hall, hoping to discover the identity of the author:

'The editor of the *Morning Chronicle* (with which I am connected) has requested from me a review of an extraordinary novel just published by your house, "Alton Locke". I have not been so struck by any work I have taken up for years, and shall endeavour to make the article upon it a decided exception to the ordinary notices one writes of fictional works. It is a gratifying thing to see that a publisher *dares* to publish such a work, an evidence of courage, which . . . promises a speedy doom to the "novel mongering" practices of the hour.'

Another approving reaction was that of Caroline Fox, who 'read it as an intensely, frightfully practical book, and bought a more expensive pair of boots in consequence!'

However strong some of the opposition to it, no one could say that *Alton Locke* was being neglected; within the year three editions had been printed. Publicity, even adverse, was what Christian Socialism needed, royalties what Kingsley needed.

CHAPTER VII

'Not Members of the Church of England'

Kingsley had a boisterous friendliness which most people found irresistible, if occasionally annoying. Hughes described him as reminding one 'of a great fullgrown Newfoundland yearling dog out for an airing, plunging in and out of the water, and rushing against and shaking himself over ladies' silks and velvets, dandies' polished boots, or schoolboys' rough jackets; and all with a rollicking good humour which disarmed anger, and carried away the most precise persons into momentary enjoyment of the tumbling'. The important word is 'momentary', for in his headlong and impetuous fashion, he sometimes struck up acquaintances that ripened into friendship in a few hours, flourished for a short time, and then slowly fell into decay. It is probably the mark of an adult attitude toward friendships to realize that one must outgrow many of them, and that it is useless to prolong them after their vigour is gone. All the same, there is something pitiable in a man who has lost almost all the friends of his earlier life by the time of his death. It can only reflect something basically unstable in the quality of his own friendship; in Kingsley's case it was not only his inability to make friends easily with members of a different social class which was at fault, but also his inability to maintain friendship, once established, on a basis of equality and easy interchange of ideas.

The first part of this attitude is easy to understand. Although his own family was good, if not particularly distinguished, his wife's family disapproved of him, for they were still rising socially and financially. It was only natural, then, that he should become unduly conscious and occasionally assertive of his own gentility. Much as he worked to help the labouring classes, and however deeply he sympathized with them, he was never in any doubt about the distinction between their social position and his own, nor was he hesitant about pointing it out. At the other end of the social scale, his excessive consciousness of social distinction and his genuine admiration for royalty and the peerage made his excursions into society stiff and joyless. Lord Goderich was frequently embarrassed by the insistence with which Kingsley used his title when other friends had long since adopted a less formal address, Froude deplored his manners as at once too rigid and too coarse. It was only with men of his own station that he could relax comfortably and lose his self-consciousness.

Even among his social equals, however, Kingsley was harassed by a lack of assurance that sometimes swelled into self-assertiveness. For a time he would be borne along by the delight of making a new friend, but as the novelty wore off, instead of settling down to the calm give-and-take companionship which most men know, he was compelled to discover which of his friends he could master and which he could not. His combative nature was not like the school bully's, willing to take on all comers, but more like the behaviour of chickens in determining 'peck-order'. In the fowlyard a new bird soon has a series of skirmishes until her own place in the hen hierarchy is found, and after that she may peck with impunity all those below her and must accept with humility the nips of those higher in the scale. Once established, the order is never varied. That is precisely how Kingsley would have been happiest, could he have regulated the establishment of his relationships with friends. With some he immediately accepted with patience and admiration the role of an intellectual subordinate—his relationships with Maurice and with his scientific acquaintances are good examples of how he could defer to those whose minds he knew to be more profound or better informed than his own. Other friends tacitly took their places as his inferiors and the peace was kept. Of course some were either unconscious of the place assigned them or ignored it, and the result was sometimes unpleasant. When he felt it necessary, no one could deliver a home-truth with more enthusiasm than Kingsley. When he heard that Kingsley was dead, Monckton Milnes remarked that he had 'literally *rowed* himself to death, and everybody about him'. With old friends like Ludlow, Kingsley eventually quarrelled; with others like Hughes, the lack of real community of interest finally became apparent.

With younger men, however, Kingsley was almost universally successful. Mrs. Kingsley's biography of her husband is full of letters from former curates who worshipped him. His first pupil's biography is called *John Martineau: The Pupil of Kingsley* in tribute to the affection he felt for Kingsley.

Young Martineau came to Eversley on 21st January 1850 and stayed until the end of June the following year. Because he was considered too delicate to go anywhere so rough as the public schools were in those days, John was put to live and study with Kingsley. The Martineaus were Unitarians, but they were persuaded to let their son study with an Anglican parson because they were politically liberal and admired him for his reputation as a radical. Kingsley scupulously avoided proselytizing but John absorbed the religious ideas around him and eventually became a member of the Church of England. Even in this matter Kingsley was patient and moderate, for he and Maurice decided that confirmation for John was not essential and that it would only accentuate the difference between his views and those of his family.

Kingsley heard Martineau's lessons in the study after breakfast and after dinner. Naturally, the formal work was largely in Latin and Greek. In the afternoon came the lessons which both master and pupil enjoyed more. The fifteen-year-old boy and the Rector would walk around the parish, occasionally visiting the poor, more often talking, talking about nature, watching birds, learning plants, or, to the delight of both, doing a bit of angling in the Blackwater. Kingsley was at the height of his physical powers at thirty, and once in a long time there was hunting on a borrowed hack. Young John found the Rector grave and unlaughing on first acquaintance, but his impression may have been a reflection of his own nature, for two days after his arrival Mrs. Kingsley wrote her sister: 'Our boy came Monday & we like him very much, he is so teachable & conscientious, his only fault seems gravity & Exclusive devotion to his studies; wh. at *just* 15 does not seem natural. I think he will be no trouble only an interest to Charles.' Mrs. Kingsley petted John, mended his braces, saw to it that he had a fire in his room, and generally gave him the motherly affection a fifteen-year-old needs without ever admitting his need. John was frequently taken out to dinner with the family and helped entertain Mansfield, Parker, Ludlow and the other visitors who streamed to Eversley. Even the Scotch terrier Dandy adopted him, following him around the house and once trotting contentedly into the church at his heels in an attempt to enter the door of the family pew.

Kingsley's terms for pupils were £250 per annum or £5 a week. In asking Hughes to help him get another pupil, he wrote: 'I need not say that we are a jolly household, & not at all in the Squeers or Blimber line.' Martineau was joined in August 1850 by a twenty-three-year-old companion, William Lees, who came for four months immediately after taking his degree from Christ's College, Cambridge. Lees, an orphan of some means, studied theology with Kingsley in preparation for taking holy orders. He was generous with his money and once loaned £100 to help with the work on Jacob's Island; at one time he even thought of trying to buy up the whole area and replace it with model dwellings. A good deal of his money seems to have gone toward the purchase of fine hunters at Tattersall's (where he was 'done brown') and in other forms of youthful wildness which kept him from being ordained until 1854. After his ordination Lees saw little of Kingsley; Martineau was one of the family so long as the Kingsleys lived, he settled near Eversley, and at his death he was buried at Kingsley's feet.

Martineau and Lees were both at the Rectory during the Frimley outrages of 1850. Work was scarce, and bands of thieves and robbers wandered around the southern part of England. Mr. Hollest, the clergyman of nearby Frimley, was murdered in his own garden as he tried to chase away a group of thieves. Martineau wrote home in delight at the excitement at Eversley. A prowler was seen several times in the neighbourhood, so additional bolts were added to the doors, and wires from the doors were connected to the maids' bells so that they would ring if the doors were tried. Kingsley slept with a loaded gun and two pistols, Lees with a rifle and two pistols of his own; Kingsley asked to be sworn in as a special constable. On one occasion there was an alarm while Maurice was visiting, and the entire adult male contingent gave chase, leaving John importantly guarding the women and children with a rifle. There were marks of a crowbar on the door, but the thieves escaped. The danger was so great that John and Mrs. Kingsley stayed at home to guard the house when Kingsley was holding service in the church, and even then he seldom stayed for the entire service, but came home to help guard while Percy Smith preached the sermon. The same thieves molested John Parker at nearby Farnham, and Ludlow, visiting him, wrote Kingsley that Parker had 'ranged all his necessaries of defence in due order upon his table, beginning with his spectacles'.

Finally Kingsley sent to Odiham for a 'blue-bottle', to help guard the Rectory, and other police were stationed around the neighbourhood, for normally there were no police in the parish. When Mrs. Kingsley returned at seven o'clock in the evening from Reading, where she had bought additional bells to put on the front shutters, the Rector met her on horseback and escorted her home with pistol drawn. There were several other attempts to enter the house, and Kingsley fired at one of the intruders. To Martineau's intense disappointment the pistol was loaded with slugs rather than a bullet, so that the prowler was not killed but escaped into the darkness. Eventually one of Mr. Hollest's murderers was caught by the London doctor to whom he went to have shot removed from his back, the countryside settled down to calm once more, and the clergyman's widow consoled herself by marrying the detective who had been investigating the case. Later that year Kingsley wrote a series of four articles, 'Thoughts on the Frimley Murder', for the *Christian Socialist.*

During the next two or three years Kingsley tried several times to get pupils, but his own reputation seems to have kept them from coming to Eversley. To Hughes he wrote: 'As a good Socialist, you should try & help me—for *my Socialism prevents my getting pupils*—I am a martyr to my opinions! ! !' To Maurice he told another story: 'Martineau leaves me in June, perhaps so much the better for me, for I do not doubt that his presence has kept away more than one pupil.' In January 1851, at Maurice's suggestion, he offered to take Archdeacon Hare's difficult nephew Francis as a pupil. His letter to Maurice is some indication of the shockproof side of Kingsley's nature: 'I do *not* mind a lad's having been a scapegrace about girls, or even having tried to lie himself out of a scrape, if there is any tolerable substratum of tenderness & chivalry, to which one can appeal. The selfish, silent, sly animal is the only one for which I see nothing but "jackass's medicine". If you think there is a soul in the lad which will wash, I will try to wash it. I should make no secret of knowing his faults, & try to put it to his honour not to corrupt Martineau.' Young Hare never came to Eversley; seventeen years later he died after one of the most colourfully profligate careers of the century.

The reason, of course, for Kingsley's anxiety to get pupils was that he was once more desperate for money; after he had made several appeals to Hughes for help, a £500 loan was arranged, which was finally paid in full early in 1857 with the proceeds from *Two Years Ago.*

At the beginning of 1850 Kingsley and Ludlow had begun corresponding about the necessity of a new periodical to replace the defunct *Politics*; on November 2nd appeared the first number of the *Christian Socialist, a Journal of Association, Conducted by Several of the Promoters of the London Working Men's Associations.* It was a weekly, quarto-size, with eight pages, and cost a penny; Ludlow was the editor. There was some controversy over the title, but Maurice insisted on the frank one adopted because critics would then be unable to complain that either the Christian or the Socialist aspect of the movement was brought in under cover of the other. Kingsley's first contribution to the new journal was the four-part 'Thoughts on the Frimley Murder'. In all, he contributed thirty-nine poems, articles, or stories to the magazine before it finished publication at the end of 1851. It was succeeded by the *Journal of Association*, and during the six-month life of this last of the three Christian Socialist periodicals, Kingsley contributed only three poems and one article.

Kingsley's own favourite work in the *Christian Socialist* was a long and rambling series in nine instalments called 'Bible Politics', which aimed at 'showing that Democracy *is* the idea of the Bible and the cause of God', and at demonstrating the falsehood of the belief that 'the Bible is the book which, above all others, supports priestcraft, superstition and tyranny'. His fellow Christian Socialists liked the series less, but they could scarcely complain of what he wrote, for he was already established as their most influential writer. The 22nd November 1851 issue contains proof of his popularity: an advertisement which announces that 'With the present No. of this journal is given away a correct Likeness in lithography of the Rev. Charles Kingsley (author of "Alton Locke," &c.) with autograph on superior Plate Paper.'

Another indication of Kingsley's growing reputation was a request from Charles A. Dana of the New York *Tribune*, offering to pay liberally for a novel. Kingsley had to answer that he had no suitable work in hand, but recommended in his place his 'most intimate friend, & brother-in-law', Froude. Clearly, the Rector was beginning to make his way in the world.

Already the distinguished foreign visitors were asking to meet him. One of those who came to see the Great Exhibition was the Swedish novelist, Frederika Bremer, who declared that the Crystal Palace was secondary to meeting Kingsley. Her wish was granted, and she was invited for a weekend at Eversley, where she asked to see a furze bush because when Linnaeus had seen one for the first time he fell on his knees and thanked God;

neither Miss Bremer nor the bush was a disappointment, and she, too, knelt before it with tears in her eyes. The Kingsley children were particularly interested to note that she had trouble at family prayers in slipping into a kneeling position because she was so tiny that her feet would not reach the floor from her low armchair. The serious Miss Bremer thought the trip worthwhile just 'to meet the author of *Alton Locke*'.

The same year Tennyson stayed at Eversley Rectory. He came to look at Brick Hill House, a fine Jacobean farmhouse up the hill from the Rectory, as a possible place in which to settle with his bride, but while he and Kingsley smoked their pipes in the study, the Rector, although it went against the grain, pointed out that the house looked due north and that it was kept permanently damp from the springs draining into it from the hillside in which it was set. During his stay Tennyson sat for a pen-and-ink portrait by Kingsley, but the drawing has since disappeared. It was Tennyson's only visit to Eversley, but he and Kingsley frequently met in London, and the Kingsleys stayed at Faringford in November 1860, when Tennyson read 'Maud' in its entirety to Mrs. Kingsley 'with the extraordinary and illuminating emphasis with which he could read his own works—a never to be forgotten experience'.

On the front page of *The Times* of 21st June 1851 appeared an innocent advertisement:

> THE Rev. C. KINGSLEY, M.A., Jun., Rector of Eversley, Hants, will PREACH To-morrow evening, at St. John's Church, Charlotte-Street, Fitzroy-square, the Third of a Series of Discourses on the Church and its Message to Different Orders of Society. Subject—'The Message of the Church to Labouring Men.'

The Rev. G. S. Drew, Rector of St. John's, had planned a series of six Sunday evening sermons, primarily for the young professional men of the neighbourhood of Charlotte Street and for the many working men who came to London that summer for the Great Exhibition. Maurice had given the first of the talks and was to give the fifth of the series; F. W. Robertson of Brighton delivered the second; Kingsley the third; Septimus Hansard was to follow Kingsley; and after Maurice's second sermon, the incumbent was to give the last of the series. The sermons had been well advertised, and on June 22nd, there was a large crowd gathered to hear Kingsley. The general tenor of the sermon was no surprise to the congregation, and it can hardly have been so to Mr. Drew. The heart of it was Kingsley's assertion 'that all systems of society which favour the accumulation of capital in a few hands—which oust the masses from the soil which their forefathers possessed of old—which reduce them to the level of serfs and day-labourers, living on wages and on alms—which crush them down with debt, or in anywise degrade or enslave them, or deny them a permanent stake in the commonwealth, are contrary to the kingdom of God which Jesus proclaimed'. It was an effective setting-forth of the principles of Christian Socialism in precisely the tone the congregation expected. As Kingsley was about to give the blessing after the sermon he was interrupted by the voice of Drew, rising at his reading-desk to protest against what Kingsley had said as largely dangerous and untrue, and quite unlike what he had been led to expect. Somewhat to the surprise of everyone, Kingsley merely bowed his head and after the blessing left the pulpit without a word, pushing his silent way to the vestry through crowds of his hearers who spontaneously ran forward to wish him well. Robertson and Hansard took his sermon from his hands, then went out to calm the working men who were beginning to hiss Mr. Drew; eventually the church was emptied without any further incident.

Before Kingsley went back to Eversley that night, he went with several others to Maurice's house for a calming cup of tea. Only Kingsley seemed undisturbed; Ludlow, in particular, felt somewhat guilty, for it was through him that his acquaintance Drew had approached the Christian Socialists. Kingsley preserved his sang-froid, as he had through the whole evening. When talk fell on Francis Newman's *The Soul, Her Sorrows and Aspirations*, he burst in with good-natured contempt: 'Oh, yes!

the s-s-s-soul and her stomach-aches!' and the resulting laughter reduced some of the edginess of the group. Kingsley arrived in Eversley late that night and paced up and down the lawn outside the study. Mrs. Kingsley knew he must be composing, and the next morning he recited to her the beautiful little ballad, 'The Three Fishers', the result of his chagrin.

Everyone else connected with the Drew affair was less calm. Maurice and Hansard naturally refused to lecture for Mr. Drew, who announced that on the following Sunday the sermon would be by 'the MINISTER. Subject—The Message of the Church to the Poor'. Hansard and Robertson rushed Kingsley's sermon off to be printed exactly as he had delivered it; it appeared on July 5th. Meantime the press began on Kingsley. The *English Churchman* described the scene in St. John's: 'After Prayers, Mr. Kingsley, whose appearance was that of a somewhat conceited, literary, intellectual young man, entered the pulpit. . . . Mr. Kingsley has become somewhat notorious as the author of "*Alton Locke*, Tailor and Poet," a book of doubtful principles we understand, but which we have never seen.' The *Daily News* demanded in its leading article that the Bishop of London investigate Kingsley's fitness to preach. Bishop Blomfield wrote to Kingsley to forbid him to preach in London. Kingsley replied at once:

My Lord

I beg to acknowledge your letter, which I have just received, & to thank you for the considerate & kind tone of it. I am most deeply pained at finding that any hearsay reports should have given you an impression of my sermon, quite contrary to that which the perusal of it will, I trust, & hope, produce in your Lordship's mind. I am emboldened to hope this from the gratifying acknowledgements which I have already received from clergymen of all parties, many of them utterly unknown to me. I have therefore taken the liberty of directing a copy to be sent to you.

I must express my great sorrow for having, however innocently or unconsciously, added a moment's trouble to your

Lordship's numerous anxieties; but as I am fully aware that I have said or done nothing whatsoever contrary to the doctrine or discipline of the Church of England as by Law established, I must venture to express a hope that your Lordship will reconsider your request, & thus relieve me from my present delicate & humiliating position.

I remain your Lordship's most obedient servant

Charles Kingsley

When Blomfield had read the sermon, he at once invited Kingsley to visit him and withdrew his prohibition.

Although he was cleared of all blame in the Drew affair after talking to Blomfield, the whole business had exhausted Kingsley. His mother, who was always solicitous for his health, persuaded him to accompany Henry, Mr. Kingsley, and herself on a two-month vacation in Germany. It was Kingsley's first trip across the Channel and it was the longest time he had been separated from Fanny, who was to take Rose and Maurice on a round of visits to her relatives while Charles was gone. The church and Rectory at Eversley were left in the charge of the curate, Percy Smith. The suddenness of his leave-taking made preparations difficult, but Kingsley had time to buy a new brown high-crowned wide-awake hat to match that of Henry, who was taking his long vacation from Worcester College, Oxford.

The packet-boat left London Bridge in a drizzle, but the dismal weather was forgotten when Kingsley discovered that their travelling companions were to be Thackeray and his daughters. Anne Thackeray, then thirteen, was less interested in the literary conversation than she was in the splendour of the Kingsley brothers' wide-awakes, which quite eclipsed her father's new grey hat; her enthusiasm for headgear was probably sharpened by her own new bonnet, for in later years her memories of the Kingsleys on that crossing seemed to be concerned primarily with their poetic appearance in their new hats. The crossing to Antwerp was rough, but Kingsley stood sailor-like while women were sick all around him; Thackeray wisely retired under a table in the saloon to rest.

When the Kingsleys reached the Continent, they set out for the Rhine; Charles wrote home constantly on letterheads which Fanny had prepared for him by writing in the names of the cities from which she expected notes. Kingsley naturally missed the whole sense of peace which he felt with Fanny, and he found that when he was with his family he was constantly chafing against the aloof impoliteness with which his father treated his mother:

'I do think I am a comfort to my poor mother. I am as attentive to her as possible. . . . But I confess it is hard to keep one's temper, when one sees her so bullied—& yet slaving on. It makes my blood boil; but I have not had any unpleasantness as yet. Oh pray for me, that I may not quarrel with him. He is as kind as possible to *me*, & at heart, I know well, there is nothing that he would not do for her. But it is the *little* things which make up life, as you often say.'

Of his mother he wrote: 'What a woman that is! I know not which is the larger, her heart or her head. Except you, I know no human being to whom I dare say so much of my inner heart about *you*, & poetry, & Popery, & the old Saints, & all the forbidden depths.'

Mrs. Kingsley, in her turn, sent encouraging messages to her daughter-in-law to report that 'Charles is so well & grown fat', and then indicated her sensitivity to his kindness: 'How happy he is!—and he deserves it—It shall be the *last* joy of my life & my only self indulgence, to introduce him to God in Nature, where he has never seen him before, & where He is so grand & beautiful.' When Charles wrote from Ems: 'I have just had my first sight of the basalt opposite the Kurhaus of all Kurhaus—so lovely one longs to *kiss it*,' his mother could not resist a teasing postscript: 'Think of his *kissing* the curhouse! Don't be jealous.'

The entire family was too tired to travel far from Antwerp, so they went through Cologne to Ems, where they settled for a fortnight, making local excursions in the vicinity of Coblenz in the intervals between mineral baths at Ems. On a steamer trip to Bingen Kingsley climbed the face of the Lurlei 'to the Nymph's own seat' to pick a little bouquet for Fanny, which he dried with several other souvenirs. Ehrenbreitstein was utterly disappointing, for 'the lying painters paint it just three times as high as it is'. To Rose and Maurice he sent playful letters, telling of climbing the mountains near Ems with his parents and their friend Louisa Plum. 'Grandmamma and Louisa Plum had donkeys, and Grandpapa had a mule. . . . Coming down the mule squealed out, & tried to kick Daddy when he was doing nothing at all to it. The donkeys are very good here, but the mules are very naughty.' By good fortune they were in Ems during the birthday celebration of its ruler, the Duke of Nassau, and he told Rose and Maurice of seeing the school children carrying their blue and yellow flags, the little girls with garlands of flowers and oak leaves around their heads, marching off with their masters to spend the day in the woods. In the evening there was a 'grand ball, & the great room at the Kurhaus dressed up with lovely flowers, & all the houses lit lamps, red & blue & green, & lights floating on the river in the dark'.

His letters to his wife during this trip are a different story. All of them are full of his desperate loneliness for her, many of them are too intimate for printing. From Ems he wrote: 'You do not seem to recollect how dreadfully I long for you in *body*—as well as mind. I kiss those two locks of hair till I am ready to cry, & think of you *all day long*—I don't believe you are out of my head for half an hour together by day—& I am always talking about you, & at night, unless I have walked myself tired, I cannot sleep for thinking of you, & if I wake I begin longing & thinking & picturing you to myself.'

Most of Kingsley's correspondence from Germany, the largest single group of love letters to his wife that has survived, is now in the Parrish Collection at Princeton. Turning the brittle blue sheets with their broken vermilion seals, one frequently has the feeling of a trespasser, reading the still-vivid messages of love in fading brown ink. The intensity of the physical passion is startling, not for its existence but for its expression, particularly by an earnest young clergyman of the 1850s. One of the letters, considerably less specific physically than the others, shows how thoroughly inseparable were his religious belief in the spirituality and beauty of temporal life and his strongly passionate nature. The letter indicates better than volumes of his sermons do the reason he hated spiritualism, monasticism, Roman Catholicism, and all the other apparent denials of the flesh which he lumped indiscriminately together as Manicheism:

'I shall now doubly thank God for this trip, since it has taught thee as well as me, so much. I feel most thoroughly what you say about thee & thou. One cannot help instinctively using it in the higher poetry. It seems the only true way of addressing the person. But I have now a new fear. After reading all the deep & dear spiritual wisdom in your letter, I fear you may think mine too exclusively physical—that I love your body—rather than your mind. But it is not so—only I cannot & will not analyze. I love *thee*—& I cannot divide thy body from mind or thy mind from thy spirit. Thou art *one*—as it is written—my love, my dove, my undefiled is but *one*, & I know no parts or distinctions in you—therefore it is that I think of you as in the body so much . . . simply because it is thou—& that will endure through old age, & death, on to the resurrection, & so for ever & ever & ever. I cannot tell you what I mean—words are very cold—But your body to me is the sacrament of *you*, and thou art one!'

Naturally, much of Kingsley's loneliness was transformed into poetry written for his wife. Among the several he sent home was one of his most successful poems, seventeen lines of verse which he rather perversely called 'Sonnet':

The baby sings not on its mother's breast;
Nor nightingales who nestle side by side;
Nor I by thine: but let us only part,
Then lips which should but kiss, and so be still,
As having uttered all, must speak again——
O stunted thoughts! O chill and fettered rhyme!
Yet my great bliss, though still entirely blest,
Losing its proper home, can find no rest:
So, like a child who whiles away the time
With dance and carol till the eventide,
Watching its mother homeward through the glen;

Or nightingale, who, sitting far apart,
Tells to his listening mate within the nest
The wonder of his star-entrancèd heart
Till all the wakened woodlands laugh and thrill——
Forth all my being bubbles into song;
And rings aloft, not smooth, yet clear and strong.

With the poem he sent a note to tell Fanny: 'I have shewn it my father & mother, & they like it—*so perhaps you will.* I was forced to shew it them, for I had written a great deal that I would not shew, so they were a little jealous—& wondered what it could all be about! ! ! you understand.'

The first week in August Kingsley and Henry set out for a fortnight in the Eifel and the country around the Moselle. Kingsley was only a little cast down because Fanny had not received his earlier letters, which Mr. Kingsley had mailed via France 'for oeconomy' rather than by the faster Ostend route. Kingsley looked forward to the walking, for by now he was 'in very rude health, & enjoying everything to the full extent of his powers, moral & physical'.

While her two sons were in the Eifel, Mrs. Kingsley planned on staying at Ems but finally went east to Dresden. 'In after years [she] used to be fond of telling her grandchildren how another lady and herself had been extremely terrified, when they were once walking together in the vicinity of Dresden, by the sudden appearance, around a bend in the road, of a ragged, resolute, ruffian-looking young vagabond, who, fixing his wild gray eyes on them, and uttering an exclamation which they interpreted as a menace, had approached them with, as they had thought, the intention of peremptorily demanding alms; and how a close inspection had revealed that he was none other than her own son George, returning literally from Bohemia, with his clothes in tatters, the remnants of his boots tied together with pieces of string, and his face burnt as brown as a gipsy's, radiant, with his freedom and his joy at seeing her again.'

As her other two sons were leaving for their own trip, Kingsley sent off a last letter to Fanny:

'I am just off this afternoon for the Eifel for a fortnight. I take (you may like to hear) a knapsack with a plaid, 2 clean shirts, clean trousers, clean brown holland coat, 2 prs. of worsted socks, a little paper to write to you *twice* a week, my pipe, fishing tackle, a pair of slippers for the evening, a little German testament, word-book, map of the Eifel, & note book. And so we start—& in a fortnight appear at Bonn with *beards*, I suppose, for shaving is out of the question. I get better & better, though your letter made me very unhappy—But I have written lots more poetry, & most of it about—*you*. Oh how I love you!—I take my money, £5, which my mother *will* furnish, whether I like or not, & *your locks of hair*, in a little bag round my neck.'

The next two weeks were hard walking. At one point Kingsley and Henry found themselves at the top of a 500-foot cliff at night, 'with a roaring river at the bottom, and *no* path. So down the cliff-face we had to come in the dark, or sleep in the forest to be eaten by wild boars and wolves, of which latter, one was seen on our route yesterday "as high as the table". And down we came, knapsacks, fishing-rods, and all; which process must not be repeated often if we intend to revisit our native shores.' After the richness and softness of the 'perfectly exquisite' Moselle, Kingsley found the Eifel 'the loveliest place you can imagine', the whole country a jumble of 'Cambridgeshire ugliness (only lifted up 1,200 feet high) with all the beauties of Devonshire'. The inhabitants of the country were equally interesting; at Birreborn they found the landlord of their inn, 'a dirty pothouse-keeper', capable of both good fishing and informed judgment on the stained glass at Cologne. 'Really this Germany is a wonderful country—though its population are not members of the Church of England—and as noble, simple, shrewd, kindly hearts in it, as man would wish to see.'

The physical hardship was just what Kingsley needed to make him recover from his mental exhaustion and the indigestion which inevitably accompanied it. He was 'lean as a lath, as any one would be, who carried two stone of baggage daily increasing in weight from the minerals and fossils I find, on his back through broiling suns. We are both worse than the "hollow pampered jades of Asia, that cannot go but thirty miles a-day", for with our knapsacks we can only make fifteen, and then a sight-seeing walk in the evening.' But in spite of losing weight, he reported to Fanny:

'I am exceedingly well & strong, though I did dine yesterday off *raw ham & hock at 9d a bottle*.—Oh! and had no katzenjammer after it! ! ! My knapsack & plaid weigh about 2 stone, which is very heavy; but I go well enough under it, having got a pair of elastic cross straps, which divide the weight over the breast bone. Henry's kit is lighter, but I am getting old & luxurious & cannot move without little comforts—which of course one's non-taking friends *borrow* after all.'

At the end of the walking trip the Kingsleys found themselves involved in low comedy at Treves, where they were brought under arrest by a constable sent by the mayor of Bitburg, who had been alarmed by the two foreigners speaking German with an accent and carrying over their shoulders fishing-rods which he took for some sort of deadly weapon. Even the famous wide-awakes which Anne Thackeray had so admired were taken not as the garb of poets but as Italian hats, so it was clear to the befuddled mayor that they must be emissaries of Mazzini engaged in distributing political tracts. The pair was thrown into prison at Treves, where they had the pleasure of spending a night 'among fleas and felons, on the bare floor'. Luckily, the police inspector of Treves 'was a gentleman, and his wife and daughter ladies, and they did all they dared for us'. Liberation came the next morning 'with much laughter & many curses on the Dogberry of Bitburg from the Police' at Treves. The constable, 'who, after all, poor fellow, was very civil', was sent back to Bitburg with a reprimand. The same evening the elder Kingsleys appeared unexpectedly and found their sons 'at the Trierischer Hof, the lions of Treves pro tempore—for the affair has made considerable fuss'.

The reunited family travelled slowly to Bonn, Brussels, Waterloo, Ghent, and Bruges before sailing once more from Ostend. For Fanny, Kingsley bought 'some chamois gloves & little washing silk handkerchiefs' and 'a bit of trumpery'. In his last letter to her from the Continent, Kingsley told her how much he longed for the hour of their reunion, when he hoped she would not be wearing spectacles: 'I *do* hate them so! I sat next the *first* woman today I have seen in them, & behold she was an Englishwoman! & I *shuddered.* Don't be angry, there's a darling love for I love you better than all the world beside!'

CHAPTER VIII

The Historical Novelist

Kingsley's Continental trip was restful to him, but when he returned to England, he was once more in the midst of controversy. The year of 1851 was a bad one generally for his reputation with the press. W. R. Greg attacked the Christian Socialists in an article in the *Edinburgh Review*, taking them to task for establishing the Working Tailors' Association and its parallel organization, the Needlewoman's Association; Greg singled out for particular wrath *Alton Locke* and *Cheap Clothes and Nasty*. In indignation Kingsley wrote Ludlow:

'The man has grossly insulted me, in language which he dared not have made use of to my face. He has tried with all his might to do harm to the good cause and that not in a letter to an editor, or a pamphlet, but with the whole corporate force of the Edinburgh Review. . . . I am perfectly sick of the new editorial cant of "misunderstanding". Men lie now, & excuse it by saying that they cannot understand *you*, & then when you call their lies by the right name, they turn round, & say that you have misunderstood *them*.'

All through the year the high church *Guardian* took potshots at the Christian Socialists, whom it accused of wanting a new Church and of interfering with the natural law of supply and demand in their setting up of co-operative associations. On May 7th the *Guardian* carried an anonymous review of the newly reprinted *Yeast*. Although the reviewer conceded that the social criticism was valid, he felt that 'it is, on the whole, a trashy and mischievous production. . . . Lancelot, a "healthy animalist", who has gone through that course of profligacy which is considered necessary to develop the nature and impart breadth and manliness to the intellect of the latest and most philosophical phase of Christianity. . . . Professing to aim at religious earnestness and high morality, its tendencies are really toward the destruction of both. . . . All practical religious convictions [Kingsley] endeavours alike laboriously to unsettle. . . . Above all, we are utterly at issue with him in an opinion that a certain amount of youthful profligacy does no real and permanent harm to the character: perhaps strengthens it for a useful and even religious life; and that the existence of the passions is a proof that they are to be gratified.' In her personal copy of her biography of her husband, Mrs. Kingsley wrote many years later in purple ink: 'John Duke Coleridge, now Lord C., confessed 1880.' Of course Kingsley wrote a hot reply to Coleridge, disdaining to argue, merely repeating: 'Mentiris impudentissimé.'

Later that year the *Guardian*, in 'The Social Regeneration School', deprecated Kingsley's connection with the *Leader*, whose advertising placards listed him as a contributor. Primly the *Guardian* noted that the *Leader* had printed a funeral oration for a Mrs. Emma Martin, who was both a communist and a woman who had contracted a common-law marriage—and that Kingsley wrote for such a periodical. To this kind of reasoning Kingsley could only reply truthfully that his sole connection with the *Leader* had been a letter protesting against the paper's communist doctrine.

Over and over Kingsley and his friends had to submit to this sort of muddle-headed criticism, and if it did not wear down his enthusiasm, it taxed his patience to not very distant limits. The cause of Christian Socialism, he complained to Ludlow, 'wants notoriety. In plain English we haven't had row enough yet.' Knowing that Ludlow was inclined to caution, he confessed that the writing of *Alton Locke* and *Yeast*, his avowal of Chartism at Drury Lane, and his sermon for Mr. Drew were all acts to which he felt impelled, however foolish others might think them.

'But I do humbly think that these vagaries of mine which might, I know well—though I have not yet wisdom to see how—have been done just as effectually *without* a mess, have helped us on really. I do think my speeches & sermon have given the workmen a confidence in us, which they might not have had, had I been less reckless about committing myself. I do think Alton Locke's plain speaking has smashed its way into more than one heart, which you could not have conquered on the usual plan of killing a flea recommended by Charles Matthews . . . viz. "Tickling a flea gently till he opens his mouth & then cramming your elbow down his throat." '

Hoping to curry favour for their social reforms by being friendly to the high church party would not work: 'I cottoned to the Guardian & found that I had been doing very much like the gentleman who asks for a kiss out of window in Chaucer's tale, and gets to kiss—you recollect what.' What remained was to concentrate attack on a periodical, not a religious paper, and to be so offensive as to be publicly noticed. Once more Ludlow had to dampen his ardour, to steady him down.

Kingsley's own situation as spiritual adviser at Eversley was secure enough, however dangerous he might seem to outsiders; increased notoriety merely meant increased sales for his books. There were others who had to worry more over reputation. Dr. Jelf, Principal of King's College, had already refused to allow Kingsley to teach at the College, and now he became fretful over Maurice's associations: 'Mr. Maurice is identified with Mr. Kingsley, and Mr. Kingsley is identified with Mr. Holyoake [of the *Leader*], and Mr. Holyoake is identified with Tom Paine. . . . There are only three links between King's College and the author of the "Rights of Man".' On the basis of this dubious reasoning Jelf appointed a committee to investigate Maurice's opinions and fitness to teach. The committee expressed its regret that Maurice was 'mixed up with publications . . . which they consider to be of very questionable tendency', but found no reason to dismiss him. The gentle Maurice was deeply wounded by the notoriety and the implications of the investigation; Jelf was hurt, too, but only because he had failed to get rid of Maurice. However, he could afford to wait, for sooner or later Maurice or one of his friends would make a misstep.

In spite of all his friends' counsel to write no more novels, in spite of Fanny's pleas to give them up, in spite of his own resolves, Kingsley had begun reading in 1850 and 1851 in preparation for another story, but before he began it, he took a practice swing at the subject by writing a 'Socratic' dialogue, *Phaethon; or, Loose Thoughts for Loose Thinkers*, to attack 'Emersonian pseudo-spiritualism'. The central figure is an American, Professor Windrush, 'a rampantly heterodox spiritual guerilla', who is intended as an incarnation of Emersonian doctrine, which Kingsley thought was Neo-Platonic at the core. Kingsley's delight in demolishing Windrush was greater than his skill, and the reviewers naturally fastened on the unfortunate subtitle of the book to describe his method of thinking.

'Hypatia: or, New Foes with an Old Face' appeared in sixteen instalments in *Fraser's* in 1852–3 and was issued in book form by Parker as soon as the last instalment had appeared in the magazine. As if to foreshadow his later withdrawal from political and social matters, Kingsley turned from the contemporary England of *Yeast* and *Alton Locke* to set the new novel in fifth-century Alexandria, 'a very hideous, though a very great age'. As the subtitle indicates, he is still concerned with the dangers of celibacy and Manicheism, but the close observation of the society around him which gave life and spontaneity to the first two novels is replaced by the re-creation of the turmoil and daily upheaval of the 'last struggle of the Young Church and the Old World'. Kingsley wrote Maurice: 'I have exhausted both my stock & my brain, & really require to rest it, by turning it to some new field, in which there is richer & more picturesque life, & the elements are less confused—or rather, may be handled more in the mass than English ones now.'

Perhaps all historical novels tell as much of the contemporary life of their authors as they do of past periods of time; certainly, *Hypatia*, like many Victorian novels of the genre, seems as much of the nineteenth century as of the period it purports to record. The fault lies in Kingsley's attitudes, rather than in his research, for he had spent much of his free time for more than two years in adding to his knowledge of the theology, the philosophy, and the daily life of the Alexandrian Christians, the Neo-Platonists, and the invading Goths. Before he had finished preparing *Yeast* for republication, he was writing to Maurice to ask: 'Can you tell me something about those later Alexandrian Platonists in the 4th. & 5th. century? or where I can find out about them?' Of William Cope, still at Westminster Abbey, he asked the loan of several Latin histories of the period, for 'second-hand authorities are as bad as second hand dinners—one's neighbours' leavings—if not worse'. Of necessity he had to use Gibbon's *Decline and Fall of the Roman Empire*, although he did not like the book.

When Maurice wrote to congratulate him on the first instalment of *Hypatia*, Kingsley explained its genesis: 'My idea in the Romance is to set forth Christianity as the only really Democratic creed, & Philosophy, above all Spiritualism, as the most exclusively aristocratic creed. Such has been my opinion for a long time, & what I have been reading lately confirms it more & more.' A year later he told Hughes that the moral of the novel was 'that all "philosophy" is essentially aristocratic, & that Xtianity, even its *lowest* form, has the only true Gospel for the people'.

The plot of the book is woven around the young monk Philammon, who leaves his desert community to go to Alexandria, where he forsakes Christianity when he submits to the charm of the beautiful Hypatia and becomes her disciple in Neo-Platonism. He recognizes the seductive Pelagia, mistress of the leader of the Goths, as his long-lost sister and tries to win her away from her sinful life. Hypatia is eventually murdered by a Christian mob at the very moment when she seems to be reaching out for Christianity. Philammon returns to the desert and becomes a hermit until he is made abbot of his monastery; he remains true to his monastic vows but is made aware of the limitations of celibacy. Pelagia dies as a Christian anchorite, still faithful to the memory of her Goth lover.

Philammon is a wooden character, Pelagia too much the nineteenth-century courtesan of good heart, and Hypatia too like the beautiful high church Argemone of *Yeast*; the most vivid of the characters is Raphael Aben Ezra, a vital and cultivated Jew who becomes a Christian convert. Raphael is an articulate cousin of Lancelot Smith, and like him represents Kingsley's own point of view.

The model for Raphael was a brilliant Jewish barrister, Alfred Hyman Louis, ten years younger than Kingsley, who had been drawn into the Christian Socialist movement by his lawyer friends and eventually converted to Christianity by his association with the group. Kingsley baptized him at Eversley two months before the first instalment of *Hypatia* appeared. Kingsley told Hughes: 'Raphael was suggested to me by Louis, & I am so fond of him that he who touches him, touches me.' Subsequently, Kingsley found Louis rather difficult to work with, as he continually sided with Ludlow in what Kingsley thought were hare-brained schemes. Louis, who later claimed friendship with George Eliot and insisted that he was her model for Daniel Deronda, contributed to the *Spectator* and the *Fortnightly*, wrote poetry and several books on English foreign policy. He was a close friend of the Meynells and through them met Cardinal Manning, who received him into the Roman Catholic Church. As he aged, Louis had intermittent periods of insanity and became something of a tramp. On one of his trips to the United States he became part of another literary group, including Edwin Arlington Robinson, for whom he was the original of still another fictional character, the title figure in *Captain Craig*. When he died in 1915, Louis had returned to the Jewish faith and was buried in a Jewish cemetery in London.

It is not always easy to see how Kingsley is serving Christianity in *Hypatia*, because, as always, his allegiance is to the physically vital, regardless of religion: to Raphael, to Synesius ('The Squire-Bishop' who hunts ostriches in a fifth-century version of the foxhunt), most of all to the band of drinking, plundering Goths, uncouth but with the 'new and healthier blood' which 'those wild tribes were bringing with them into the magic circle of the Western Church's influence [as] the very materials which she required for the building up of a future Christendom'. Kingsley's allegiance is indicated less by overt statement than by the exuberance with which he writes of the Goths and of the Jew. The monks and priests, who obstinately refused to make themselves into Victorian Protestants, are by contrast a sorry lot. In their paganism Hypatia and Pelagia are considerably more attractive than is Victoria, the pretty young Christian who converts Raphael. Actually, it is the vividness of the crowded city, full of conflicting groups, which gives the novel life, rather than the ideas for which those groups stand.

The curious mingling of elements in the novel was recorded by Lewis Carroll in his diary: 'Finished *Hypatia*: it is powerful, like all that Kingsley writes—outrageous to taste in some parts, which is a new fault (to me): I mean especially the sneers at Christianity which he puts into the mouths of some of the heathen characters, and the undisguised horrors of the gladiators' show in the theatre, and the death of Hypatia. It bears out the theory of the affinity between things dreadful and things beautiful, that he displays the most perfect sense of beauty, and some of his English reads like unmetrical poetry.' Tennyson was somewhat shocked at the novel; he found it powerful and tragic, but he hated the use of the word 'naked', and he said that he 'really was hurt at having Hypatia stript' at her death.

The large number of characters gave some trouble to Kingsley, and they are frequently difficult for the reader to keep straight. They also forced him into a mechanical alternation between the strands of his story; all but two of the instalments in *Fraser's* contained two chapters each, and the necessity of advancing at least two lines of the story each month makes the original periodical publication too evident in the novel as a whole. As usual, Kingsley began publishing the early chapters before he was sure of the plan of the entire book.

There was some initial trouble over the publication of the novel, for Kingsley felt himself indebted to Chapman, who had published *Alton Locke* when Parker refused it. When Parker suggested publishing *Hypatia* in *Fraser's*, Kingsley wrote him:

'As for your proposition about Hypatia, I like it entirely. But I do not know how far Chapman may consider me bound to him. I have therefore written to him, without mentioning from whom the offer comes, but frankly stating the case, & asking him how far he considers me bound, & openly asking him to let me off, if he thinks right. That is the honest thing, & the honest thing always pays. But I have many reasons for preferring your plan to any other. By bringing it out piecemeal, I should get passing criticisms on the *plot*, which would help me to weave it better & better as I went on, & that it would be better in a pecuniary point of view is self evident.'

Chapman agreed to release him, but Kingsley was still touchy because Parker had turned down *Alton Locke*. When Parker asked for a preface to make the moral intent of the book clear, Kingsley replied: 'As for a preface *I think*; & what is *a great deal more, Mrs. Kingsley* thinks, that it would only set peoples' ears & tails up, & make Mrs. Grundy suspicious. So just begin quietly, & trust me not to play the fool. If I do, you can but point out the locum suspectum. I should like to have the proof back as soon as possible; for I cannot tell what the *style* looks like, unless I see it in print . . .'

Parker had for some time been slipping away from his early sympathy with Christian Socialism. In February 1852, in the issue of *Fraser's* containing the second instalment of 'Hypatia', there appeared a discussion of Christian Socialism which concluded:

'We know the purity of intention by which these able and honest men are actuated; we believe their objects to be in the highest degree benevolent and elevating; that, practically, they would be as unwilling as we should be ourselves to sanction revolutionary or communist views. If, however, in the pursuit of a contingent good, they seem to sanction opinions and dogmas dangerous to the repose of society, or if they leave their actual convictions on these agitated questions open to misconstruction, they cannot be relieved from the responsibility of indirectly promoting a crusade against order and property, of which we believe, thus plainly set before them, no men in the kingdom would more conscientiously disapprove.'

In rage Kingsley wrote to Parker: 'The editor of Frazers' has put me in a very delicate position, by the last page of the February number. . . . But as a man who is before the public, as one of the members [of] a certain clique, I cannot allow that page to go forth in the same magazine with any writings of mine without a very strong & peremptory explanation of my own opinions about it. To do so, would be to fail as a gentleman & a man of honour, & to lose the whole of that influence with the working men for which I have ventured reputation, caste, even my position as a clergyman.

'I shall send, through you, a formal letter to the Editor of Frazer's, which I shall submit to the opinion of experienced friends first. On the way in which that letter is received, must, I am afraid, depend my future relations with Frazer's magazine.

'As far as Hypatia is concerned, I am of course, utterly bounden to it, & I need not tell you, that whatever happens will make no difference in my earnest endeavour to make Hypatia the best I can, & to fulfil my engagement. But all beyond that, will depend on your editor.

'I should tell you that I talked over Hypatia with Wilmott of Bearwood. That he approved entirely, & saw no anachronism in the style whatsoever; that agreed with my plan of rendering ancient slang into modern.'

Although no retraction of the offending words seems to have been printed, Kingsley and Parker arranged some kind of truce. Probably even this would have been impossible had Kingsley known that the anonymous editor, whose name even Maurice did not know, was Parker himself.

When the serial publication of *Hypatia* was attacked by George Henry Lewes, literary editor of the *Leader*, and by the *Guardian*, Kingsley wrote to defend himself to Parker. In January 1852 Lewes had written that 'on the whole the story excites little interest. The *wilful* mingling of the quite modern with the ancient colouring—for it must be wilful—we cannot help regarding as a mistake.' The following month he wrote of 'Kingsley's ambitious, but somewhat wearisome, *Hypatia*', and in April pronounced that '*Hypatia* (with a fine translation from Homer) is still the failure of a remarkable writer'. Kingsley wearily wrote

Parker of the May instalment: 'I should think the last no. would have satisfied the Guardian & respectability. As for the Leader. Don't mind it. Lewes is an ignorant charlatan, who dislikes me, because I have boldly shaken off the Leader, & therefore snarls & snaps. Froude still asserts that my costume is right. And I have been reading Ben Johnson [*sic*], & find that He, the most learned dramatist we have ever had, found mine *the* plan for reproducing a past age.' Before the last instalment had appeared, Parker took fright once more and complained to Kingsley that the magazine's reputation was suffering.

When Kingsley came to make terms with Parker for the book-publication of *Hypatia*, Parker shilly-shallied, saying that after all Kingsley had left him for other publishers. Kingsley wrote at once:

'I don't think that you can say, my dear fellow, that I left you. You yourself declined Alton Locke, when I offered it to you, & sent me kindly enough to Chapman, but you can't call that leaving you. And you declined also the sermons when I offered them you. And you declined Phaethon when I offered it to Frazer's. I would much sooner publish with you than with most other publishers: but I don't think that in a single case, *I* have left *you*.'

After this time Kingsley continued to contribute to *Fraser's*, and Parker continued to publish some of his sermons and minor writings, but *Hypatia* was the last novel which Kingsley offered to Parker.

In February 1851 Kingsley met for the first time the twenty-four-year-old Viscount Goderich, who, in spite of his family connections, was probably considerably more radical in his politics than any of his Tory-Chartist Christian Socialist friends. Kingsley was delighted to have a young nobleman in the movement, and he liked Goderich personally. Until Goderich's conversion to Roman Catholicism some years later, Kingsley maintained a respectful friendship with him, even supporting him on occasion against Maurice, and sticking loyally by when he was accused in 1852 of bribery in his election to the constituency of

Hull. Before Goderich was acquitted, Kingsley wrote Hughes: 'As for bribable gentlemen of course they exist—& syphilitic ones do too—& it is equally easy for either rich or poor to be bribed or p.x.d.' The whole Hull business Kingsley thought might cure his friend of ultra-democratic tendencies: 'It will be a good lesson to Goderich, too, and cure him of wanting to call himself "Jack Robinson"!' In his own letters Kingsley constantly addressed Goderich as 'My Lord'. If it was difficult for Kingsley to believe ill of the aristocracy, he could still worry about the bad influence of his own friends on Goderich. 'I am glad to hear good reports of Lord Goderich,' he wrote Hughes. '*Do* keep him in your hands, & make him *obey* Maurice; & don't, *don't* let Ludlow & Louis fanaticise him—pray don't!—Don't tell them I said soo——." Hughes was a close friend of Goderich, but Ludlow shunned his acquaintance.

More and more Kingsley turned for consolation to the undemanding, sportsman's common sense of Hughes: 'Your letters delight me, because you are the only man of our lot except Maurice, who seems to have the wildest sense of which way the cat jumps. All owing to three of the four royal F's; fishing, fowling, & foxhunting. . . . Hit Louis behind the ear, & Ludlow too. They are fine fellows, but, we who have read Bell's Life, know that a man can never fight well, till he has had one good licking.'

Ludlow seemed increasingly difficult; at times Kingsley could scarcely contain his temper. When Ludlow ventured to reprove Maurice for his opinions on strikes, Kingsley's reaction was as vehement as if the reproof had been for him. Although he wrote to 'Dearest Ludlow' and signed himself 'Yours affectionate ever', the tone of the letter is anything but affectionate:

'Between ourselves, I was perfectly shocked at the tone of your letter to Maurice. How a godly man like you, remembering your youth & inexperience, can write so to a man much older, better & wiser than yourself, & one who has done & suffered more in God's service a hundred-fold than you or I ever shall, I cannot conceive. As a mere question of modesty & reverence, I cannot conceive it, let alone the question of delicacy toward one who has just been through so fiery an ordeal as that King's College business. . . . My dear friend, when will you learn that severity & violence of expression are not always either true wisdom, strength, or honesty. . . . Do, for God's sake, repent of that letter. I would sooner have cut off a finger than have written it.'

Even Mansfield was no comfort to Kingsley now. Several years of living with his 'Magdalen' had produced the inevitable conflict in a man of deep Christian principles and strong sexual drives; somewhat belatedly he wanted to divorce the wife who had deserted him and to marry his 'female person'. 'I see nothing in the case at all complicated,' Kingsley told Ludlow. 'They *must* keep physically apart. She *must* leave the house where she lived as his mistress, & he *must* try for a divorce.' Finally Kingsley had to turn to plain speaking in an attempt to make Mansfield face his situation realistically:

'I have been trying hard to make him believe that his sorrows come from himself & the Devil, just because he *has* been believing that they come from God. He has been believing, & telling me that he is under a curse. That God's wrath is permanently abiding on him for acts committed at school years ago, which never can be undone, & that therefore—"If God be *against* him, what matter who is for him?" Now I have been trying to tell him, as I do everyone, "If God be for you, what matter who is against you?" . . . Am I to tell him that it *pleased* God that he should marry a harlot? or am I to tell him, "It pleased the devil, into whose power not God, but you yourself put yourself, when you, in days & deeds to which I was privy years ago, deliberately separated your own will from God, & determined to be a law unto yourself, & do exactly what was right in the sight of your own eyes?" '

Mansfield was unable to get a divorce, so in 1852 he left for an extended trip of exploration in South America, to try to forget what was incapable of resolution.

During this period Kingsley spent some time with a rather surprising admirer of his, a handsome young man named George Meredith. When *Yeast* appeared, Meredith wrote: 'I am driven with a spur to tell you the delight and admiration with which I read your last book, "Yeast", and the positive "Education" I have derived from it. It was the very book I was in want of and likely to do me more good than any that I know. May it do as great service in the world.' John Parker brought Meredith down to Eversley to stay with Kingsley, and they all gathered for Tuesday evening tea-drinking at the Parkers' shop. Ludlow had heard of Meredith only as an interesting young man with no particular promise, and when they met he was disgusted with him because 'there was such striving for effect in all he said'. Kingsley was delighted with Meredith,[1] but he thought rather less of his wife. If Mrs. Meredith actually had been Mansfield's mistress, as has been conjectured, there is good reason for the tone Kingsley took when he read 'Gastronomy and Civilisation' in the December 1851 issue of *Fraser's*. The piece was signed only with the initials 'M.M.', although it is probable that Meredith helped his wife in writing it. 'I hope the cookery article in the last Frazers' is not by Mrs. Meredith,' Kingsley wrote Parker. 'It is clever enough, of course; but a great deal of *bosh* about the Greeks—as wrong as it can be; very pedantic style; incoherent scraps of information shoved in on purpose; & bold confession of having read books (Petronius to wit) which no decent woman should touch with a pair of tongs. It is all hypocrisy to talk of Petronius, yet be ashamed to confess to Fanny Hill or Harriet Wilson, which are chaste & clean compared with him.'

Besides his other new friends, Kingsley had a new patron, Sir William Cope, to whom Kingsley had written when Sir John was dying: 'Sir John remains in status quo. That is he is often ill from over-eating. But he is quite helpless, & his mind never of the clearest, is in a state which would be ludicrous, were it not so painful—I may almost say, humiliating, to see what this poor four pounds of brain may become, when it is getting worked out, & "the silver cord" of mental harmony is loosed. God help him! I often reproach myself for not having spoken more earnestly to him when he could have understood! But

[1] For an interesting comparison of *Westward Ho!* and Meredith's burlesque of it in *Farina*, see A. H. Able, *George Meredith and Thomas Love Peacock*, pp. 31–2.

those who know his reserve, & suspicion, & alas! his ungovernable temper, will perhaps be lenient to what I cannot help feeling a neglect—however hopeless the attempt might have been.'

For years Kingsley had been looking forward to a new squire in Bramshill, but he was shocked to find that Sir William's coming was by no means the millennium he had expected. Kingsley was full of advice for his new patron, whose business sense he distrusted; Cope was not disposed to look with much favour on the Rector who held the very living he had expected himself to be given by Sir John. There was no open trouble, but Kingsley confided in Ludlow:

'Well, I sometimes regret old Sir John. This man is thoroughly well-meaning, but he is fussy and worries the people about trifles. The old man at all events left them alone.' To Mr. Stapleton in London he sent the parish news: 'Poor Cope is finding out more & more the difficulty of living at Bramshill (with every farm & cottage in ruin) on 3000 a year—& looks by no means a happy man—I do hope he will have courage to go to Italy for 7 years & save £15000.' A year later he wrote that 'Sir William's exceeding Puseyism—(he is far more a Papist than anything else, & why he stays in our church I cannot conceive)—gives me a great deal of anxiety: but we have kept all smooth as yet, thank God.'

In the spring of 1852 Kingsley left in high spirits to visit the Froudes at Plas Gwynant, near Snowdon. There were three weeks of shooting, fishing, and walking in one of the most beautiful parts of Wales. In spite of their poverty the Froudes had constant houseguests, one of whom Froude warned: 'I can't give you any wine, because I haven't a drop in the house, and you must bring your own cigars, as I am come down to pipes. But to set against that, you shall have the best dinner in Wales every day—fresh trout, Welsh mutton, as much bitter ale as you can drink; a bedroom and a little sitting-room joining it all for your own self, and the most beautiful look-out from the window that I have ever seen.' Kingsley was in 'perfect paradise', although the fishing was disappointing; 'I am enjoying here a state of utter animalism,' he wrote Ludlow, 'devoting myself to the comforting of my five senses, & taking care to go to sleep if I see any symptoms of the malady of thought approaching.... There is such a pool at the bottom of the garden into whose liquid ice Froude & I take a header every morning.' Enchanting as the visit sounds, one senses in the constant stream of visitors the loneliness of the Froudes and wonders about the domestic comforts of such an existence. Some clues to Mrs. Froude's feelings are given in a piece of advice written by Mrs. Kingsley some years later to Ludlow, who contemplated moving to Wales:

'Let me beg no one with a Family of children to go where the Froudes were. Their nearest butcher was 10 miles off & came once a week—so they had to live on *veal* from stray calves—& trout. Their nearest doctor was 10 miles & dead drunk from morng. till night. The only rational doctor was 17 miles off, & by the time the 34 miles had been crossed, the patient was dead or well.

'I wd. rather have a Butcher & a Doctor near my children than the Most Exquisite Lakes & Mountains in the World, but perhaps this is a matter of *taste*!'

CHAPTER IX

The World of Letters

When the *Journal of Association* ceased publication in June 1852, Kingsley said farewell to it in his verse 'Epicedium' ('meant, of course, as an imitation of In Memoriam—I like trying my hand at my neighbour's tools—so only one learns to be really master of one's own').

So die, thou child of stormy dawn,
Thou winter flower, forlorn of nurse;
Chilled early by the bigot's curse,
The pedant's frown, the worldling's yawn.

Fair death, to fall in teeming June,
When every seed which drops to earth
Takes root, and wins a second birth
From steaming shower and gleaming moon:

Fall warm, fall fast, thou mellow rain;
Thou rain of God, make fat the land;
That roots, which parch in burning sand,
May bud to flower and fruit again.

To grace, perchance, a fairer morn
In mighty lands beyond the sea,
While honour falls to such as we
From hearts of heroes yet unborn.

Who in the light of fuller day,
Of loving science, holier laws,
Bless us, faint heralds of their cause,
Dim beacons of their glorious way.

Failure? while tide-floods rise, and boil
Round cape and isle, in port and cove,
Resistless, star-led from above:
What though our tiny wave recoil?

The note of farewell was not only for the passing of the *Journal*; it was also Kingsley's real leave-taking of Christian Socialism. There was no sudden break, but from that time Kingsley gradually ceased thinking as one of a group. The reasons behind this are not hard to see, although it is difficult to assess their relative importance. First of all, there was the matter of personal relationships, particularly with Ludlow. Gradually the tone of the correspondence between the two men became less friendly, more concerned with poetry than politics, anxious to avoid conflict if possible. In the bundles of letters Ludlow kept is a note that 'C.K. does not seem (with the exception of a few letters about C[harles] M[ansfield]'s death) to have kept my letters after 1852.' And without a curate, Kingsley found it more and more trouble to keep up with his other friends in London.

Another reason for his gradual severance from the group was that, after 1852, the Christian Socialists became increasingly systematized and institutionalized; whatever else Kingsley's mind may have been, it was not systematized. The Associations which had been founded were flourishing, and at the end of June, their position was eased by the passage of the 'Industrial and Provident Societies Act, 1852', which allowed them to do business without registering under the Joint Stock Companies' Act of 1844. The passage of this measure was the most important victory of the Christian Socialists, and the end of their real fighting days. Kingsley loved the excitement of battle; had he been a soldier he would have been an admirable cavalryman, sweeping in on daring raids, but it is doubtful that he would have been of much use in an Army of Occupation. The peaceful organization of more Associations and the foundation of the Working Men's College, which took the later attention of the Christian Socialists, could not be expected to interest Kingsley for long.

As a literary figure Kingsley had made his mark, if not his fortune. There is no reason at all to think that he had consciously used Christian Socialism for publicity, but the knowledge that his name was famous would be a good reason for him to seek to consolidate his position rather than to look for further notoriety. Besides, his literary interests were becoming less and less political.

There is another possible reason for Kingsley's retreat into respectability in 1852, although it can only be conjectural. One of his biographers has mistakenly stressed the snobbishness of Fanny Kingsley, for which there is no real evidence. All the same, it is perhaps worth noticing that it was 1852 when Fanny's brother, Charles Pascoe, bought Taplow Court from the Earl of Orkney and proceeded to rebuild the old house in splendour, with cut-stone finishings in the Tudor manner, a roof of oak and plate glass, spirelets, and a large square centre tower which concealed a water tank. One need not sniff out snobbishness if Charles and Fanny saw the incongruity between Grenfell and his radical brother-in-law; simple family feeling explains it as well, or, more probably, the natural growth of conservative tendencies in a man now thirty-three years old and aware of the advantages for his family in avoiding a bad reputation.

For any or all of these reasons, 1852 marks a real change in Kingsley, the end of the Parson Lot phase, the beginning of the period of the eminent Victorian.

Not that it was an easy year. Mrs. Kingsley's health, never strong, was particularly bad during pregnancy. 'We are shocked to hear of all Mrs. Hughes's sorrows, & we both entreat her to keep to the sofa, & Do, do *put* her *stays* into the fire,' Kingsley wrote Hughes; 'they are the causes of boundless misery & disease, & 100 years hence, they will be looked back on as more barbarous folly than Chinese feet or Indian Flatheads. My Fanny, thanks to *no stays* goes on getting better & better.—God bring her well through it.' A few days later he told Hughes that he had nearly caused Fanny to lose the baby 'on my return from a county dinner party, by making her over-laugh herself'. For a time it looked as if she might lose the child in any case, but Dr. Foster prescribed 'quinine & less baby', and on June 4th, Kingsley told Ludlow: 'I have gotten a daughter. Thank God, Fanny is safe through all her troubles, wonderfully well, & the baby too!' The birth of Mary left her mother weak, however, and it was many years before Kingsley could be free of worry about Fanny's health.

One pleasant recreation Kingsley had this year, riding on the superannuated mount Hughes lent him, but even this was not without its perils: 'Conceive that young horse falling on his head with me today, Heaven only knows how on a road as smooth as this paper, & smashing his sanguinary knees to atoms.' 'I am a mass of aches,' he reported another time. But like anything with which he was associated, the horse grew in Kingsley's esteem: 'My old horse is turning out a trump. I have mended his legs & will back him in a forest country with double banks against any horse of his size—and age.' On a particularly rainy day, one of 'everlasting sludge, & a Tophet of dirty water,' he wrote: 'I had a grind today: but I couldn't do anything: It was all neck & money, & a cheap screw like mine had no chance. I did some grewsome things in the first two miles, but the ground beat me, blew the old man before he could get his second wind, & trod his fore shoes almost off, & I had to go to the nearest forge, & was beaten off beastly—horrid done & sold, & passed by base road riders who hadn't crossed a fence all day. . . . My bones ache—having ridden many miles. My backside is sore, having ridden in a new saddle. My feet hot, having walked to Bramshill afterwards to look after the orphan & widdy. I am as sulky as a bear, having been thrown out, & as stupid as a pot, having just dined; so farewell.'

When Fanny fell ill, Kingsley lacerated himself for having used her as amanuensis in writing his novels, and repeatedly he would renounce fiction. In the middle of August 1852 he told Ludlow: 'When I have done *Hypatia* I will write no more

Maurice Kingsley, 1869

Rose Kingsley, 1866

Mary and Grenville Kingsley, 1863

novels. I *will* write poetry—not as a profession, but I will keep myself for it—& I do think I shall do something that will live.' Hughes reported a visit from Kingsley, who was 'forswearing all manner of political writing & other effort for the present. He is going to devote himself to looking after old women & writing poetry.'

Kingsley had the true poetic instinct for verse on a small scale, although too often he could not see how intrusive his moralizing could be. During this year he worked hard at poetic theory for the first time, and he and Ludlow wrote each other constantly on the subject. Ludlow had published several poems in *Fraser's* and the *Christian Socialist*, but when he wanted to bring out a volume of his verse Kingsley told him gently that his work was only second-rate. After this rebuff it was real generosity for Ludlow to tell him: 'I don't believe you ever will write such a novel as Uncle Tom's Cabin. But you can write poetry, & do beat everybody living, not as a genius *in* poetry, but as a poet. There is no comparison between you & Tennyson, because Tennyson is a sunset poet, & you a sunrise one, brightening fast into midday. He is gorgeous, tingeing everything with his own splendour; you are mighty, shewing everything in its own colour & beauty. . . . So do throw that d——d prose (its you who make me swear) overboard, & stick to poetry.' Kingsley answered impetuously: 'What you say about my ergon being poetry is quite true. I couldn't write Uncle Tom's Cabin. And I can write better poetry than any Englishman living. I don't say I have written it: but I know I can write it; there is no denying it. I do feel a different being when I get into metre—I feel like an otter in the water, instead of an otter ashore.'

At other times he would lament: 'Poetry is not *my* line. I have none of the exuberant fancy which seems to be the very first, & almost lowest sub-stratum of a poet,' or 'Unrhymed blank verse is very bald in my hands, because I *won't* write "poetic diction", but only plain English—& so I can't get mythic grandeur enough. Oh, for the spirit of Tennyson's *Oenone*!'

When he and Ludlow corresponded about hexameters (sometimes writing their letters in that difficult form), he criticized others who had attempted them: 'Ovid always makes me inclined to vomit, so I'll pass him over. Lucretius is like a great noble *cart*-stallion, but always noble: and Homer—greater & greater every day, in soul & in sound. . . . Whewell & his school make base noises in their hexams.'

The long interchange of letters was made worth while when he wrote 'Andromeda', which is sometimes considered the best use of hexameters in English. The myth of heroic salvation of maiden from monster must have had particular relevance in the Victorian mind to the perils of family disapproval through which lovers must pass before marriage. It is surely more than coincidental that Kingsley and Browning each used the story as the central motif of his most ambitious poem,[1] that each had to triumph over the ogre of family opposition before marriage, that 'Andromeda' was written for Mrs. Kingsley and *The Ring and the Book* in memory of E.B.B. The legend had long been in Kingsley's mind; he had been touched by the beauty of John Bell's bronze statue of Andromeda at the Great Exhibition, and he had made more than fifty drawings of her rescue. 'The beauty of that whole myth' he found 'unfathomable'.

Although there are places in the poem which make Andromeda seem as if she would be more at home in Kensington than in antiquity, Kingsley uses the hexameter easily, particularly when he moves away from characterization to nature, as in the extended simile describing Perseus' dive on to the monster:

As when an osprey aloft, dark-eyebrowed, royally crested,
Flags on by creek and by cove, and in scorn of the anger of Nereus
Ranges, the king of the shore; if he see on a glittering shallow,
Chasing the bass and the mullet, the fin of a wallowing dolphin,
Halting, he wheels round slowly, in doubt at the weight of his quarry,
Whether to clutch it alive, or to fall on the wretch like a plummet,
Stunning with terrible talon the life of the brain in the hindhead:

[1] Professor W. C. DeVane first pointed out the importance of the Andromeda legend in *The Ring and the Book*. There has been no notice taken of the possible influence of Kingsley on Browning.

Then rushes up with a scream, and stooping the wrath of his eyebrows
Falls from the sky, like a star, while the wind rattles hoarse in his pinions.
... Thus fell the boy on the beast.

The same summer he wrote 'Saint Maura. A.D. 304', the long monologue of a martyr as she and her husband hang dying on twin crosses. 'I don't feel I can lose a line of it,' he wrote, but for most readers it is more interesting as a revelation of his views on the marital state than as a work of art.

When 'Andromeda' and 'Saint Maura' were finished, he reminded Parker of an old suggestion for bringing out a book of poems. He had 'in all 29 pieces', enough for a '12mo of 70 pages . . . (I presume it would be a 2/6 one). . . . This is to be said. That there is *no* trash in it, that everything is of my best, & has been polished over & over until I hate the very sight of them.' Parker only reminded Kingsley that his own suggestion was some time in the past, when he could still count on exclusive rights to what Kingsley had written. Not until 1858 did Parker issue Kingsley's poems, and then only after Ticknor and Fields had produced an American edition.

Kingsley's views on some of his contemporary poets probably indicate as much his own preferences and prejudices as they do the quality of the poetry under discussion. When Matthew Arnold published *Empedocles on Etna and Other Poems*, Kingsley wrote in disgust to Ludlow: 'Empedocles & the rest of it is worse than the Strayed Reveller. 3/4ths. of it is a mere rechauffée, I happen to know, of old things written in his asinine period: but he makes a most excellent & child-loving school inspector —so there is "*humanity*" as Confutzee would say—great forgotten word!—in him after all. But if he has no more to say than that, he had better hold his tongue.'

One of Kingsley's traits at once maddening and lovable was his willingness to change his views. 'A fool, when once he gets an opinion, sticks to it like grim death, because he does not know when he shall ever get another,' he once wrote in defence of his own tergiversations. 'But a clever man knows that if he parts with an opinion he can always get another just as good, and so he is always ready to change on cause shown.' By the time Arnold published *Poems, 1853*, Kingsley was willing to recant:

Eversley
Decr. 3/53

My dear Sir

Let me thank you for your new volume of poems, & above all for Sohrab & Rustrum [*sic*], for which I have no words to express my admiration—not however my surprise—for I have always felt sure that the man who could write 'The forsaken Merman' must be capable of very great things indeed; & if I was once somewhat saucy to you in Frazer's Magazine, it was, believe me, out of good will, in the hope of spurring you up to do better, because I thought that you seemed to be frittering away great talents. But now I have nothing to say, but to ask you to forgive & forget. Go your own way, & God be with you. I don't quite agree with all of your preface, wise & true as much of it is; some of your metres, that of 'Consolation' for instance, I cannot scan —& your view of the relation between man & nature seems very opposite to my own: but all these are slight matters; & if, as I hope, I review your book in Frazer, I shall do very little but praise with my whole heart.

I think you were right in relinquishing Empedocles. The subject seemed to me too remote from the thoughts of men in general, & (pardon me) too vaguely & obscurely delineated; I frankly confess that I carried away no impression whatsoever from it of a human character & its struggles: but the bit about Cadmus & H[armonia] which you have kept is an exquisite jewel. I am sorry that you have thrown away the beautiful bit of description—the ascent of Aetna—& in the name of all infanticides, what is become of 'The Sick King in Bokhara' in my eyes one of the healthiest & most racy of your poems?

I hear from Froude that you are doing good work as a school-inspector. You will learn many things there; & have beside the inestimable blessing of some fixed unpoetical drudgery; the best school for a poet.

I trust that some day you & I may be jostled against each other in this little English world. Till then believe me

Yours very faithfully
CKingsley

. . . P.S. I have seen the Spectator's Review, & though I agree with its doctrine on the whole, think it very unfair to your powers.

Arnold must have smiled at the use of 'racy', and the condescension of the advice can hardly have been palatable, but he recognized the sincerity of the admiration. He wrote, after Kingsley's death, that 'he was the most generous man I have ever known; the most forward to praise what he thought good, the most willing to admire, the most free from all thought of himself in praising and in admiring, and the most incapable of being made ill-natured or even indifferent by having to support ill-natured attacks himself.'

In the autumn of 1852 Kingsley wrote to Mansfield of his first meeting with the Brownings, at the home of John Paine in Farnham: '*He* won't wash: he is very clever, but low-bred, effeminate, & ἄρρυθμος, a man who fancies that a man can be a poet by profession—& do nothing else—a wild mistake. She is wonderful; but very obstinate in her bad taste, & considers Socialism as stuff, and Competition as the Divine Cheese. Not that I argued with her. I never argue with anyone.'

The year before meeting them Kingsley had written a joint review of the Brownings in *Fraser's*. Mrs. Browning was 'the best poetess, in our humble opinion, whom England has yet produced', and her husband was 'distinguished from the herd of scribblers, by vigorous and manful, often profound thoughts, jaciness of expression, and an amount of learning on the subrects which he handles, which is becoming more and more rare these days.' Kingsley found him 'never weak, never commonplace: but we must add, too, never pleasing'.

Years later Gerard Manley Hopkins compared Kingsley and Browning, and neither his opinion of Kingsley nor the likeness he discerned between the two writers would have pleased the

Rector of Eversley: 'Now he [Browning] has got a great deal of what came in with Kingsley and the Broad Church school, a way of talking (and making his people talk) with the air and spirit of a man bouncing up from table with his mouth full of bread and cheese and saying that he meant to stand no blasted nonsense. There is a whole volume of Kingsley's essays which is all a munch and a not standing of any blasted nonsense from cover to cover.'

Like most of his countrymen, Kingsley reserved the position of greatest poet of the age for Tennyson, whom he admired equally as poet and as man. When *In Memoriam* was published anonymously, he reviewed it in *Fraser's*, first asking Parker:

'Do you wish me to review The Princess, &c. *with* In Memoriam? I had rather not; for though everyone knows that the latter is Tennyson's, I do not like breaking the incog, especially as *he* told me, & told me, too, private histories connected with the book, so that I should be hampered, *if* I mentioned his name, with the fear of anything like a breach of confidence. . . . Now I think that the mag. may never have again such a chance of reviewing a first rate work of art simply as such without the prestige of the author's name—& you need not fear my not praising the book for I am utterly lost in admiration of it.'

Presumably acting on Parker's advice, he reviewed the long poem as the work of Tennyson. The poem he found 'in our eyes, the noblest Christian poem which England has produced for two centuries', and he thought that Tennyson had surpassed 'the rich fulness of Keats, and the simplicity of Wordsworth'. While working on his own poem 'Sappho', Kingsley told Ludlow: 'I thoroughly feel what you say about getting out of Tennyson's way with his Oenone: but as for comparing Sappho to Oenone—stuff! I was reading Oenone through last night & thought it more wonderful & glorious than ever.' Of course he liked the ending of 'Maud', with its exhortation to fight in the Crimea, but his review of the poem compared it unfavourably to 'The Brook' and demanded *à propos* of the 'Byronic' hero: 'Would an Englishman in earnest talk thus?'

All his admiration for Tennyson must have made it doubly

painful for Kingsley to be so grossly misunderstood as he was after the publication of *Two Years Ago*. One of the chief characters in the novel is Elsley Vavasour, a vain poet, obviously a thrust at the 'Spasmodics', who deserts his wife and dies of the effects of opium. For some reason Tennyson was told and believed that Vavasour was a caricature of himself, although the reason for his credence of the story is not apparent. It is true that Vavasour is not unlike the 'gloom-pampered' hero of 'Maud', whose character Kingsley thought had a 'tone of effeminacy' about him, and Tennyson was morbidly sensitive about the opium addiction of one of his brothers and the alcoholism of his father and another brother, but there is no reason to think that his family affairs were common knowledge and certainly none to believe that Kingsley would have indulged in low personal attack. On 16th October 1858 Maurice wrote a shocked note to Ludlow:

'I should be grieved beyond expression if I thought that Kingsley had written anything against Tennyson, worst [of] all on the score of his private life. Were he to do anything so unnecessary & unusual, I should be bound to say everywhere & as publicly as I could that I believe Tennyson's life to be a perfectly simple & innocent one, & the charge about opium which I suppose Kingsley accepts to be utterly false. I know no reason to think there was any foundation for it in past years—he declares solemnly that there was not—I feel as convinced as I can be that he is entirely free from the sin now. If Kingsley—as Tennyson has been told—meant to strike at him in his Vavasour, he never made a greater blunder. I have seldom seen a man who so little affected to be *l'homme incompris*, who more intensely accepted [?] his wife's appreciation of him as the very best that he could know & who was more indifferent to the homage of other women. He is, of course, acutely and morbidly sensitive. His thinness of skin lays him open to the scorn of all the thick skinned. But I cannot throw stones, much as I can regret such a fault & such a misery in a friend whom I reverence. But I am satisfied that the treatment of this disease . . . is not contempt but sympathy.'

There is no further reference to Tennyson's misunderstanding and one can only assume that the Poet Laureate's invitation to Faringford in 1860 is clear proof of his satisfaction with Kingsley's innocence.

A genuine Spasmodic poet for whom Kingsley had a passing admiration was the young Glasgow lace-maker, Alexander Smith, whose first book of poems Kingsley reviewed in *Fraser's* in 1853. One of Kingsley's chief reasons for admiring Smith's work was that he was a self-taught labouring man. But let him beware of his 'evil angel', P. J. Bailey, Kingsley counselled. To Ludlow he wrote: 'I have nothing to tell you, except that I wish some of you would knock that Furnivall on the head. And the worst of it is, the fellow will go on writing to me, though I never answer him if I can help; but as I am full of that charity which rejoices in evil, if you have a good story or two to tell me about his bearleading that hapless Alexander the Great send them down to amuse Darby & Joan here in their solitude. By the bye, & what do *you* think of Mr. Smith? I can't make head or tail of his capabilities. Tennyson wrings his hands, & says that he will end like Festus Bailey. Froude says he is the most egotistical heartless writer he ever read. I think I don't know nothing.'

Part of the reasoning behind some of Kingsley's personal likes and dislikes of poetry becomes clearer in his essay on Shelley and Byron, where he distinguishes between the two on the ground of 'healthiness'. Shelley was introspective, therefore 'effeminate', therefore probably headed for Romanism:

'The age is an effeminate one; and it can well afford to pardon the lewdness of the gentle and sensitive vegetarian, while it has no mercy for that of the sturdy peer, proud of his bull-neck and his boxing, who kept bears and bull-dogs, drilled Greek ruffians at Missolonghi, and "had no objection to a pot of beer"; and who might, if he had reformed, have made a gallant English gentleman; while Shelley, if once his intense self-opinion had deserted him, would probably have ended in Rome, as an Oratorian or a Passionist.'

Kingsley's prejudiced pronouncements sometimes served merely to alienate his readers. One of them, George Gilfillan, noted in his journal when he had finished the essay:

'His judgments on Byron and Shelley are most unjust. Tennyson is his idol. He talks of Shelley being "girlish", &c., which was not the case. Childlike is a far truer epithet. He was to the end an impassioned and inspired child, and this is perhaps as good as "muscular Christian". Again, what Kingsley says about his exquisite lines written in dejection at Naples, is absolutely contemptible. Altogether, I begin to think Kingsley destitute of true taste, a very narrow pre-Raffaelite.'

When he was not concerned with poetry, Kingsley was caring for 'the orphan & widdy'. As soon as little Rose could sit Dicky, the brown donkey, when he kicked, she was promoted to a pony and accompanied her father around the parish. At the services in the church, more and more often scarlet flashes showed that officers from Sandhurst had walked over to sit among the soberly dressed gentry and the labourers in their white and green smocks embroidered with cart-wheels in coarse thread. Kingsley was a born preacher, vivid, colloquial, intimate, but with great dignity. His stammer was a thorn in his flesh: 'A man has no right to be a nuisance, if he can help it,' he once remarked, 'and no more right to go about amongst his fellows stammering, than he has to go about stinking.' Although his stammer kept him from talking too much in company, he was completely free of it in the pulpit, and in later years it lessened considerably at other times. His preaching voice was a 'strange, rich, high-pitched, musical monotone', and as his sermons progressed, his hands would escape from the cushion which he habitually clasped to avoid gesticulation and would be lifted in the air, the fingers of his right hand working with a peculiar hovering gesture, while his eyes flashed and his body swayed and vibrated. All observers, even those who disliked him personally, agreed on his reverence and humility in the pulpit.

That year a new national school was built in Eversley with money given by Sir William and Mr. Stapleton. It was opened in November, and Mansfield wrote to London that 'there will be grand doings at Eversley, the new school to be opened—a full choral service in the church, Sir John Harrington &c &c &c are to come from London—the Bishop of Oxford is to preach

. . . and the next day in the evening there is to be a concert in the Hall at Bramshill, where there is to be some very fine music'. Bishop Wilberforce's visit was an indication of his growing intimacy with Kingsley, and another frequent guest at the Rectory was Bishop McDougall of Labuan. Kingsley told Hughes: 'The Dougall critter is a trump. And his moonkey stories are cold water to a thirsty soul.' That year he became still closer friends with his neighbour Miss Mitford and with Mrs. Gaskell. With the latter, an 'entirely loveable creature', his admirer ever since the publication of *The Saint's Tragedy*, Kingsley sympathized when her novel *Ruth* was attacked for coarseness, saying that he had 'heard, but one unanimous opinion as to the beauty & righteousness of the book; and that, above all, from real *ladies*, & really good women'. He was beginning to meet the social lions as well. Lord Carlisle thought him 'pleasing' when they met at a Grenfell wedding and was happy to see him the next day at Bridgewater House, where Kingsley was visiting Lord Ellesmere.

In March 1853 old Mrs. Kingsley of Dulwich, widow of a stockbroker cousin of Charles's father, died and left her estate divided among her husband's relatives. Charles, George, and Henry each received £500, and their father £1,500. It was welcome to Charles, but doubly so to Henry, who was badly in debt at Oxford. Thanks to his legacy, he was able to leave with a clear name, but without a degree. While at Oxford, Henry is said to have won the Diamond Sculls; he certainly learned to smoke too much, and was one of the founders of the misogynist Fez Society, but of more academic accomplishments he showed little mastery. With three or four others he formed a group who affected careless dress and so earned themselves the name of 'The Intellectual Bargees'. Presumably the lack of elegance in his dress did little for the looks of Henry, who was known as one of the three ugliest men in Oxford, sharing the distinction with another unfortunate known as 'The Exasperated Oyster' and one called 'Curius Dentatus' because of his curly teeth. After paying off his debts, Henry purchased a passage to Australia, where he hoped to find the good fortune which had so far eluded him.

Fanny Kingsley wrote in September: 'Poor dr. Henry started with good prospect & capital introductions from Captn. Sturt —he & Captn. Sturt's nephew went together. His Father & Mother are just arriving here.' Five long years passed before the Intellectual Bargee's parents heard from him again.

Ever since the King's College enquiry into his orthodoxy in 1851, Maurice had been subjected to continuous criticism from the religious press, including the *Record* and the *Guardian*. Dr. Jelf was a timid, frightened man with all the unreasoning cruelty of a man who lives in terror of what is said of him, and he waited for an opportunity to rid himself of Maurice and his frighteningly radical associates. When in 1853 Maurice published *Theological Essays*, the *Record* urged Jelf to another enquiry. The pretext was the final essay in the book, on 'Eternal Life and Eternal Death', the argument of which was that the words 'eternal punishment' do not necessarily mean that the objects of it are in endless torture. When he published the book, Maurice told Kingsley: 'I knew when I wrote the sentences about eternal death that I was writing my own sentence at King's College.' Jelf was stampeded into asking for another enquiry, and the council found Maurice's opinions 'of dangerous tendency, and calculated to unsettle the minds of theological students'. When Maurice did not resign at once but reasonably asked which of the articles of belief of the Church of England condemned his teaching, the council declared both his chairs vacant. Kingsley's first emotion was sympathy for Maurice, but he could scarcely help seeing that it was also a concealed blow at himself. Personally, he cared little, but the Jelf business was to stand in the way of his promotion for some years.

The notoriety which frightened London worried Edinburgh not at all; on the strength of *Hypatia*, Kingsley was asked by the Philosophical Institute to come for a series of four lectures on the Alexandrian Schools. He was afraid of offending Unitarians by his speech, but he was so excited by the thought of his first visit to Scotland that he could not turn down the flattering offer. He was treated most hospitably, met 'the very best society in Scotland', and was 'much cheered and clapped' for his lectures, although he was so upset before the first of them that he cried with sheer nerves. Even the lecture which he feared might irritate the Unitarians went off without unpleasant incident. It was heartening after seeing how cruel the religious world of Jelf and the *Record* could be.

In the autumn of 1853 Mansfield told Ludlow: 'Poor Mrs. Kingsley has had a bad miscarriage, and is laid up with a bad cough and going to seaside for a month.' Actually, it was not until the spring of 1856 that Fanny returned to live in the Rectory. The winters were hard in Eversley, the house miserably cold and damp, and the doctors advised her to stay away. Kingsley installed her first in Torquay, then joined her there a month later in December 1853. He could not bear to be away from her, but it was difficult to find and to pay replacements at Eversley. A succession of curates helped him, of whom the one who stayed longest was William Lemprière, who later became seigneur of Rosel and Diélament in Jersey. Kingsley himself frequently came back on weekends to take services, although he had been given leave of absence by the Bishop.

Kingsley's notoriety had preceded him to Torquay, which suffered from all the dreary and self-righteous priggishness of a fashionable watering-place. One writer tells us that Kingsley was actually forbidden to preach by 'Henry of Exeter', the autocratic Bishop Phillpotts, who regarded him as dangerous, if not actually devilish. More probably, it was the prejudice of both clergy and congregation which kept the pulpit doors locked against him. Only once was he invited to preach in the parish church, and once at the Chapel of St. John, in a Lenten weekday service, where the high church congregation was edified by his orthodox views on the Eucharist. Bravely the Kingsleys consoled themselves by spending quiet Sundays as a family for the first time and telling themselves they preferred it that way.

If the clergy were inclined to be standoffish, there were still many of the Kingsleys' other neighbours at Torquay who enjoyed visiting them. Caroline Fox, for one, was delighted to make their acquaintance:

'We paid him and his wife a very happy call; he fraternizing at once, and stuttering pleasant and discriminating things concerning F. D. Maurice, Coleridge, and others. He looks sunburnt with dredging all the morning, has a piercing eye under an overhanging brow, and his voice is most melodious and his pronunciation exquisite. He is strangely attractive. . . . His wife's stories of him are delightful: the solemn sense of duty under which he writes, the confirming letters he has received from far and near from ardent young spirits, who thank him for having rescued them from infidelity. Such things console him greatly for being ranked amongst his country's plagues.'

The soft air of Torquay and the gentle beauty of the scenery helped Fanny on her way to recovery, and for Charles the enforced vacation meant an opportunity to return to his own boyhood bent for physical science. The bluffs and shore provided him with plenty of opportunity for geologizing, but what he enjoyed most was wandering along the shore, looking for the strange and beautiful creatures washed up there. Robert Battersby, a Torquay physician with a fine collection of shells, obligingly lent Kingsley his shell-dredge and sieves, and told him the location for good dredging, so that Kingsley need not wait for the tides to bring specimens. Each day Kingsley and the children took home creatures for the vivarium which stood near Fanny's couch, but the best specimens were shipped off in hampers to a new acquaintance of Kingsley's in London, Philip Henry Gosse.

Today Gosse is remembered as the father of Edmund Gosse, who told in *Father and Son*, with wit, if not always with understanding, of the clash between the world (often represented by Edmund himself) and his unyielding father. In his own day one of the best-known of British naturalists, the elder Gosse was a member of the sect known as the Plymouth Brethren. He spent his gloomy life torn between fear for his soul and love of sea-creatures, the claims of a literal evangelical Christianity and a liberal scientific viewpoint.

Kingsley had introduced himself to Gosse by letter in July 1853. Gosse was charmed out of his usual suspicion and reserve by the breathless energy and intelligent curiosity of his correspondent, who suggested a specimen-hunting trip to Devon. Gosse replied with a new warmth induced by Kingsley's infectious enthusiasm: 'How pleasant it wd. be to have such a companion as yourself in the investigation of those prolific shores!... Be assured, my dear Sir, I shall esteem it a favour & a privilege to continue the correspondence you have commenced.'

With Gosse, Kingsley's acquaintance was based on shared scientific interest, and on that footing he was content to remain his disciple, just as he was Maurice's follower in matters religious, literary, and political. The warm admiration with which Kingsley approached him would have melted a heart more stern than that of Gosse, to whose work Kingsley contributed a torrent of enthusiasm quite unlike anything the shy naturalist had ever known. Kingsley could even bring himself to apologize for breaking the Sabbath when he wrote Gosse on a Sunday, although he abominated Sabbatarianism. Occasionally, however, the Anglican was condescending to the Plymouth Brother on religious questions. Gosse's faith was as outspoken as Kingsley's own, and considerably more flinty in social intercourse; by 1860 even Kingsley's habitual veneration for a man of science had waned. At last he tired of an association where principles were more important than persons, and Gosse lost the friend from the outside world whom he had preserved longest. Since he had always excluded the pleasures of society from his existence, Kingsley's going left a vacant spot in Gosse's life; there is gentle melancholy in noting that Kingsley, whom he certainly regarded for some years as his closest friend, probably never realized the part he played in Gosse's lonely life, and although only a few years separated them in age, never addressed him more intimately than 'My dear Mr. Gosse'.

When Kingsley went to Torquay, he asked Gosse if he might be useful in sending 'beasts' up to town from the shore. In answer Gosse sent a hamper of wicker-covered jars, which Kingsley returned stuffed with specimens in good condition, the first of a long series of such hampers. With no parish duties, Kingsley wrote Gosse: 'I must add my thanks to you for giving not *me* only, but Mrs. Kingsley & my children, this occupation. We are as busy as bees about the animals all day, & the little ones full of desire to find something worth sending you.' In his answer, Gosse showed his awkward pleasure:

'I have to express my thanks to your dear little boy for the specimens he has found for me, & for the zeal with which all the family have engaged in the search. I feel sure they will never have cause to regret having had an early bias toward out of door zoology. May I venture also to offer my respectful thanks to your lady for her kind co-operation also. It is a grand gala day for Mrs. Gosse as well as myself, when we get an opportunity of examining a consignment from the sea; such an array of pans & bowls, of vases & tubs come out, & the whole house is on the tiptoe of expectation.'

With the hampers from Devon went long descriptions of their contents and query upon query about the specimens. Occasionally catastrophe had to be reported: 'All the specimens were put in a hot window & died before I could send them you, with the dear lost "blue plum" Actinia which I found at Lundy, covered with a thin mucous *shirt*.' Enthusiastically Kingsley wrote Gosse of the spiritual good his books had done:

'I am glad to find you so thorough a *Protestant*. I fancy that you & I should agree there as well as we do on sea-beasts. . . . Your larvae of echinoderms have thrown me into such a state of astonishment, that, if I could make my people understand them, I would preach a sermon on them, & ask them (as I often do on other matters) how man can doubt the mysteries of grace, coming from a God who has created such mysteries of nature.'

All the time Kingsley was working with Gosse, he was hatching an article, 'The Wonders of the Shore', which began as a review of Gosse's books for the *North British Review*, November 1854. The following year he expanded the article into *Glaucus*, his first real venture into popularizing science. For this kind of work he had great talent; he had enough scientific knowledge to use the solid works of research intelligently, and he could make the description of a sea worm as beautiful as one of his passages of 'scene painting' and as exciting as the plots of his best novels. *Glaucus*, illustrated by its author, was a success and helped pay the expenses of remaining in Devon. After this Kingsley began to think of himself as a man of science, and reviews of scientific works and books on popular geology flowed from his pen.

Beside his love of nature, another feeling was stirring in Kingsley. The bristling, rampant patriotism of the Crimean War called to his blood like a trumpet. Not that the feeling was new. For years he had been defending England's right to interfere with the lesser nations; when in 1849 Sir James Brooke, the white Rajah of Sarawak, was charged in the House of Commons with inhumanity to the Dyaks, Kingsley was furious that his hero should be questioned. To Ludlow, who irritatingly complained of Brooke's bloody slaughter in stamping out piracy and head-hunting in Borneo, Kingsley snapped: ' "Sacrifice of human life?" Prove that it is *human* life. It is beast-life.' Kingsley recommended sending an iron steamer to the aid of Brooke, 'to be carried out *in pieces*, and put together'. Bishop McDougall, who had worked with Brooke and who himself rather enjoyed a good Christian rifle against the pirates, also kept the Rector's blood boiling. McDougall, whose background included a place in the University boat at Oxford and training as a surgeon, was a sporting man who shared Kingsley's contempt for Roman Catholics and foreigners. John Martineau once heard McDougall describe to Kingsley the summary treatment he had given intruders in Sarawak: 'The Bishop was much disgusted at a French ship armed with a Roman Catholic bishop on board bearing down on Sarawak with doubtful intentions, so he just sent word to his French holiness that he had better not poach on his grounds, and that if he did not take the hint he should open fire, and the French bishop sheered off accordingly.'

The subjects of the Queen were divinely inspired in their task of keeping order among inferior races, and both McDougall and Kingsley knew it. Rajah Brooke and the English heroes fighting at the Alma were the modern counterparts of the great Elizabethans who had subdued the Spaniard.

The Elizabethans had been much in Kingsley's mind, for he

had been re-reading Hakluyt in preparation for 'Sir Walter Raleigh and His Time', a review in *Fraser's*. In May 1854 the Kingsleys left Torquay for Babbacombe, in order to be near the Froudes for a month or two before moving to Northdown House, Bideford, in July. While Froude and Kingsley walked the Babbacombe shore, they talked of Froude's own investigations of Elizabethan history. Inevitably, Kingsley's mulling over a period of history meant that a novel was brewing. To Maurice he wrote: 'It seemed so dreadful to hear of those dreadful Alma heights being taken and not be there. . . . But I can fight with my pen still.' But while the war lasted, Kingsley felt unequal to poetry: 'As for a ballad. Oh my dear lad,' he wrote Hughes, 'there is no use fiddling while Rome is burning. *I* have nothing to sing about those glorious fellows except God save the Queen & them. I tell you, the whole thing stuns me so I cannot sit down to make fiddle rhyme with diddle about it—or blundered with hundred, like Alfred Tennyson.' When William Cox Bennett dedicated *War Songs* to him, Kingsley wrote Bennett: 'For beside this war, one has no heart to sing of anything but it; & of it I cannot sing. . . . As for battle-songs, I cannot write them, for I have never been in battle. I must have felt the cannon fever, & seen men drop at my side (not to mention starvation, cold, defeat, & the rest of the devils) before I can put them into words. For I am essentially a Pre-Raphaelite in poetry, & can only imagine what I have seen.'

But if Kingsley could not write poetry, his pen was not idle. In his concern for the spiritual welfare of the forces in the Crimea he turned out an anonymous tract to cheer them, *Brave Words for Brave Soldiers and Sailors*. Most of his friends agreed with Kingsley that the ministry was managing the war badly. 'What a muffy war!' he told Hughes. 'God grant that we may not fail at Sebastopol, or the ministry will go out; & muffs as they are, whom can we put in their place?' Not everyone agreed on where the blame lay; Mansfield, back once more in England, wrote Ludlow of a visit to the Tennysons: 'Mrs. T. is charming. The poet suffering from the effects of meat—as are our soldiers in the East—cucumbers falsely accused.'

The confused emotions stirred by the Crimea, Rajah Brooke, and the Elizabethans crystallized in that 'most ruthless bloodthirsty book', *Westward Ho!*, dedicated to Brooke.

In July the Kingsleys moved to Bideford as a change of climate for Fanny and so that Charles might be near the scene of the novel he was writing. Northdown House was a large and somewhat formal eighteenth-century building, set in an enormous garden in which the children played and in which Mrs. Kingsley could walk, sheltered from the wind by the curved wall of pinkish local stone which rose nearly twenty feet behind the house and then dropped low enough for the family to look from their front windows through the trees of the field before the house to the slender masts of the ships which still came into the tidal waters of the Torridge River, just as other tall ships had done in the days of Queen Elizabeth. The house has since been expanded, but the well-proportioned big rooms remain with their fine plasterwork, and in the central hallway the graceful Georgian staircase still rises without support in an oval spiral of white, gold and mahogany to the floor where Kingsley sat in his study, looking over the back garden and writing *Westward Ho!* on a table spread with a ball-and-tassel cloth.

One of the most ironic facts of Kingsley's life is that so many of his friends and relatives—even his own daughter—became Roman Catholics; Northdown House, where Kingsley wrote his most vehemently anti-Roman novel, today is a convent school.

The surrounding countryside, close to Clovelly, was still filled with stories of the Devon men who had sailed with Drake and Grenville. In Bideford itself in Bridgeland Street stood an old tobacco merchant's house with a cobbled courtyard in which the pack-donkeys had been unloaded of their tobacco brought from the ships from America. In the novel the house figures as Salterne's house. And two doors beyond stood the bow-windowed house of young Dr. W. H. Ackland, recently qualified and burning still with wrath at the squalor in which he had seen the poor living in London when he was a medical student and at their living conditions in the depths of Devon. He was what his granddaughter calls a 'red-hot radical', but he knew it was imprudent for a professional man in a remote part of the country to air such views, and they remained bottled up until Kingsley's arrival. When Ackland went his rounds, he would frequently stop at Northdown House, and at his whistle Kingsley would wave out a window above the kitchens and then race down the back stairs and out the carriage gate. As Ackland's horse plodded on its usual rounds, the two men would talk hard about reform until they nearly forgot the patients, and then drift into pleasant chatter about fishing and sailing and plans for a trip to the Isle of Lundy, where Ackland was the only doctor. It is probable that the prosperous young Ackland contributed to the cost of maintaining Northdown House, although Kingsley's own finances were improving. By the end of 1854 he asked Hughes's advice: '*Ought I to return in my income tax papers the money which I get from selling books or writing in reviews?* Having never been asked for it, I have not as yet done so: & the sum was inconsiderable, but this year I have made about £400, & it seems to me that I must be expected to return this, & pay income tax on it.'

It is one of the minor curiosities of literature that Kingsley's most violently propagandist novel has survived the century since its publication primarily as a book for boys. To be sure, it is filled with adventure, swordplay, sea-fights, treks through the jungle, and horses galloping in the night, so that adult readers returning to the book for the first time since childhood are startled at how little they remember of the bitter polemical Protestantism of the novel. If the Crimean War was the immediate stimulus to writing the book, surely a secondary one was the fright England had taken in 1850 over 'Papal Aggression' when Wiseman was named Archbishop of Westminster by the Pope. In 1851 the 'Ecclesiastical Titles Bill' was passed, forbidding Roman Catholics to establish bishoprics in England. The bill was never enforced, but it was evidence of the hysterical fear felt by some English Protestants, among them, of course, Kingsley. *Hypatia* is a warning, using third-century Alexandria as a frightening example of what might happen to an unreformed

England. *Westward Ho!* also turns to the past in its didacticism, but it uses the reign of Elizabeth as a model for England and her treatment of foes, whether political or religious.

Kingsley himself indicated that his model for the chief character, Amyas Leigh, was his own old friend Francis Penrose. Amyas, a somewhat less sensitive version of Lancelot Smith, is a physical giant, brave, reverent to women, fiercely anti-Catholic, embodying most of the ideals of the public school man of nineteenth-century novels. He is bluff, pious, unimaginative, and so sure of what he knows that Sir Walter Raleigh calls him 'Sir Monoculus' and 'Single-Eye'. A century later adults, if not boys, may wonder how satisfactory is this ideal of a completely unintellectual 'Muscular Christianity'. In contrast to Amyas is his elegant courtier-brother Frank, the soul of punctilious honour, equally ready with sword or with a torrent of Euphuistic gallantries. Perhaps Kingsley drew Frank Leigh from life as well, taking his courageous gentleness, his courtly charm, his maddening sense of fair play from Charles Mansfield. The descriptions of the manner and personality of Mrs. Leigh, the mother of Amyas and Frank, coincide almost exactly with those of Kingsley's own mother. Searching for the originals of fictional characters is seldom rewarding; in Kingsley's writing such source-hunting is important only because it demonstrates how much his ideals were determined by persons whom he loved. On the other hand, in the creation of unsympathetic characters, imagination frequently was dominant over experience, to the detriment of the credibility of the characters.

To the writing of *Westward Ho!* Kingsley brought all the knowledge of the Elizabethans he had from his reading since childhood. His primary source was Hakluyt, but he also used Prince's *Worthies of Devon* and the writings of Raleigh, Prescott, and Froude himself, as well as dipping into countless other volumes. Drake, Richard Grenville, Raleigh, Frobisher, and a dozen other Elizabethan heroes strut through the book, and Spenser and Sidney discuss the literature which paralleled the martial glory of the period. In the prominent place given the St. Legers and the Grenvilles there is perhaps indication of

Kingsley's wish to flatter his wife's family; certainly the book was one at which the Grenfells could take no offence, as they could at the earlier novels.

Throughout the book Kingsley's attitude is that which he took to be the opinion of any English gentleman: Roman Catholics may be as personally attractive and brave as Don Guzman, but their religion naturally makes them into seducers and traitors; priests of Rome are necessarily engaged in deception and plotting. The assumption that all educated men of his own class shared his prejudiced point of view was one of the reasons why Kingsley later seemed so blind when he attacked Newman; everyone knew what Catholic priests were, he thought, so it was hardly necessary to examine the particulars of any single case. In the novel he tried hard to be fair by citing his authorities for the more gruesome incidents of the Inquisition, but he was ultimately incapable of fairness to Catholicism. Constantly the whole emotional tone is of bloodthirsty satisfaction over Spanish losses. While Kingsley shakes his head sadly over Spanish atrocities, assuring the reader that it is hard to believe that they actually occurred, he glosses over the parallel cruelties of the English. He writes of Raleigh in Ireland condemning seven hundred Spaniards to a bloody death:

'It was done. Right or wrong, it was done. The shrieks and curses had died away, and the Fort del Oro was a red shambles, which the soldiers were trying to cover from the sight of heaven and earth, by dragging the bodies into the ditch, and covering them with the ruins of the rampart; while the Irish, who had beheld from the woods that awful warning, fled trembling into the deepest recesses of the forest. It was done; and it never needed to be done again. The hint was severe, but it was sufficient. Many years passed before a Spaniard set foot again in Ireland.'

At the end of the book Amyas Leigh is struck blind by lightning because his vengeance becomes personal rather than national and religious, but Kingsley's sympathy is clearly with him in his hatred of all things Spanish and Roman.

Westward Ho! is the best example of the traits which W. R.

Greg singled out in one of the most ill-natured yet shrewd criticisms ever written of Kingsley:

'What unspeakable relief and joy for a Christian like Mr Kingsley, whom God has made boiling over with animal eagerness and fierce aggressive instincts, to feel that he is not called upon to control these instincts, but only to direct them; and that once having, or fancying that he has, in view a man or an institution that is God's enemy as well as his, he may hate it with a perfect hatred, and go at it *en sabreur*! Accordingly he reminds us of nothing so much as of a war-horse panting for the battle; his usual style is marvellously like a neigh—a "ha! ha! among the trumpets"; the dust of the combat is to him the breath of life; and when once, in the plenitude of grace and faith, fairly let loose upon his prey—human, moral, or material—all the Red Indian within him comes to the surface, and he wields his tomahawk with an unbaptized heartiness, slightly heathenish, no doubt, but withal unspeakably refreshing. It is amazing how hard one who is a gladiator by nature strikes when convinced that he is doing God service. Mr Kingsley is a strange mixture of the spirit of the two covenants. He draws his sympathy with human wrongs mainly from the New Testament; but his mode of dealing with human wrong-doers altogether from the Old.'

As in his earlier books, Kingsley uses two types of women in the novel to represent antithetical attitudes. Queen Elizabeth stands in spiritual affairs as head of the English Church and in temporal matters as the inspiration of art, patriotism, and gallantry in her subjects. In religion her antithesis is the Virgin, whose worship Kingsley thought had inspired such foolishly cruel excesses; her political opponent is, of course, the Roman Catholic Mary Stuart. On the personal level the book builds toward the military victories of Amyas against the Armada and then his subsequent spiritual victory as he learns humility; on an ideological plane, the episodic plot works toward the defeat of the Armada and the Virgin, and toward the death of Mary Stuart and all that Kingsley felt that she stood for.

Yet the sense of religious unfairness one feels in the book seems to be one which Kingsley's contemporaries at large did not share, and the book was more successful than even he dared hope. The hacking of swords, the wind in the hawsers of Amyas's ship, the Spanish ambush in the jungle, the rout of the Armada: these are enough to keep the loose-jointed plot exciting. Critics admired even more the 'word-paintings' of which Kingsley was one of the great Victorian masters. As Leslie Stephen indicated, the jungle scenes are dutiful set-pieces patiently fitted together from Kingsley's reading; the best scenes are those which he had known ever since his Devon childhood. Two examples, one from the beginning and one from the end of the novel, show his style at its most vivid. The first is the opening paragraph of the novel, carrying Bideford back into history:

'All who have travelled through the delicious scenery of North Devon must needs know the little white town of Bideford, which slopes upwards from its broad tide-river paved with yellow sands, and many-arched old bridge where salmon wait for Autumn floods, toward the pleasant upland on the west. Above the town the hills close in, cushioned with deep oak woods, through which juts here and there a crag of fern-fringed slate; below they lower, and open more and more in softly-rounded knolls, and fertile squares of red and green, till they sink into the wide expanse of hazy flats, rich salt-marshes, and rolling sand-hills, where Torridge joins her sister Taw, and both together flow quietly toward the broad surges of the bar, and the everlasting thunder of the long Atlantic swell. Pleasantly the old town stands there, beneath its soft Italian sky, fanned day and night by the fresh ocean breeze, which forbids alike the keen winter frosts, and the fierce thunder heats of the midland; and pleasantly it has stood there for now, perhaps, eight hundred years since the first Grenvil, cousin of the Conqueror, returning from the conquest of South Wales, drew around him trusty Saxon serfs, and free Norse rovers with their golden curls, and dark Silurian Britons from the Swansea shore, and all the mingled blood which still gives to the seaward folk of the next county their strength and intellect, and, even in these levelling days, their peculiar beauty of face and form.'

The second of these scenes is an extraordinary mixture of

visual and auditory impressions of the cliff where the blinded Amyas makes his peace with God and nature: 'So on they went to the point, where the cyclopean wall of granite cliff which forms the western side of Lundy, ends sheer in a precipice of some three hundred feet, topped by a pile of snow-white rock, bespangled with golden lichens. As they approached, a raven, who sat upon the topmost stone, black against the bright blue sky, flapped lazily away, and sank down the abysses of the cliff, as if he scented the corpses underneath the surge. Below them from the Gull-rock rose a thousand birds, and filled the air with sound; the choughs cackled, the hacklets wailed, the great black-backs laughed querulous defiance at the intruders, and a single falcon, with an angry bark, dashed out from beneath their feet, and hung poised high aloft, watching the sea-fowl which swung slowly round and round below.'

Kingsley had published several books with the Macmillans since *Cheap Clothes and Nasty* in 1850, but *Westward Ho!* was the first novel he had offered them, and it sold better than any of his books had yet done. It also ensured the commercial success of the publishers as their first highly profitable work. The critical reception was largely favourable, even from quarters which Kingsley had expected to be hostile. Some of the enthusiasm of its readers was for the novel's timeliness; Caroline Fox recommended it to a friend as 'a fine foe-exterminating book of Elizabeth's time, done and written in the religious spirit of Joshua and David. For Spaniards read Russians, and it is truly a tract for the times.'

In the *Westminster Review* George Eliot wrote that Kingsley 'sees, feels, and paints vividly, but he theorizes illogically and moralizes absurdly'; however, her 'dominant feeling towards his works in general is that of high admiration'. One sentence in the review is strikingly reminiscent of Greg's estimate of Kingsley: 'The battle and the chase seem necessary to his existence; and this Red Man's nature, planted in a pleasant rectory among corn fields and pastures, takes in default of better game, to riding down capitalists and Jesuits.'

Not surprisingly, the perceptive Miss Evans watched Kingsley's career with a reluctant and irritated enthusiasm. Of *Phaethon* she had written: 'Perhaps you may not be as much in love with Kingsley's genius, and as much "riled" by his faults, as I am.'

Kingsley's views of George Eliot were considerably less polite. Two years later he told Maurice, who had been unfavourably reviewed: 'I do hope you will not bother your soul about what the Westminster says. The woman who used to insult you therein—& who I suppose does so now—is none other than Miss Evans, the infidel esprit forte, who is now G. H. Lewes's concubine—I met him yesterday, & lucky for me that I had not had your letter when I did so; or I certainly should have given him (he probably being the co-sinner for he pretends to know all about the philosophers, & don't) a queer piece of my mind to carry home to his lady. Let them be.'

Considering his opinion of her, one can not help wondering how Kingsley answered, or if he did, when he received one of George Eliot's seven presentation copies of *Adam Bede*; perhaps he was mollified by knowing that others went to Dickens, Jane Carlyle, Froude, and Thackeray. In any case, if he knew the identity of 'George Eliot', he must have accepted the compliment with mixed feelings when the reviewer in the *Saturday Review* said that the author had obviously 'sat at the feet of Mr. Kingsley'. John Blackwood, editor of *Blackwood's Magazine*, was also irritated with the review, but not for reasons which Kingsley would have advanced:

'Damned presumptuous ass was my mental comment on the reviewer in the Saturday. The idea of G.E. sitting at the feet of Kingsley riled me particularly. Why there is more sense in George Eliot's little finger than in Kingsley's whole carcase. With all his blustering, would-be manliness, I do not look upon Kingsley as a man of power and substance at all.' Knowing how hard Kingsley was on 'coarseness' in women novelists, one can easily imagine how completely he would have censured the seduction in *Adam Bede*.

Since Kingsley had no parish work at Bideford, he organized a drawing class of the young men of the town. He lectured on anatomy for artists, illustrating the subject with rapid chalk drawings, and brought flowers from his conservatory for the men to draw. The meetings were held in the house of Edward Capern, known as the Postman Poet, who used to think out his rustic poetry as he walked his postal rounds. Some of Capern's poems are charming evocations of the Victorian countryside, but they have been forgotten today. Among the best of them are those written on the plight of the poor postman, working while the rest of the world is in church. Kingsley peppered his friends with requests for advice on how to get the postmen relieved of their Sunday duties; still better, he circulated Capern's poems and interested Tennyson, Landor, and Dickens in them. Dickens expressed his willingness to subscribe to a volume of Capern's verse and added: 'If you should see anything from his hand that you think I could have the pleasure of printing in Household Words, at least to let me read it with that object in view.'

The winter at Bideford brought the greatest loss Kingsley had yet suffered. Charles Mansfield had returned from South America a much happier man. 'The clouds which had beset his path had all but cleared, and left sunshine and hope for the future,' Kingsley wrote. Mansfield settled down to brilliant research in chemistry; the discoveries he had already made are said to have laid the foundation of the aniline industry, and he was recognized as one of the most promising young chemists in England. While he was working in his laboratory, a naphtha still boiled over, and in an heroic attempt to save the premises and the boy who was responsible for the accident, Mansfield seized the blazing still in his arms and tried to hurl it through the window, but was burned so badly that he had to drop it; he rushed out in agony, rolled in the snow, then broke the ice of Regent's Canal and jumped in the water. For nine days he lay in the Middlesex Hospital in pain and convulsions. All his friends in London took jealous turns at nursing him, and Kingsley wanted to come up from Devon, but was told that he could do nothing further. Both Ludlow and Penrose secretly tried mesmerism when the hospital attendants were out of the room, but they had no success in relieving the pain. What impressed Ludlow most in the sad vigil was that Mansfield was 'with God constantly, gentle, tender, considerate'. He died quietly in the evening of 25th February 1855, and was buried in Weybridge cemetery, with Maurice reading the service; there was no 'hearse, or feathers, or mutes, or such like beastly paganism'. Kingsley was too overcome by the news of Mansfield's death to attend the service. Instead he wrote at once to Ludlow:

I shall use few words with you, my dearest friend. What need? We know what he was. We know what he wished to be. We know what he ought to have been. And therefore, we know what he is now. He will have work given him, in a climate fitter for those delicate soul's lungs than England, 1855; & he will do it.

But oh John Ludlow, if he was so much to you, what was he to me? He was my first love. The first human being, save my mother, I ever met who knew what I meant. To him & to Frank Penrose what do I not owe. They two were the only heroic souls I met during those dark Cambridge years. They two alone kept me from sinking in the mire, & drowning like a dog. And now one is gone; & I shall cling all the more to the other. Tell Frank Penrose so, tell him that now Mansfield is gone, he must be my friend, & I his, in a way that we never yet have been.

And yet the two men were as different from each other, as from me. Mansfield the race horse, Penrose the lion, but both noble, both somehow inseparable in my mind in spite of the utter, almost laughable differences, because both loved righteousness before all things.

Keep close to that man Penrose now, dearest Ludlow. He is cold & unimaginative: but his eye is single, & his heart is mighty in warmth, though not in heat—He is my model for my hero in Westward Ho, & I want none better, for I believe him incapable of meanness or vanity.

And for your self, dearest man, *pray* do not accuse yourself—You have *not* wronged Mansfield. None knew better, or felt more, that you had not, than he himself. You had the most frightful complication of disease & misfortune to deal with, in a patient the most abnormal, whom none of us had ever seen the like of, whom we do not understand, & perhaps never shall, & what wonder if the medicine which seemed to you the best was *not* the best? You meant the right thing; & I believe that you did him good as you meant to do, even in that for which you now reproach yourself. Was not the total & final result good? God knows it was; & he owes you much, very much. And who cares for the passing errors in an intricate campaign, provided the method has been earnest, & the sum, victory?

Never speak or think of that more. You have sadness enough (for I am sure, & have been for years) that you have some hidden sadness, which would God I could relieve, to burden your soul with one undeserved regret—But he is gone. I have had a feeling, as I have in the case of others, for a long time past, that he would go. His image, as others' have, grew fainter & more distant, I knew not why. I could not realize him to myself as a being of flesh & blood. I could not see a future or purpose for him. There was a great mist just beyond him, & he was fading away into it, dim & large. Then I knew that he would die, & denied it to myself: but it was true.

My kindest love to all who were with him in his illness, especially Power & Penrose.

CKingsley

When I am wanted to come to London as executor, I am ready. I should have been glad to have been at the funeral. But I am better where I am, for many reasons. Mrs. Kingsley has felt it much, too much. She loved him as well as any of us, perhaps better—God bless you for all you have been to him, *& to me*.

From Mansfield's estate Kingsley received all the books on magic and mesmerism. The manuscripts were taken by Ludlow, who saw them through the press. For several years thereafter, Mansfield's friends, with the exception of Kingsley, met for corporate communion on the last Sunday of each February, at Lincoln's Inn Chapel, where Mansfield's 'deepest religious experiences came to him'. Kingsley told Ludlow that he could not attend the memorial services: 'I have a shrinking from that sort of thing, into the cause of which I will not enter.' To Ludlow's edition of Mansfield's letters from South America, published as *Paraguay, Brazil, and the Plate*, he contributed an introductory memoir, but after that Ludlow and Kingsley had still less to do with each other. Mansfield's death created a hole in Kingsley's life which was never filled. Had Mansfield lived, Kingsley's later years might have been much happier, bulwarked by the love and understanding of the closest friend he had ever had. Never again would he see Mansfield flash 'down over the glebe at Eversley, with his knapsack at his back, like a shining star . . . bringing an involuntary smile into the faces of every one who met him—the compelled reflection of his own smile'.

CHAPTER X

Preferment and Fishing

The mild winters of Devon were what Mrs. Kingsley needed for the slow recovery of her health, and by the end of 1854 her husband could tell Maurice that she 'with occasional little relapses, gets steadily better & better. The glorious climate, & what is more the complete rest, are doing her wonderful good'. But the frantic dashing between Eversley and Bideford was draining Kingsley's energy. In any case, he must soon return to residence at Eversley, and it seemed inevitable that Fanny would suffer another relapse once she was living again in the low, damp Rectory, which they both loved, but which was so manifestly unhealthy. On one visit to Eversley he had written Fanny of its beauty under the deceptive sun: 'The dear old treacherous place looking as if it were really healthy. Nothing sanitary done in the parish.' He could agree to take Fanny back to Eversley only to a new house, and he began writing from Bideford to Sir William Cope of his plans for a Rectory to be built on the little hill in front of the present house, safely away from the streams that drained into it.

In difficulty as a patron Sir William proved equal to Sir John, and though intelligent and well educated, he and Kingsley could find little in common. Sir William was as hot-headed as his Rector, and their surviving correspondence constantly reveals the antagonism which was so near eruption. Usually Kingsley meekly tried to keep the peace, but on at least one occasion he had demanded and received an apology from Sir William for a personal affront; since only part of Kingsley's reply survives, it is no longer possible to know what the offence was. To Mr. Stapleton, Kingsley later wrote of his patron: 'I have suffered a good deal from his hastiness: but since his last explosion in my absence, he has been much better, & he & I got on very well the other day at Eversley. . . . As for any business complaints of him which you may have heard, my belief is that it is mere want of business habits, he having been a mere bookworm, & knowing nothing how to manage an estate.' Kingsley's constant requests to Sir William on behalf of the local Sanitary Committee, to clear up 'nuisances' in his cottages, kept the mutual irritation alive, and always there was the overt doctrinal difference between the Rector and his high church patron to separate them.

Much as he disliked asking favours of Sir William, Kingsley finally had to remind him of the unhealthiness of the Rectory and to say 'that the impossibility of keeping my Family there henceforth in the winter compels me to the alternative of either rebuilding or asking your leave to exchange the living'. In ten years Kingsley had spent over £1,000 on repairs: 'But I find that I have been only "sewing new cloth in an old garment", & vainly trying to fill the sieve of the Danaides, having spent out of my own pocket, in unsuccessful attempts to keep out wind & water, as much as would have built a new & good house. I now can do no more.' The new house which he planned would cost approximately £1,200, of which he proposed to pay £200; the rest could be borrowed from the Queen Anne's Bounty and repaid from parish funds over a period of years. Sir William tentatively let Kingsley go ahead with his plans, but he clearly took little interest in the project, perhaps because he would have been glad to be rid of his Rector and the irritation which he produced. Kingsley hired an architect, Mr. Habershon, and drew up successive sets of plans which he submitted to Sir William, who rather negligently indicated that he thought Kingsley was exaggerating the necessity for a new house. Finally, after six months of shilly-shallying, Sir William wrote in the spring of 1855 to say that he thought the old Rectory 'a pretty looking house, and all accounts agree (for I have never been over it) that it is roomy and convenient'. He could agree to rebuilding only if the front of the old house were exactly duplicated and the 'rooms in number and size not materially differing from the present. . . . I cannot help regretting (if I may say so without offence) that you did not postpone the rebuilding until a larger sum was at your disposal. . . . I certainly do not feel at all called upon to contribute to that object when I see that the parish demands a large outlay on my part, were funds at my disposal, where the living already possesses a sufficient and commodious house and where the change is one not of necessity, but of convenience. . . . The house is a good house as it stands and has been sufficient for many Rectors, and indeed for yourself for many years.'

When Kingsley knew that he could not expect a healthier house for Fanny at Eversley, he began looking at the prospects of another living. Meanwhile, for the winter of 1855–6 he rented Farley Court, in the neighbouring parish of Swallowfield, where the family could live in comfort in a large, dry house on high ground and where he was close enough to Eversley to carry on his parish duties without a curate.

Now that he was a nationally known figure, he might be offered a stall as canon in one of the cathedrals, a position which would suit him admirably, for he could keep his family there during the winters and bring them back to Eversley for the drier months of the summer. The first vacant stall for which he tried was at Hereford, and the Dean, Richard Dawes, came to London to hear him preach, but eventually the chapter decided to leave the stall temporarily vacant.

Tom Hughes, who had many influential friends in the government, offered to help Kingsley in getting a vacant canonry at St. Paul's, but this time Kingsley lost out to the popular preacher, Henry Melvill, Principal of the East India College at Haileybury. When Kingsley heard the news he wrote at once to Hughes, asking him to keep it 'private, even from *Ludlow*':

'St. Paul's is gone to Melville—& a very fit appointment, as they are going to do away with Haileybury. I am advised now to get another gun beside Charles Grenfell to bear on Lord

Palmerston. Charles Grenfell would principally urge *his own* claim—as the head of a great Whig family, who have worked for the party for 60 years. What is wanted is someone beside to make Lord Palmerston aware of what few claims I may have personally, & what effect on the working men's mind, & their feeling toward the Church . . . the government's patronizing me would have. Now do you think that Mr. William Cowper[1] would do this? He has been always civil enough to me: but I don't know him well enough to ask him, or even to "aborder" him on the point. Do you? & if not, who does? Does Lord Goderich? My notion of Mr. Cowper's feeling toward me is, that he would help if he was put up to it: but then how to do so. I am much too proud to blow my own trumpet, or state my own doings. But you know, & others ought to know, what I have done, & what I might do, were I in such a post for instance, as a Canonry at Westminster.

'. . . Now what I want is, a promise of the first Canonry at Westminster which falls vacant. I am sure that I could do good work there; & it is the sort of place for a literary man, especially one who is interested in social & sanitary questions; for no neighbourhood requires more looking after than Westminster —or perhaps, has had less.'

Hughes wrote at once to Cowper, who agreed to help Kingsley. Hughes also offered to get the assistance of Lord Goderich and of his own friends, the M.P.s Robert Lowe and Edward Ball, to second Grenfell's proposal of Kingsley to Palmerston. Kingsley was pleased at the help of Goderich, but he warned Hughes: 'Robert Lowe don't try. I know the white man well & he is not one to whom I should ever wish to be under an obligation. Ball I know not. They say he is a dissenter. If so, & you try him, you may let him know that *I* am for admitting Dissenters to the Universities, & widening tests of every kind, & will when I get power, back any such movements. God bless you for your goodheartedness.'

The first Westminster stall which became vacant was that of

[1] William Cowper (1811–88), later Lord Mount-Temple, was the stepson of Lord Palmerston, whose heir he was.

J. H. Monk, Bishop of Gloucester and Bristol, but after his death it remained unfilled until 1860. Kingsley had to wait until 1873 before he became Canon of Westminster.

To Hughes's hopeful suggestion that he get a London parish, Kingsley answered with a clear statement of what he thought his own function as priest should be:

'I could never take a London living; & were I a canon, I would never do what canons do, put myself into a chapter living —It is a very ugly process, to my mind—wouldn't I try to put Maurice into a living! . . . But I see no harm in holding Eversley, with a canonry, if the law allows. For I should only have to reside 3 or 4 months in the year in London, & the other nine I *must* spend somewhere, while we can perfectly live at Eversley for nine months in the year, Mrs. Kingsley is so much better. . . . Mr. Cowper's notion of a canon's work is mine. I want to be a popular preacher, in the true sense, & talk to the working men & cockneys in plain English, & to try gradually, & *cautiously* (for I can be cautious enough now, old lad, though I was not 7 years ago) to make a cathedral a centre of civilization, *physical* as well as moral, for its neighbourhood. I have visions of adult schools, reading-rooms, lectures, a *museum*, baths & wash houses, & what not—& if the shovel-hats don't do these things for themselves, & so fulfil somehow the purpose of a cathedral, they must expect the parliament to take away their money, & do it for them.

'But as for being a London Rector, I should be in my grave, or in a madhouse, in 12 months—what I want is a post at which I can work freely & at my own pace, without mingling with the religious (or the Ecclesiastical), worlds, & from whence I can take a part in *active politics*, a thing impossible for a London Rector, because he would have his parish foul of him at once.'

Another opening which Hughes suggested was the Golden Lectureship, which involved the delivery of a sermon every Tuesday morning in the Church of St. Margaret, Lothbury; it was worth £400 per year and was in the gift of the Haberdashers' Company. Remembering his own knocks at the haberdashers in *Cheap Clothes and Nasty* and *Alton Locke*, Kingsley answered Hughes:

'You are a dear good old cock: but I don't want no Golden Lectureships. . . . No. Would I canvass M shopkeepers? or let them be canvassed for me? . . . No—give me again my hollow tree; my crust of bread & liberty. Would I be a town mouse under a Deanery, a handsome brougham for my wife, & select dinners of six for literary friends? No. Every man has his price, & that's mine. A stall, to go up to 3 or 4 months in a year is one thing: but a Golden lectureship is another.'

Finally Kingsley had to face the knowledge that he was to get neither preferment nor a new Rectory, but by the spring of 1856, thanks to the dryness of Farley Court and a trip to the seaside to stay with her sister, Mrs. Kingsley's health had improved so much that the family decided to move back to Eversley at Easter. Probably if Sir William had consented to a new house, more of the rest of Kingsley's life might have been concentrated on Eversley; as it was, he still felt the need of making himself better known in the hope of eventual clerical advancement.

Actually, by 1856 his books were doing well in making him famous. *Westward Ho!* and *Glaucus* were selling well, he was reviewing constantly for *Fraser's*, and his first book for children, *The Heroes*, had come out in time for the 1855 Christmas trade.

While writing *The Heroes* he asked Macmillan to have it read 'by scholars & sensible people; for otherwise I have no heart to go on in a thing really important in my eyes'. To Ludlow he explained: 'I have adopted a sort of simple ballad tone, & tried to make my prose as poetical as possible. . . . You must remember as to modernisms, that we Cambridge men are *taught* to translate Greek by its modern equivalent even to *slang*.' His retelling of the stories of Perseus, Jason, and Theseus seems emasculated to adult readers, who may also be surprised by the Christian overtones he finds in the Greek stories. For children to whom action is enough, however, *The Heroes* has the same direct appeal as the Lambs' *Tales from Shakespeare*, and, like that other little masterpiece of simplication, has interested generations of children in the originals from which the stories are taken.

Kingsley dedicated the book to his three children, Rose, Maurice, and Mary, and in keeping with the informality of the story-telling he contributed his own illustrations, which are much less successful than the stories they accompany.

As it had been ever since his days as an undergraduate, the remedy for Kingsley's troubles was still a good day's fishing. The hard winter of 1855–6 was tempered with dreaming of a fishing trip the following summer, when he planned to go with Froude and Hughes to Ireland for salmon fishing. The day after Christmas he suggested that their trip be to Wales instead: 'I wish you would make a wow & keep it strong: for Mrs. Kingsley says that if you will, I may: & that is, not to cross the sea like Sophia, but to go with me to Snowdon next summer for a parson's week, i.e. 12 days.' The prospect of physical hardships was exhilarating, if only he could get away from the worries of civilization:

'We must depend on our own legs, & on stomachs which can face braxy mutton, young taters, Welsh porter—which is the identical drainings of Noah's flood turned sour, & brandy of more strength than legality. Bread horrid. Fleas MCCCC ad infinitum. Bugs a sprinkling; Ditto a worse complaint if you sleep in cottages: Inns are safe; for baths, ye. mountain brook; for towel, a wisp of any endogen save Scirpus triqueter, or Juncus squarrosus, & for cure of all ills, & supplement of all defects, baccy.'

Throughout the spring his letters to Hughes were full of references to 'the happy fishing ground', of the gudgeon recommended by his 'most poaching man of all work', of flies, of oolite and chalk, of dozens of fish landed, of hundreds that got away. The frivolous language of the letters Hughes wrote made Kingsley forget his tribulations: 'You are almost the only cove I care to hear from, because you don't *write* wisdom, but write nonsense, & does wisdom—which is the blessed silent sow as sups all the milk, & works afore faith, & what's the odds of being eloquent if one's useful? Blow genius & give me a brick.'

One of his fishing jaunts with Hughes was in the company of

that phenomenon of Victorian poetry, Martin Tupper. Like most of his fellow literary men, Kingsley had expected Tupper to be a ridiculous little man, conceited to the point of fatuity, but he was pleasantly surprised. Because he, too, had suffered from a bad stammer, Tupper liked Kingsley immensely:

'With *Charles Kingsley*, however seldom we met, I had strong sympathy in many ways, as a man of men, to be loved and admired; but chiefly we could feel for each other in the matter of stammering,—a sort of affliction not sufficiently appreciated. Kingsley conquered his infirmity, as I did mine, and rose to frequent eloquence in his public ministrations: privately his speech would often fail him, and was his "thorn in the flesh" to the end.

'I remember a most pleasant day spent with him about the fishponds and cascades of Wotton—and I noted how skilfully he threw the fly some five-and-twenty feet under the bushes, to the wonder of a gaping trout, soon to find its lodging in the creel.'

Elsewhere Tupper wrote of Kingsley's 'abundant charity for all sorts of miserable sinners . . . for there never lived a more universal excuser of human imperfection than Charles Kingsley'. After the fishing trip, Kingsley told Hughes: 'Tupper is a good, feeling little fellow. I have been unjust to the man: & we have made great friends.'

At the last moment Froude had to back out of the trip to Wales, so Hughes suggested as the third fisherman his good friend Tom Taylor, the popular playwright. Kingsley replied with pleasure: 'Of all men on earth I should like to have Tom Taylor for a third—entreat him to make it possible, & come & be a salvidge man with us.'

Before leaving for Wales, Kingsley visited Hughes's chambers in London, and finding him away, left a long rhymed invitation:

Come away with me, Tom,
Term and talk is done;
My poor lads are reaping,
Busy every one.

Curates mind the parish,
Sweepers mind the Court,
We'll away to Snowdon
For our ten days' sport,
Fish the August evening
Till the eve is past,
Whoop like boys at pounders
Fairly played and grassed. . . .
Down, and bathe at day-dawn,
Tramp from lake to lake,
Washing brain and heart clean
Every step we take.
Leave to Robert Browning
Beggars, fleas, and vines;
Leave to mournful Ruskin
Popish Apennines,
Dirty Stones of Venice
And his Gas-lamps Seven;
We've the stones of Snowdon
And the lamps of heaven. . . .
See in every hedgerow
Marks of angels' feet,
Epics in each pebble
Underneath our feet;
Once a year, like schoolboys,
Robin-Hooding go,
Leaving fops and fogies
A thousand feet below.

When the long-awaited day came, Kingsley and Hughes met Taylor in Wolverhampton, where they took the Holyhead mail train, which dropped them at Bangor at 5 a.m. They fished all that day and walked to Capel Curig to spend the night; the following day they went to Pen-y-Gwryd, where they stayed the rest of the holiday at the hospitable inn run by Mr. and Mrs. Owen. Each day they started at daybreak, spent the day climbing and fishing, then back to the excellent food of Mrs. Owen.

To Rose Kingsley her father wrote of the climb above the vale of Gwynant:

'Such a place! All tumbled about with cliffs & rocks, & great heaps of stones, & little vallies full of heath & grass, & white sheep who squeak at you just like a squeaking doll, & then gallop away down cliffs where you would fancy only a goat could climb, each of them with a beautiful lamb as white as snow, & looking back every minute to see if the lamb is coming, & we went by the place where the poor gentleman was found dead. He lost his way in a fog, & was not accustomed to climb, so at last when he came to the cliffs, he was afraid to go down, & he made a bed with heather in a cave; & there the shepherds found him with his book open on his knees, quite stiff & cold & dead: and if he had even called out, the people below might have heard him; & if the cloud had cleared for a minute he would have seen Gwynnant lake, & all the farms & houses, only 2 miles off, right under his feet.' The incident furnished Kingsley with the material for the central chapter of *Two Years Ago*, his new novel for which he was seeking backgrounds in Wales. Mr. and Mrs. Owen, the owners of the inn, appear in the story under their own names.

In the evenings the trio sat in the dark-beamed kitchen of the inn, hung with bacon, fishing rods and drying stockings. Tom Taylor was in beard and red flannel shirt, his torn breeches patched across behind with a piece of Welsh red and blue flannel cut from an old petticoat belonging to Mrs. Owen. Hughes, too, had suffered from rough climbing, and the remains of his walking wardrobe were a flannel shirt and dirty, ragged trousers. Over these, Oxford Blue to the last, he wore an old boating coat. Hughes wrote that Kingsley was 'stealing everybody's paper to dry plants in, and jogging of the table in an unchristian manner so that parties can't write a bit; his neck half-broken by a rock in the stream where we bathed this morning, and otherwise much knocked about by wind and weather, but struggling still into respectability by reason of the common domestic linen collar and a clean shave.'

Taylor declared that he was in fear of his life 'between this

Socialist lawyer and this Socialist parson—two unnatural varieties of the genus professional man, each caring more for his neighbours than himself or his cloth, and thus departing from the wholesome rules of his craft. . . . But if I am left a demd unpleasant body on these mountains, don't say I didn't expect it, and inform my relatives and have Thos. Hughes and Chas. Kingsley tried as murderers before the fact.'

Occasionally Kingsley's overly serious manner grated on Hughes, and he was glad to find that 'The Parson has all the prophecy knocked out of him and can only talk slang, which is very refreshing.' When the three joined in a letter to Lord Goderich, who had lent them his salmon tackle, Kingsley's section was stiff and quite out of keeping with the playful parts written by his companions. He wrote to 'My dear Lord Goderich', thanked him for the use of the tackle, hoped that he was enjoying in Italy 'a somewhat more genial climate than we', and closed with 'Yours truly ever, C. Kingsley'.

In answer Lord Goderich wrote Hughes from Venice: 'I wish the Parson wouldn't go for to stick the "Lord" before my unfortunate name; but ever since Ludlow cut up so rough upon that subject[1] I've been afraid to suggest such a thing to anyone.'

'I don't wonder at your grunting and grumbling over the "Lord" dodge, but one must take folk as one finds them,' Hughes, who could be aware of the difficult personalities of his friends without ceasing to love them, commiserated with Goderich. 'Who'd have thought 6 or 7 years ago, when *Yeast* came out . . . that *the* Parson, Parson Lot the Chartist, and the "Black Man", [Ludlow] wd. be *the* two who never really believed in equality and brotherhood, for if they did they wd. practise it, I suppose, as much toward folk who are conventionally above them as below, seeing that the former is out and out the hardest of the two. However, you was born a Lord and bred a Lord, and I suppose must take the consequences of being found in that dreary and disgusting situation.'

[1] In his unpublished autobiography, Ludlow noted that he shunned intimacy with Goderich 'as I always have shunned through life such intimacy with persons much above me in position or fortune'.

Kingsley and Dandy

versley Rectory
ıd Church
ıring Kingsley's
ˈetime

The Snowdon trip refreshed him wonderfully, but Kingsley was not the man to remain buoyant for long; particularly during 1855 and 1856 he touched the depths. He was worried over his wife's health, over money and preferment, and he also felt himself farther and farther from the friends and interests of his youth. He tortured himself with shame over his mixed motives as a Christian Socialist, and ended by doubting the sincerity of his religious belief, as he had done when he was an undergraduate.

From the vantage point of a century later, it is easy to see that one of the most characteristic Victorian afflictions was the alternation between pessimism and optimism of men like Arnold, Clough, and Tennyson. The dizzy exhilaration of the flight to absolute confidence was always followed by the sickening plunge into doubt, and the cycle seemed endless. Kingsley, too, was infected with the *maladie du siècle*. With the light-hearted Hughes he could share an uncomplicated belief and feel assured of the blessed state of the world. 'The long and short of it is, I am becoming an optimist,' he wrote. 'All men, worth anything, old men especially, have strong fits of optimism—even Carlyle has —because they can't help hoping, and sometimes feeling, that the world is going right, and will go right, not your way, or my way, but its own way.'

For the straightforward Hughes this was sufficient proof that Kingsley had moved out of his Christian Socialist phase simply because his optimism had convinced him that things would come right without human intervention.

But Kingsley's confident moods never lasted long, and soon he was questioning his own motives again: 'I've often thought what a dirty beast I was. I made £150 by Alton Locke, & never lost a farthing by anything—& I got, not in spite of, but by, the rows, a name & a standing with many a one who would never have heard of me otherwise.'

With Ludlow Kingsley abased himself even more than he did with closer friends. Because he thought Ludlow was arrogant he consciously strove for humility himself. In considering the Parson Lot period of his life, he achieved a despairing clarity to Ludlow about his own motives:

'For myself, on looking back, I see clearly with shame and sorrow, that the obloquy which I have brought often on myself and on the good cause, has been almost all of it my own fault—that I have given the devil and bad men a handle, not by caring what people would say, but by *not caring*—by fancying that I was a very grand fellow, who was going to speak what I knew to be true, in spite of all fools (and really did and do intend so to do), while all the while I was deceiving myself, and unaware of a canker at the heart the very opposite to the one against which you warn me—I mean the proud, self-willed, self-conceited spirit which made no allowance for other men's weakness or ignorance; nor again, for their superior experience and wisdom on points which I had never considered—which took a pride in shocking and startling, and defying, and hitting as hard as I could, and fancied, blasphemously, as I think, that the word of God had come to me only, and went out from me only.'

But it was to Maurice that Kingsley could reveal himself most fully. Few of his letters to the older man tell us much about the externals of Kingsley's life, but to his 'Dearest Master' he could show without shame the naked, cowering fear which all men know. Naturally, between these two despair manifested itself in religious terms.

'I am losing a zest for work. Every thing seems to me not worth working at—except the simple business of telling poor people, Don't fret, God cares for you, & Christ understands you, & that I can't tell fully, because I daren't say what I think—I daren't preach my own creed, which seems to me as different from what I hear preached & find believed, everywhere, as the modern creeds are from Popery, or from St. Paul—and as St. Paul—horrible thought!—seems to me at moments from the plain simple words of our Lord. . . . When my trust in the Bible seems falling to pieces it is—you must feel it is—terrible work for a poor soul to know where the destructive process must stop; & one feels alone in the universe, at least alone among mankind, on a cliff which is crumbling beneath one, & falling piecemeal into the dark sea.'

Many of the old guides no longer satisfied him. Carlyle, his literary model at the beginning of his career, now disgusted him, he told Maurice in November 1856: 'I was with him the other evening, with Froude & Parker; & never heard I a more foolish outpouring of Devil's doctrines—Raving Cynicism which made me sick. I kept my temper with him: but when I got out I am afraid I swore with wrath & disgust—at least I left no doubt on my 2 friends' minds of my opinion of such stuff. All the ferocity of the old Pharisee without Isaiah's prophecy of mercy & restoration—the notion of sympathy with sinners denounced as a sign of innate "scoundrelism"—a blame I am very glad to bear: I must tell you all vivâ voce. If I can temperately. I never was so shocked in my life—& you know, I have a strong stomach, & am not easily moved to pious horror. Meanwhile his wife is pining, poor creature, for want of sympathy & attention from him, & is very ill. Whatever her faults may be, *he* has no right to neglect her. I am sick of his present phase, moral & intellectual, though I never can forget what he has taught me: but where should I have been, if you had not brought me on *The* step beyond him?'

Even such revulsions from the old idols were only temporary, and eventually Kingsley resumed his pleasant visits to Carlyle, with whom he loved to talk, particularly of politics and literature. Mrs. Kingsley says little in her husband's biography of his friendship with Carlyle, but several of their contemporaries have left records of it. Walter White wrote a long account in his daily journal of a characteristic evening in March 1860, when the two men talked at Carlyle's house. White went after dinner to tea with the old Scot in Chelsea, and found Carlyle wearing a long dressing-gown, his face of a 'youthful and fresh-coloured appearance, remarkable in a man of sixty-three'.

After some talk, Carlyle took down a book. 'His face was a good study while he read, wearing no spectacles, shadows thrown on one cheek, bushy eyebrows, moustache and beard masking the massive underlip. A cheerful tone of voice, the more reason by its occasional manifestations of native Scottish. Then Kingsley was announced: entered in hat and overcoat and with a hoarse voice from a cold: in mourning for his lately deceased father. Enquiries as to health led to his telling us that for three years to come he was forbidden to write or undertake severe intellectual work, he having had warning and acute pains in the head, accompanied by great heat.'

After Kingsley's arrival, he and Carlyle took over the conversation from the other guests. The bellicose Carlyle and the equally militant Kingsley talked for some time of the advantages of the military life and agreed on the volunteer movement that it was 'a good thing for all that number of men to get themselves washed and cleaned and used to punctual habits'.

'Then some general talk on Macaulay's falsification of history; then literature generally, and K., "How long will this jackassery, this flood of books written by people who have nothing to say, continue? Look at Dickens, a man who might have been a Defoe if he would but have restrained his pen, who has degenerated ever since 'Nickleby', whose Christmas stories are gloomy and depressing."

'C. "I find the humour of his 'Pickwick' very melancholy."

'. . . Then sermons were talked of and the strictures on books applied to them. "I hate the sound of my own voice," said K., "especially if I have to speak beyond a quarter of an hour. 'Tis a torture to me."

'Then I: "Then every Sunday is to you a martyrdom."

' "It is, and judge of my feelings when I am obliged to listen to somebody else's sermon for thirty-five minutes. Think of 15,000 clergymen having to stand up Sunday after Sunday with nothing to say. Ah! the Reformation has much to answer for." Turning to C. "You and your Puritans have much to answer for. Those men first started the notion that the way to heaven was by infinite jaw: and see what infinite jaw has brought us to."

' "Ay," said C. " 'Tis wonderful how men will go on talking with nothing to say." '

In 1866 Kingsley wrote to congratulate Carlyle on becoming Rector of Edinburgh University, and in his letter he acknowledged all that he had learned from the older man, saying that in his youth he had learned many truths and had been delivered from 'phantoms & superstitions, which have made me bless the day when my dear & noble wife first made me aware of your existence. What I owe to that woman God alone knows; but among my deepest debts to her is this—that she first taught me to reverence you. Amid many failings & follies, I have been at heart ever true to your teaching.'

Many of the Christian Socialists who were not intimate with him wondered why Kingsley continued to hold aloof from the Working Men's College. Lord Goderich, who had given a good bit of 'tin' to its foundation, said that Kingsley's 'healthy animalism' would have been welcome among some of the staff whom he thought effete. It is difficult, however, to imagine Kingsley working, for instance, with Ruskin, whom he disliked on first meeting as being essentially feminine; when the Ruskins separated, Kingsley's sympathies were naturally with 'his hapless ex-wife'. Ruskin turned on Kingsley the bland and baffling good nature with which he could ignore any enmity, and told Furnivall how much he admired Kingsley's views on art. Caught off guard by the compliment, Kingsley wrote to Furnivall: 'Your letter pleased me exceedingly, & made me a little ashamed of myself, for I certainly have not spoken of Ruskin as he has spoken of me, & I fear I have been very unjust to him.' As a teacher Ruskin was charming, but Ludlow felt that he was too dictatorial and sometimes too disparaging, on one occasion by a single remark killing a modelling class under Thomas Woolner and causing Woolner to leave the College. Kingsley's own satirical descriptions of Pre-Raphaelitism in *Yeast* and *Two Years Ago* make it improbable that he would have got on easily with the master of the advanced class in painting, Dante Gabriel Rossetti. Ludlow thought that Rossetti had painted no single satisfactory picture and that his conception of woman was 'simply morbid. The man, himself, slight, weakly, narrow-browed, had to my mind not an element of greatness about him'.

One of the visitors to Eversley Rectory in 1856 was Harriet Beecher Stowe, who brought her sister Mrs. Perkins with her. Mrs. Stowe wrote home of being 'ushered into a large, pleasant parlor lighted by a coal fire, which flickered on comfortable chairs, lounges, pictures, statuettes, and bookcases'. Kingsley she described as 'tall, slender, with blue eyes, brown hair, and a hale, well-browned face, and somewhat loose-jointed withal. His wife is a real Spanish beauty.' Later she and Kingsley went to his study, in which she sank into a low armchair which so pleased her that she christened it 'Sleepy Hollow'.

During Mrs. Stowe's stay they were all sitting at lunch when the local pack passed the Rectory. The American visitor launched out into a violent attack on fox hunting, saying that 'hunting a man would be far better sport than a poor fox'. The Kingsleys were a little shocked, and Maurice's nine-year-old face turned crimson with silent fury. The moment he and Rose were alone and could speak of the blasphemy against the sport they loved best, he burst forth: 'I thought I should have thrown the water bottle at her head!' Mrs. Stowe did not realize her own *faux pas* and wrote home with pleasure of her stay: 'How we did talk and go on for three days! I guess he is tired. I'm sure we were. He is a nervous, excitable being, and talks with head, shoulders, arms, and hands, while his hesitance makes it the harder.'

At this time Kingsley was particularly interested in the abolition of slavery in the United States, on which he intended having his say in *Two Years Ago*. Besides Mrs. Stowe, another American whom he saw in the autumn of 1856 was W. H. Hurlbert (born Hurlbut), who was writing abolitionist propaganda in the English journals. He was a friend of James Russell Lowell, and Kingsley recommended him to Hughes as 'one of us to the back bone'. Hughes welcomed him to his house in Wimbledon with open arms; he was a charming guest and taught Hughes and his friends such useful tricks as the making of a sherry cobbler, but slowly the hospitable Hughes realized that his guest had no intention of leaving. It was not without difficulty that he finally shook himself free of Hurlbert. Wryly, Ludlow wrote of Kingsley's enthusiasm for new friends, that his 'swans sometimes turned out a different kind of bird'.

Before beginning work on *Two Years Ago* Kingsley had planned a novel on the Vaudois massacre of 1655 and had expected to go to Italy to 'get up' his background. When the trip fell through, plans for the novel were abandoned as well. As the title indicates, in *Two Years Ago* he returned to the contemporary scene. The novel takes place in 1854, when England was occupied with the Crimea abroad and cholera at home. Nowhere in his writings does Kingsley better exemplify his idea, expressed to William Bennett, that he could imagine only what he had seen. Most of the action is laid in Devon at Clovelly (here called Aberalva), in Wales near the Owens's inn at Pen-y-Gwryd, in Germany at Bertrich, and in the south of England in a village much like Eversley. The life of the central character, an adventurous, cholera-fighting doctor, Tom Thurnall, is a mixture of the character and interests of George Kingsley, the medical practice of William Ackland, and the frustrating experiences in sanitary reform of Charles Kingsley himself. Scattered throughout the book are short sketches (under fictional names, of course) of Henry Kingsley, Tom Hughes, and Tom Taylor. The absurdly improbable poet, Elsley Vavasour (born John Briggs), is probably modelled on Shelley and the poets Kingsley considered his successors, the Spasmodics; certainly, Vavasour is not a caricature of Tennyson. Kingsley's friend Hurlbert sat for the portrait of the dilettante American, Stanlake, and, with Mrs. Stowe, probably supplied many of the ideas of the novel about slavery. At the time Kingsley was completely abolitionist in sympathy, although this was to change by the time of the Civil War in America. In the novel Stanlake finally marries a beautiful American quadroon actress who passes herself off as Italian, presumably showing how easy the answer to slavery really was.

There are plenty of familiar Kingsley characters: the lovable and unintelligent young nobleman, the bluff country squire, the corrupt squireen, the patient Dobbin-like army man who loves hopelessly, the foolish high churchman (although this one is redeemed from his stupidity by the love of a good woman), the superstitious Dissenter, and the old pairing of two women, one passionate, one grave and thoughtful. Even Thurnall is Lancelot Smith or Amyas Leigh with a medical degree, and like them, he is eventually converted to true Christian belief through love.

When Kingsley discarded the trappings of the historical novel, his doctrines stood naked to view, so that in a sense *Two Years Ago* is the best of his novels as a test of his ideas. It indicates transparently what he thought of as common sense.

In religion works appear to be more important than faith; Tom Thurnall's fight against cholera is made to seem more spiritual than the prayers of the orthodox. It is slight wonder that many of Kingsley's contemporaries were shocked by the religious ideas of the novel. What they missed was that Kingsley was showing physical laws as manifestations of God's spiritual laws, that there was no essential conflict between science and religion, and that those who thought those two great forces were in opposition were themselves guilty of stupidly narrow Manicheism. Darwin's *Origin of Species* did not appear until 1859, but *Two Years Ago* shows how ready Kingsley was to accept the doctrine of evolution without losing his faith in God. It was to men like him that the Church of England owed its continued existence when Darwin's book plunged orthodoxy into warfare with the scientists.

Even more surprising in *Two Years Ago* than the priest's views on religion are the views of art indicated by a man who was novelist and poet, and here the modern reader is less apt to sympathize. The only two purposes of art seem to be to reproduce faithfully and to instruct. Claude, the painter, is frankly a useless member of society (although Kingsley finds him delightfully so) except when he paints realistic and didactic scenes which elevate the morality of the viewer. Significantly, by the end of the book, he has deserted painting for photography, which Kingsley indicates can do everything which paint can achieve—and better. In heavy sarcasm about the Pre-Raphaelites, Claude says that 'the only possible method of fulfilling the pre-Raphaelite ideal would be, to set a petrified Cyclops to paint his petrified brother'.

In answer to some complaints about the book by George Brimley, Kingsley underlined his views on art as instruction: 'People are too stupid and in too great a hurry, to interpret the most puzzling facts for themselves, and the author must now and then act as showman, and do it for them. Whether it's according to "Art" or not, I don't care a fig. What's "Art"? I never saw a little beast flying about with "Art" labelled on its back. Art ought to mean the art of pleasing and instructing, and believe me, these passages in which the author speaks in his own person do so.'

As a poet Vavasour's chief sin is that he makes his art the focus of life. Kingsley told Alexander Macmillan that 'all the best poems have been written by men whose vocation was not poetry. Shakespeare was an actor, Spenser a private secretary, Milton ditto, Pope a man of the world. Poetry as a profession succeeds no better than it pays.' Too much writing has cramped Vavasour's chest, ruined his digestion, and weakened his muscles; the state of his physique can lead only to introspective and unhealthy poetry. Three months of exercise would make him 'fresh as a lark, and able to sing like one'. Kingsley's definition of poetry is implicit in his description of two unintelligent, rough-and-ready Cambridge undergraduates, who 'are simply brave honest men; and who are, perhaps, far more "poetic" characters at this moment than Elsley Vavasour, or any dozen of mere verse-writers, because they are hazarding their lives on an errand of mercy'.

In small things as well as large, Kingsley's attitudes are shown in the novel. Some months before, he had composed a little poem, 'Farewell', for his wife's niece, verses which are probably his best-known today. The third stanza of the poem originally read:

Be good, sweet maid, and let who can be clever;
Do lovely things, not dream them, all day long;
And so make Life, Death, and that vast For Ever,
One grand sweet song.

In the novel the stanza was printed for the first time, and deliberately or not, Kingsley altered the first line of the stanza to give the poem an even more decidedly anti-intellectual bias than it originally had: 'Be good, sweet maid, and let who will be clever'. It is an attitude which informs the whole novel and which is central to Kingsley's thinking. Near the end of *Two Years Ago* the question is asked: 'Why should people be born clever, only to make them all the more miserable?' Kingsley's only answer is: 'Perhaps they learn the more . . . by their sorrows, and so they are the gainers after all.'

Kingsley's distrust of religious faith, of art, of intellect is the kind of materialism which Matthew Arnold called Philistinism, a judgment which would perhaps be unimportant except as it shows the reason for the final failure of Kingsley as a writer. He tried to combine the emotional drive of the artist with the intellect of the Philistine; Pegasus and the plough-horse seldom pull together in harness.

The contemporary reviewers were most complimentary about *Two Years Ago*, partly because Kingsley had managed the complications of his plot better than ever before, partly because he had served his apprenticeship and the time had now come to recognize him as a man of letters. Froude thought that 'Charles has written his best book and all the world knows it'. As an indication of his own opinion of the book, Mudie sent an order of 1,000 copies for his lending library, which he later increased to 1,200. The advances from Macmillan enabled Kingsley to pay off his old debts and he told Hughes: 'I am better off than I have been for years! God be thanked!'

CHAPTER XI

Muscular Christianity

On his birthday, 12th June 1857, Kingsley paused to take stock. 'Eight & thirty years old am I this day, Tummas,' he wrote Hughes, 'whereof 22 were spent in pain, in woe, & vanitie; & 16 in very great happiness, such as few men deserve, & I don't deserve at all. . . . Well, Tommy, God has been very very good to me; & I can't help feeding a hope I may fight a good fight yet before I die, & get something done. I've done little enough yet. The best work ever I've done has been my plain parish work.'

The fourteen years of his marriage were of a perfection particularly precious because it had been threatened early that spring, as he wrote Hughes: 'You have heard, I suppose, how we have been in trouble by Mrs. Kingsley's premature confinement. A bitter disappointment—and for a few hours a very great fright.' Once more Mrs. Kingsley had to leave her husband behind in the Rectory and, accompanied by nurses and children, go to the sea coast to wait for summer and the return to Eversley. Kingsley told Lord Goderich that one 'never truly understands the blessed mystery of marriage till one has nursed a sick wife, nor understands, either, what treasures women are'.

In the autumn he asked Fanny wonderingly: 'And now—what shall I say of my delight at your news? It seems too good to be true. Surely God is Love, & gives with one hand, if he chastises with the other!' The following spring, 1858, their fourth and last child, Grenville Arthur, was born and named for his mother's ancestor, Sir Richard Grenville, and for Arthur Penrhyn Stanley.

'I am so well and really married on earth, that I should be exceedingly sorry to be married again in heaven; and it would be very needless,' he told John Bullar. 'All I can say is, if I do not love my wife, body and soul, as well there as I do here, then there is neither resurrection of my body nor of my soul, but of some other, and I shall not be I.'

Physical love in marriage was for Kingsley a holy thing, for to him man's love of woman was tangible expression of the indivisible unity of his two-sided nature, and in his correspondence on the subject he was frank and sometimes surprisingly outspoken for a Victorian. 'Here the natural body can but strive to express its love—its desire of union,' he wrote in one of his many letters about marriage. 'Will not one of the properties of the spiritual body be, that it will be able to express that which the natural body only tries to express. . . . And what if earthly love seems so delicious that all change in it would seem a change for the worse? . . . The expression of love produces happiness; therefore, the more perfect the expression the greater the happiness! And, therefore, bliss greater than any we can know here awaits us in heaven. . . . Do I undervalue earthly bliss? No! I enhance it when I make it the sacrament of a higher union!' His views on second marriage, he admitted, were 'peculiar', for he considered that it was 'allowed for the hardness of men's hearts, but from the beginning it was not so, and will not be so, some day, when the might of love becomes generally appreciated!'

One of the clearest statements Kingsley made on the relationship between body and spirit was written in a letter to a clergyman advising a woman parishioner who contemplated joining the Roman Catholic Church. In a quite impartial fashion Kingsley tries to show why Roman Catholicism could never be meaningful to him. 'Now, there are two great views of men. One as a spirit embodied in flesh and blood, with certain relations, namely, those of father, child, husband, wife, brother, as necessary properties of his existence. . . .

'Those of them who are spiritually enlightened, have learnt to believe that these relations to man are the symbols of relations to God. . . . They deny that these relations are carnal, *i.e.*, animal, in essence. They say that they are peculiar to the human race. That being human, they are spiritual, because man *quâ* man is not an animal, but a spirit embodied in an animal.' It was, of course, this first view of man which Kingsley held.

'The second class . . . hold an entirely different anthropology. In their eyes man is not a spirit necessarily embodied in, and expressed by an animal; but a spirit accidentally connected with, and burdened by an animal. The animal part of them only is supposed to be human, the spiritual, angelic or diabolic, as the case may be. . . . The ideal of man, therefore, is to deny, not himself, but the animal part which is not himself, and to strive after a non-human or angelic state.' If a man held this second view, it was impossible in Kingsley's eyes for him to be a true Christian, let alone a Protestant, for it seemed automatically to negate man's duty to his fellow creatures and certainly to make a mockery of both the marital and the familial relationship.

The hypocritical cruelty of the Rev. Theobald Pontifex to his children in *The Way of All Flesh* admittedly should not be taken as typical of the ways of Victorian parsons as fathers; still, it seemed so to Samuel Butler, and one need only turn to that mordant commentary on Victorianism to know what an extraordinary father Kingsley was for his day. Remembering his childhood and the antagonism he had felt for his parents, he banished corporal punishment from his own home, for fear that it might produce lying, unhappiness, and lack of love. Instead of making many small rules for the children, he tried to lay down only broad, distinct principles of conduct: 'It is difficult enough to keep the Ten Commandments, without making an eleventh in every direction.'

As soon as they were able, the children accompanied their father on his walks around the parish, and as they walked, Kingsley taught them his own love of nature, pointing out to them with equal enthusiasm plants, birds, a fox's earth, green tiger-beetles, and the rocks that lay beneath the moor on which they walked. Almost as if to demonstrate his own closeness to the physical part of his parish, he would occasionally stop by a furze bush and whip out a clay churchwarden pipe which he had hidden there in case of sudden need. All the children were taught to follow the Bramshill Hunt on foot or on horseback, and by the time he was ten, Maurice was riding with his father, who was usually mounted on the old mare appropriately named Puff.

Around the house there was always at least one cat, and more in the stables. Dandy, a Scotch terrier noted for his cheek in accompanying the children to church, lived with the family for thirteen years before he was buried in the pets' graveyard on the Rectory lawn. Sweep, a black retriever, and Victor, a Teckel given Kingsley by the Queen and named for her, succeeded Dandy at the Rectory. Other pets, less orthodox but equally loved, were a family of toads, whose home was annually protected from the scythe; a pair of sand wasps who made their nest in the window of his dressing-room; a flycatcher; and even a favourite slow-worm in the churchyard. The pets were apt to make guests nervous, but they taught the children an undifferentiated love of natural things.

Kingsley tried, too, to save his children from the gloom of the Victorian Sunday. After church he would draw them pictures and show them picture books saved as a special treat (not as a penance) for this day, and then take them for a long walk, frequently stopping to watch village cricket, reminding Maurice that the boys who worked all week had no other chance to play. The keeper of the local public house once told visitors: 'Eh, Paason, he doan't objec'—not ee—as loik as not 'e'll coom and look on, and ee do tell 'em as it's a deal better to 'ave a bit o' elthy play o' a Sunday evenin' than to be a-larkin' 'ere and a-larkin' there hall hover the place a-courtin' and a-drinkin' hale.' Kingsley was always strongly anti-Sabbatarian in his beliefs; in 1852 he had associated himself with the movement to keep the Crystal Palace open on Sundays in order to cut down on drunkenness. 'I have often fancied I should like to see the great useless naves & aisles of our cathedrals turned into museums & winter gardens,' he wrote Maurice in 1856, 'where people might take their Sunday walks, & yet attend service.' When he went to Westminster as a canon, he supported the Sunday opening of the British Museum.

When the boys left for school, Kingsley wrote them delightful letters, gently encouraging them when they were lonely or doing poorly in their studies. When Maurice first went away to St. Neot's, where Cowley Powles was Headmaster, his father wrote him: 'Keep up your heart & be a good boy, & never mind if boys bully a little; they mean no harm. And you shall have all the fun you like when you come home.' A later letter indicates that Maurice made the necessary adjustment: 'Dad is so pleased at your defending the *weak* from the strong—but I advise you not to throw boys *downstairs*, for fear they should arrive at the bottom with their skulls cracked, which I have heard of one boy doing. I would never fight on *the stairs*, for fear of concussions of the brain.' On another occasion: 'Mr. Powles says there is no chance at all of your being caned. That you are a very good boy, & have not been reported to him since he cannot tell when: & that no boys are ever caned unless they have been reported again & again, & will not mend for any reasonable management. So put such stuff out of your pate, & get along.'

Frequently he would report on the local hunting and fishing, or on the condition of their own horses, illustrating the letters with amusing drawings. In 1859 he wrote Maurice: 'The grey is lame, & Mamma had to hire Marlow's horse to go to Reading, & he stopped at every public house on the road. Oh ho ho says your Ma, That vulgar conduct won't do for me. So she got out & walked past the publics!' Another time he wrote: 'I galloped Puff today: but she made as much noise as a railway engine; not having been out of the stable for a week, & as fat as a pig.'

Kingsley told Peter Wood that he was bringing up Maurice as both naturalist and sportsman, so that 'whether he goes into the army (Engineers), or emigrates, he will have a pursuit to keep him from cards and brandy-pawnee, horse-racing, and the pool of hell.' Once when Wood arrived for a visit at Eversley, Kingsley was out fishing. When he came home, Wood went with Mrs. Kingsley and the children to meet him at the door.

With little more than a greeting to the adults, he at once lay down at full length on the floor of the hall and let the children romp over him, whooping with delight. Kingsley was always careful to be even tempered with the children and to treat them with courtesy, humour, and informality. In later years their dominant memory of childhood was of riotous laughter with their parents.

As Kingsley suggested to Hughes, his parish work was going extremely well, whether in the pulpit or on his rounds of the cottages, in and out of which he could sometimes be seen going with huge stone bottles of gargle under his arm, to teach his parishioners to gargle their throats as a preventive against diphtheria. His sermons were increasingly effective, partially because he had found new help with his stammering. In January 1857 he spent ten days in London, visiting 'Hunt the stammering man every afternoon'. Kingsley consulted Dr. James Hunt frequently in London and spent a fortnight with him in Swanage. Hunt told Kingsley that the trouble with his speech had been improper breathing, and so convinced was the patient that he wrote to many stammerers, suggesting deep breathing and exercise with dumb-bells, and then imitation of the speech of others by opening the mouth wide, by reading aloud, and by watching as well as listening to good speakers. Also they must be careful to keep the tongue firmly in check: 'I know a beautiful great lady who lets her tongue fly about in her mouth, and consequently you often cannot understand her.' Kingsley told his correspondents that Hunt could cure without fail except when the patient was too young or too great a fool to pay attention and practise. His own speech was so much improved that his stammer seemed to him entirely gone, although he did still hesitate. However, one young lady who met him disliked his speech: 'In ordinary conversation, Mr. Kingsley stammers a good deal, but, being conscious of it, he has taken pains to overcome the defect by speaking very slowly—almost too slowly—for when we heard him make a speech on one occasion, we felt inclined to goad him on, it became so tiresome.'

The mere fact of his stammering, he told Maurice, was proof

that he had a Father in Heaven, and he thanked God each day 'for this paralytic os hyoides of mine, which has kept me low, & makes me refrain my tongue & my soul too, whenever I try to be witty & eloquent, & a flunkey & a peacock, under penalty of stuttering dumbness.'

His sermons were now filling the church not only with members of the parish but with visitors who came especially to hear him. It was particularly pleasing to him to see the increasing number of officers and men who came from neighbouring Sandhurst and Chobham and from the new camp at Aldershot, where he had gone to see the splendid sight of the Queen on horseback reviewing the survivors from the Crimea. Frequently the officers in the congregation were invited to lunch at the Rectory, and in return he was a constant guest at the mess in the new Staff College, talking equally well and amusingly on fishing, geology, or military history. Among the military heroes he now counted as friends were Sir William Napier and Sir William Codrington, who settled near Eversley after his exploits in the Crimea.

Just as Kingsley had been excited to the bursting-point by the Crimean War, so he now found himself exploding to all his friends over the China War and still more over the Indian Mutiny. He was naturally heart and soul with England in these wars in 1857 and 1858 as a loyal subject. Beyond that, however, he felt a natural antipathy toward the coloured races, and in wars between white nations, his allegiance automatically was with the Teutonic side. His race pride and his patriotism, which sometimes amounted to jingoism, combined in one of his least attractive aspects.

When England went to war with China over the illegal boarding in 1856 of the *Arrow*, Kingsley corresponded with Stapleton, who suggested that the English attitude was not above reproach. Kingsley answered sadly: 'It is really painful for me to differ from you: but I must. It seems to me that every one, in the House or out, who has any personal knowledge of the Chinese, is unanimous on the malus animus of that nation's government—a thing one never heard doubted before. And I do ask you again, to read the proclamation quoted by Ramsden commanding the Chinese to kill the English wherever found on shore outside the Factory (& this in the face of the treaty) & to judge for yourself.' The war he felt was necessary 'for the preservation of English life & property along the *whole* Chinese coast' because the Chinese would soon have been intolerable had they found that they 'could tyrannize & insult with impunity at Canton'.

The Indian Mutiny was even harder for Kingsley to bear, particularly after the terrible news came through to England of the massacre of women and children at Cawnpore. 'Never before could I "realize to myself", as the slang now is, what the thing meant,' he told John Bullar. 'It was hearing of English women of my own time whom people knew, who drest, talked, lived as we do, who might have been my wife, my children.' To Mr. Maurice he wrote that he could hardly bear to look at a woman or child, even at his own beloved ones: 'It raises such horrible images, from which I can't escape.' On another occasion he told Bullar: 'My brain is filled with images fresh out of hell and the shambles.'

As usual Ludlow proved to be a source of irritation, by arguing over the morality of the treatment of the Indians by the British troops and by worrying over the fate of Indian women and children. At last Kingsley had to tell him: 'I have not your fears that our Soldiers will commit atrocities similar to those of the Sepoys. I dare say some of them, being blackguards will try to do, & will be stopped. I fear that women & children will be killed. It is an unavoidable evil. . . . Shall we give up taking Delhi for fear of hurting the women & children?'

When 'Clemency' Canning issued his proclamation assuring the Indians that only the guilty would be punished, Kingsley was still more angry: 'Of course he is right in saying "You must not punish innocent people" & in restraining the anger of civilians, however just: but if he had been *a man* that proclamation would have begun with a thundernote of *vengeance* against the really guilty, before it began to speak of the innocent.'

Wearily, the two men argued the decades away, over the Dyaks, the Crimea, China, India, the American Civil War, and

Governor Eyre. For Kingsley the Englishman first, then the white man, was always right; Ludlow, who had lived abroad so much, seldom agreed. In 1866 Kingsley told him: 'Be sure that whatever you may think of me, I shall always think of you with love & respect, in spite of the divergence—which I do not deny —which comes out whenever you have to deal with colonial questions, as between the English man & the savage or foreigner.'

Since he must chafe at home, Kingsley could only ease the militant ache in his heart by preaching at Aldershot and Woolwich, by lecturing to the troops, by tramping the hills near Eversley and plotting their 'attack and defence during a possible invasion', by reading books of military history, and, as usual, by fishing. How much outdoor life could relieve his pent-up mind is indicated by a letter to his son Maurice during this period: 'Would you think? There was a little jack basking in the upper pond after all, among our trout. I called George [the Eversley man-of-all-work], & he shot at it, & wounded it, & then I slew it with a big stick. So we served the nasty sepoy out.'

A less martial occupation during 1857 was the preparation of the volume of poems which had been so long projected with Parker. Parker had some trouble keeping him at it, for his mind tended to wander, this time to sanitary reform, which he was anxious to give a push: 'I will throw my whole soul into it, please God, and forget India in Cholera. That's better than rhyming, surely.'

The reviews of the *Poems* were very favourable, and Kingsley was pleased to see how much attention (some of it, to be sure, disparaging) was attracted by 'Santa Maura', in which he intended to 'exhibit the martyr element, not only free from that celibate element which is so jumbled up with it in the old myths; but brought out and brightened by married love'. When Ludlow wrote a flattering review in the *Leeds Express*, Kingsley warned:

'You are not wise in rating my work so high. I feel in myself a deficiency of discursive fancy, which will prevent my ever being a great poet. I know I can put into singing words the plain things I see & feel: but all that faculty which Alexander

Smith has—(and nothing else)—& which Shakespeare had more than any man—the power of metaphor & analogue—the instinctive vision of a connexion between all things in heaven & earth, which Poets *must* have, is very weak in me; & therefore I shall never be a great poet. And what matter? I will do what I can: but I believe you are quite right in saying that my poetry is all of me which will last.'

'It took that metre instinctively in my ears,' Kingsley wrote to Professor Blackie of the hexameters in 'Andromeda', '& went its own way, I following it'. His method of composing poetry is indicated in the rest of the letter: 'Poetry always comes to me first as music without words—to think a thought in prose, & then look about for a tune to set it to, is what I can't do—though I suppose my betters can.'

Matthew Arnold's opinion was somewhat different from that of the reviewers. In August 1853, he had written to Clough when he heard that Kingsley was working on a classical subject: 'His poem is in hexameters, and on *Perseus and Andromeda.* Eh? Froude says much of it is very good. Now I think, a priori, the man is too *coarse a workman* for poetry.'

The truth was that a drought had fallen on Kingsley; most of the poems had been written some years before, and he told Maurice: 'I have no novel in my head just now. I have said my say for the time, and I want to sit down and become a learner, not a teacher.' To a magazine editor who asked for a novel he said that he had 'an especial dislike to the serial form. . . . Twice have I written serials: but never again will I try it.' When Daniel Macmillan suggested the idea of a 'common life novel' to Kingsley at the time *Two Years Ago* was appearing, he turned it down with the request to wait two years for another book.

Then in April 1858 he became excited about writing a novel on the Pilgrimage of Grace, and he made a summer trip to Yorkshire to get the mood of the background before progressing with the story. By the end of the year he had sent Macmillan some sections of the novel, but his heart was clearly not in it, and he proposed to go ahead with the modern story instead. Even Macmillan's offer of £2,000 for either novel was not enough incentive to get him to finish his ideas, and they were gradually abandoned. The completed sections of the modern novel were probably those which his daughter Mary finished in 1916 and published as *The Tutor's Story*.

'I had been, by continual creation, using the grey matter of the back of the brain a little too fast, till it got hot and aching,' he told John Bullar in October 1859, 'and I found that the novel which I had been wearily trying to write was twaddle and a failure. So I have just stopped, and shall write nothing but sermons, and read hard. . . . I am only like a spider who has spun all his silk, and must sit still and secrete more.'

In 1859 Macmillan suggested that Kingsley and three or four of his friends, including Froude, should undertake a series of historical sketches of English heroes for boys, with Kingsley responsible for the Elizabethan heroes, but even this seemed too much, and Kingsley had to content himself with writing occasional sermons and reviews, with prefaces to other men's works, and with new editions of his own novels.

It must have been doubly difficult for him to find that he had 'spun all his silk', for two of his intimates were suddenly and unexpectedly famous novelists during this period.

In the spring of 1857 Tom Hughes had sent Kingsley the nearly complete manuscript of a boys' novel which he had shown only to Ludlow and the Macmillans; he proposed to call it *Tom Brown's School Days*. With all the generosity of his unbounded friendship for Hughes, Kingsley went to work to help him, by reading the manuscript, by making suggestions only when he was asked for them, and by advising Hughes: 'So finish the book your own original way, & never mind Ludlow.' When it appeared, he wrote Hughes that he was 'puffing it everywhere', including the *Saturday Review*, where he had 'written a sufficiently stupid & bald review' because he had had 'especial orders "not to lay it on too strong"—the cantankerous critters hate being genial, & fancy they shew their superior critical powers by picking & paring & balancing & snubbing'. But if his review was restrained, his enthusiasm elsewhere was not; there is no better measure of the essential magnanimity of Kingsley than his unfettered joy over Hughes's success at the very time he was having most trouble in his own writing.

Five years with almost no word from him had passed when Henry Kingsley came home in 1858 to the Rectory in Chelsea and paced up and down outside afraid to ring the bell for fear of what might have happened to the parents who did not even know that he was coming to England. Rather anticlimactically, when he did ring the bell, his parents were not at home; the curate told him that they had taken a cottage at Eversley because of their ill health, and that he had been left in charge. To Eversley Henry went, and when he joined his family, he was full of stories of five years of living as a gold-prospector and a 'sundowner'. Rather more importantly, since none of these adventures had made him any money, he also had with him the partly completed first draft of a novel. Kingsley, of course, was delighted and introduced him to the Macmillans, who were as impressed as Kingsley with the novel, to which they bought the rights. *Geoffry Hamlyn*, which came out in 1859, is a first-rate adventure novel, set primarily in the bush of Australia. It was followed in 1862 by *Ravenshoe*, an even better book, which Henry dedicated to his brother; after that, the quality of his novels declined sharply, until he was writing pathetic hack-work at his death. Between his return from Australia and his unwise marriage in 1864, Henry lived chiefly in a cottage in Eversley, where his unorthodox writing hours began late at night, when he would sit with rum jug at elbow working until dawn. After his marriage he was in continual money troubles and frequently borrowed from Charles, a practice which naturally cooled their relations. Henry's wife, too, took to writing begging letters which Fanny resented, so that by the time of Charles's death the two families were estranged. There is no evidence that Fanny was ever jealous of Henry or that she seriously disapproved of him before he became a maddeningly persistent borrower. Nor is it a 'cold, queer fact' that none of Kingsley's family plays any part in Mrs. Kingsley's life of her husband, as one of his biographers states, nor is it true that only old Mr. and Mrs. Kingsley are mentioned by name. It would be useless to assert that

Mrs. Kingsley wrote an intimate account of her husband; she was above all concerned with his public career and with his influence on 'souls rescued from doubt, darkness, error, and sin', and with that forbidding ideal in mind, produced a lifeless book by modern standards. It is with the Victorian conception of biography—or rather, the conception held by Victorian widows—that we should quarrel rather than seek malice in the fact that Kingsley's brothers are seldom mentioned.

Some critics have suggested that Henry was a better writer than the Rector, and even their brother George said that 'Henry was the great man, not Charles'. It is worth remembering that George had given up Christianity by the time he said that, and that he would hardly feel much sympathy with Charles's religious works. At his best Henry wrote more sensitively, more poetically than did Charles, but his best was hopelessly dispersed in the numbers of mediocre novels he wrote. Alexander Macmillan said truly that his style in *Geoffry Hamlyn* 'is wonderfully quiet and yet powerful—a kind of lazy strength which is very charming'. There is a close family resemblance to his brother's writing in his loving descriptions of the countryside.

The works of Henry Kingsley, Tom Hughes, and Charles Kingsley all display the admiration of athletic, upper-middle-class, somewhat Christian young men which inspired the term, 'Muscular Christianity'. Who first used it is no longer known (Leslie Stephen thought it was a writer for the *Saturday Review*), but by the time Henry and Hughes had published their first novels, it was already applied to Charles Kingsley, much to his irritation. In 1858 he complained to one of his reviewers of the use of 'that to me painful, if not offensive term, Muscular Christianity'. When tiny John Parker died in 1860, Kingsley wrote: 'Those who know how I loved him, know what a calumny it is to say that I preach "muscular Christianity".' Occasionally he would try to shrug it off: 'I have to preach the divineness of the whole manhood, and am content to be called a Muscular Christian, or any other impertinent name.'

It is obvious that Kingsley never saw why his critics found his a limited view; when he preached a Christmas sermon at Cambridge on David, in 1864, he said with some disgust: 'We have heard much of late about "Muscular Christianity". A clever expression, spoken in jest by I know not whom, has been bandied about the world, and supposed by many to represent some new ideal of the Christian character. For myself, I do not know what it means. . . . Its first and better meaning may be simply a healthful and manful Christianity; one which does not exalt the feminine virtues to the exclusion of the masculine.' The second possible meaning he could find was simply that of chivalry; if that was what was meant, 'then the expression is altogether unnecessary; for we have had the thing for three centuries'. Like most good tags, the label is partial, but it was sufficiently accurate to stick, and a century later it is the phrase which immediately springs to mind to describe Charles Kingsley.

Although his writing was not going well, and though he still kicked as lustily as ever against the pricks, the years had treated Kingsley well, and he could look forward on Christmas 1858 to the new year, content with his career, unaware that in a few months he would finally secure the prestige and the respectability he had always wanted.

CHAPTER XII

Royal Favour

Unknown to Kingsley, *The Saint's Tragedy* was a favourite work of the first gentleman of the land. Twelve years after its publication the Prince Consort remembered it so well that he recommended it to his daughter, the Crown Princess of Prussia, for its approach to Roman Catholicism. And Kingsley's attitude toward marriage and his admiration for the bluffer Teutonic virtues surely did not lessen the play's appeal for the Prince. In 1856 Kingsley told Alexander Macmillan that '*Glaucus* seems to have pierced the "august abodes" of Windsor, and to have elicited the present of a handsome book from H.R.H. Prince Albert'. The princely admiration of *Two Years Ago* resulted in a still more important reward for Kingsley.

The day after Palm Sunday 1859 the 'Court Circular' in *The Times* noted: 'Yesterday the Queen and Prince Consort, the Princesses Alice, Helena, and Louisa, the Ladies and Gentlemen of the Court, and the domestic household attended divine service in the private chapel, Buckingham Palace. The Rev. Charles Kingsley preached the sermon.' Presumably the Queen was trying out Kingsley to see how she liked his pulpit manners. She was not easy to preach to; she liked sermons short and uncontroversially Protestant, and she wanted a written copy of the text to hold, to see that the preacher did not depart from his announced subject. Kingsley passed his ordeal by royalty, and on May 7th he was offered the appointment of chaplain-in-ordinary to the Queen. The annual salary was £30, for which his simple duty was to preach once a year in the Chapel Royal at St. James's. In the autumn of 1859 he was invited to preach before the court in the private chapel at Windsor and afterwards was presented to the royal family. Although he was nervous, his simple and natural bearing commended itself to the Queen and her husband, who were soon to bring him into much closer relationship with their family. As he had expected, Kingsley was delighted with the Queen and told John Bullar: 'I know one more strong good man than I did—and that is the Prince Consort. I have fallen in love with that man.'

Kingsley, who was an unabashedly sentimental royalist, felt for Victoria all the uncritical worship he attributed to the Elizabethans in their veneration of their own great Queen. On the personal level he was particularly moved by her devotion to the Prince Consort, which reflected in a royal sphere all the domestic virtues he found in his own humbler but equally happy marriage. With the Prince Consort he shared an unbounded belief in the progress of science, admiration for the manly and military virtues, and the clear confidence that God had created the Anglo-Saxon as the summit of human life. The two men also had a common interest in education, although the Prince believed far more sternly in the advantages of hard and unrelieved academic work than did Kingsley. In 1859 Maurice Kingsley, with the approval of Cowley Powles, left St. Neot's to enter the newly founded Wellington College, in which the Prince Consort took so much interest, and of which Kingsley's friend, E. W. Benson, was Headmaster.

What the appointment as chaplain meant to the Kingsleys is indicated reticently by Mrs. Kingsley: 'From this time there was a marked difference in the tone of the public press, religious and otherwise, towards him: and though he still waged war as heretofore against bigotry, ignorance, and intolerance, and was himself unchanged, the attacks on him from outside were less frequent and generally less bitter.' The religious and political views of the chaplain to the head of the Church and State could hardly be attacked as dangerously unorthodox.

The royal appointment naturally meant that Kingsley was more in demand as preacher and as lecturer, and the increased control over his stammer had made him a much more effective speaker. By now his reputation was sufficiently widespread that he could choose his own topic for lecturing, and he usually chose not to talk about religion. He lectured on Chaucer, geology, Flodden Field, Darwin (whose *Origin of Species* appeared this year and was accepted at once by Kingsley), and we find him in July at Willis's Rooms urging the romance of drains on the first meeting of the Ladies' Sanitary Association. The money that came in from his lectures was welcome, but they took a great deal out of him, and he usually came home strained in brain and heart, feeling painfully that his startling mode of saying things had produced antagonism rather than agreement in his audiences.

Perhaps it was the wide range of subjects on which he lectured and the ease with which he spoke on non-religious subjects which convinced the Prince Consort (for once more he seems to have been behind the invitation) that Kingsley would be the ideal man to fill the chair of Regius Professor of Modern History at Cambridge, recently vacated by Sir James Stephen. On 9th May 1860, one year and two days after his appointment as chaplain to the Queen, Kingsley was invited by Palmerston to accept the professorship. Since he knew his own shortcomings as a scholar, he took the chair with great diffidence, aware how hard he would have to work to prepare his lectures. Kingsley had in the past hoped for many clerical advancements, but how surprised he was by this academic offer is indicated by the fact that so far he had not bothered to scrape together enough money to take his M.A. degree, an omission which he repaired in a fortnight by going up to Cambridge to stay with Dr. Whewell, Master of Trinity, while he was being made a senior member of the University. It had been a long time since he had seen Cambridge, and it was with the knowledge that it was soon to be part of his daily life that he looked with new pleasure at the beauty of the ancient stonework and the casual elegance of life in the combination rooms. The annual salary for the chair was £371, almost as much as his income from Eversley.

During the summer of 1860 he spent the time preparing for his inaugural lecture and in settling the estate of his father, who had died in February. Old Mrs. Kingsley settled permanently at Eversley, living part of the time in her own house with Henry and part in the Rectory. Mr. Kingsley had been in a state of mental and physical collapse, and Charles could find his death nothing but a blessing. To Mr. Maurice he wrote of his feeling that he had not behaved during his father's life as a son should: 'I have this comfort, that he died loving me, & satisfied with me & my small success, & happy in his children as he said, again & again.'

Before the beginning of term he went for a vacation in Ireland with Froude, to rest and, one presumes, to get pointers from one of the greatest historians of the century. The letters home were of the beauty of the country and the killing of his first salmon; he also 'saw a mighty seal close here the other day, rolling about, with a black head as big as a calf, salmon-hunting. There are whales here and grampuses, but we have seen none. We have plenty of sea-boating and yachting, but I don't care for that since I have caught salmon; I can think of nothing else.'

The only flaw in Ireland was the population: 'I am haunted by the human chimpanzees . . . to see white chimpanzees is dreadful; if they were black, one would not feel it so much, but their skins, except where tanned by exposure, are as white as ours.'

The summer was a wet one, with almost incessant rain for three months. When his parishioners asked why he did not use the prayer for fine weather, he preached a sermon which he published as 'Why Should We Pray for Fair Weather?' The rains, he said, were a gift from God to ward off cholera, by cleansing drains and sweeping away refuse, by increasing the supplies of clean drinking water. Like other physical phenomena, the rains were dependent upon fixed laws, and he objected to attempted interference by the prayers of the ignorant. He received many approving letters on the sermon from scientists, fewer from the clergy. Sir Charles Lyell wrote to tell him of two processions of peasants at Bonn thirty years before who had climbed to the top of the Peter's Berg, one composed of vinedressers going to give thanks for sunshine, those toiling up the other side from a corn district to pray for rain. Each was eager to get first to the shrine of St. Peter to ask the good offices of the saint, so they came to blows with fists and sticks 'much to the amusement of the Protestant heretics at Bonn'.

Since he was innocent of any scholarly equipment, Kingsley stated in his inaugural Cambridge lecture the intention of teaching history with an essentially Carlylean emphasis on the heroic men who made history, the direct servants of God. He called his first lecture 'The Limits of Exact Science as Applied to History' (published with other lectures in *The Roman and the Teuton*, a volume whose title would indicate to anyone who knew him where his sympathies lay). In it he said of budding students: 'If they wish to understand History, they must first try to understand men and women.' On that humanistic note, discounting all theories of economic and social history, he began an eight-year tenure as Professor.

John Martineau, who attended the first lecture, wrote home that the whole building was crowded for the occasion. Before the lecture began, Mr. Maurice came in and was recognized by an undergraduate, who gave 'Three cheers for Mr. Maurice', which was well received. The undergraduates continued amusing themselves by 'Three groans for Mr. Bright', also quite unanimous. 'Three cheers for Garibaldi' came off moderately well in spite of scattered groans and hisses. 'The Lecturer was received with deafening cheers upon the mention of his name before he came in, again when he came in, and a third time when he ended his lecture.' Although he had a strange half-frightened look on his face as he went to the desk, Kingsley's nervousness wore off and he spoke well. 'Think of noisy undergraduates', wrote Martineau, 'listening with intense silence to a lecture at boating hours for one and three-quarter hours.'

As yet there were neither faculty nor students in history at Cambridge, and it was hoped that Kingsley might start a movement in that direction. Other historians were quick to show how inept many of his judgments were, how immature his whole approach to history, and they were essentially correct. As one might expect, Kingsley's greatest contribution was in his relations with the undergraduates, who filled the halls in which he lectured, although his talks served little function save as adornment to the intellectual life of the University. The undergraduates found him approachable in a way quite new in senior members of the University, for his constant hope was to bridge the gap between the young and their tutors. He closed his inaugural lecture with an invitation to any interested undergraduate to come form part of a class at his own house on Mondays, Wednesdays, or Fridays, and an offer to 'tell them what books it seems to me they ought to read: always premising, that Gibbon whether I may agree or disagree with him in details, will form the text-book on which they will be examined by me'. If they sometimes received opinions few historians would support, the undergraduates also got from Kingsley an enthusiasm they looked for in vain in their other teachers. Max Müller, who said that Kingsley's were the most popular lectures in Cambridge, noted shrewdly: 'History was but his text, his chief aim was that of the teacher and preacher.' The success of his method was testified by the scores of his former pupils who wrote to Mrs. Kingsley after his death, recalling how he had treated them as adult friends and equal companions.

It was surely his great skill as teacher rather than his historical acumen which once more recommended Kingsley to the Prince Consort when he was looking for a tutor in history for the Prince of Wales at Cambridge. The young Prince had already spent nearly a year at Oxford being instructed by the eminent: Arthur Stanley was in charge of his religious studies, Max Müller taught him German, and the Regius Professor of Medicine watched over his sniffles and head colds. That eccentric genius Goldwin Smith taught him English history in the dining-room of New Inn Hall with several other carefully picked undergraduates, chosen more for social position than intellectual sparkle. None of Smith's seemingly radical opinions had rubbed off on the Prince, perhaps because Smith's idea of teaching was to stand flipping silently through the interminable pages of his text, W. E. Flaherty's *Annals of England.* Understandably, the Prince had learned little, even when Smith in desperation at what he considered royal stupidity suggested that perhaps the future king might absorb more history from reading Scott's novels. Smith seems never to have realized that the Prince was not stupid, merely burdened with too many subjects to master, cut off from normal contact with other young men, weighed down under the heavy restrictions of his father, who frequently descended on Oxford to watch over his progress, and, in short, having all the drudgery of the University with few of its pleasures. A young man so unacademic in his natural tastes could hardly be expected to make progress in such circumstances. He left for an extended tour of North America, and on his return even the Prince Consort realized that further imprisonment at Oxford would do him little good.

At Cambridge, where he came into residence in February 1861 the Prince was still not allowed to live in a college but went with his suite to Madingley Hall, some four miles from Trinity, of which he was a nominal member. Besides history he studied French, German, chemistry and law. Three times a week he rode in to Kingsley's house, twice to meet in a class with eleven other undergraduates, and alone on Saturdays for a review of the week's work.

To Herbert Fisher, who had been the Prince's tutor, Kingsley offered his complete co-operation, 'both as the expounder of the Prince Consort's wishes, and as the Prince of Wales's tutor'. He was disappointed at Fisher's orders to concentrate on English history between the reigns of William III and George IV, for he had been working hard on early German history. 'The Professor declares he knows nothing of eighteenth-century history,' wrote John Martineau, 'but he considers it and its kings, the Georges, to be maligned, and so will soon take up the subject *con amore*.'

Kingsley and his royal pupil got on famously, for they shared a curiosity about persons which fitted well into Kingsley's mode of teaching. The first impression was good: 'The Prince is very interesting, putting me in mind of his mother in voice, manner, face, & everything. I had him in private today, & we had a very interesting talk on politics, old & new, a free press, & so forth. I confess I tremble at my own responsibility: but I have made up my mind to speak plain truth as far as I know it. It would be bad not to do so, when such confidence has been reposed in me.'

Later in the year he told Hughes that he would 'be content, at least for this year, to help to train up that jolly boy HRH in the way he should go.

'1. by preaching to him thorough & sound Liberal doctrine.

'2. by trying to make him admire & respect all great & good men of the English nation. He is ready enough to take in both lessons: & if I can even teach a little of them to him, I shall not have lived in vain. Nothing can exceed the generous confidence toward me of those who have the right to say what opinions he shall be taught: & God give me grace to deserve it.'

Mrs. Kingsley was somewhat apprehensive about her husband's health, but the Master of Trinity suggested that his duty was more important and reminded her: 'It can only be once in a Dynasty that such a thing can occur,' so she had to be satisfied. Several of the Kingsleys' friends came to Cambridge to see the Prince; Frederick Marshall, the Eversley schoolmaster, watched him come to Kingsley's house, made a bow and received 'a most gracious one in return'. He then 'followed H.R.H. into this house, listened at the door to the whole Lecture & got out in time to see him leave'.

Sometimes the Prince would rebel against the restrictions of his father and run off to London for an evening; one biographer tells us that as often as not his absence would be found out and communicated to the Palace, so that on his arrival at the London station, he would find a royal carriage waiting for him. On one occasion he is supposed to have accepted the carriage gracefully and then gravely to have directed the coachman to that monument of non-conformist morality, Exeter Hall. Kingsley, with his tolerance of young men's wildness, was not shocked at such expeditions, and they certainly cast no blight on his affection for the young man. At his death, Rose Kingsley wrote that after his own family there was no one whom Kingsley so loved as he did the Prince of Wales.

At the end of November 1861 the Prince Consort went to Cambridge on one of his periodic inspection tours. The stress of the cold journey contributed to his already weakened state of health, and he died a fortnight later. The Queen, who secretly believed that he was responsible for his father's death, then removed the Prince from the University. After leaving Cambridge the Prince made Kingsley his own chaplain.

Because of his position in the royal household Kingsley and Mrs. Kingsley were invited to the Prince's wedding in 1863. Rose Kingsley, who bought a new white dress in expectation, did not get the invitation for which she hoped, so she led the festivities of celebration at Eversley. A sheep was roasted whole, there were hurdle races and a lobster supper for a large party at Dr. Heynes's house, and Mrs. Parfett's cook amused the company by entering so whole-heartedly into the hilarity as to ask Sir William to dance. The Kingsleys arrived home in time for the bonfire with tar barrels blazing gloriously on top. In the cocked hat of his court dress Kingsley brought bonbons and wedding cake for the children. Rose wrote Theresa Stapleton a breathless, much underlined account of her parents' excursion:

'They had the most charming day you can imagine. Mama was in the gallery the Queen had erected over the stalls of the Knights of the Garter, close to the Queen's box, so she not only saw the whole of the service, being about 20 yards from the Altar, but *heard every word* the bride & bridegroom said. She thinks & so does Papa, that the Princess is *perfectly lovely*. Please do not believe what is said in the Newspaper about the Queen sobbing & crying. Papa was exactly opposite to her the *whole* time, & says she was *perfectly calm*, except when the Prince Consort's chorale was sung, & then Papa said she threw her head back & looked up & away with a most painful look on her face, & Norman McLeod touched Papa, & said with the tears in his eyes, "See she is worshipping him in spirit."

'As soon as the Prince of Wales came up to the Altar, the Princess Royal burst out crying, & set Princess Alice, (who looked quite beautiful) & all her sisters off crying & blubbering too: but it was only from affection so they soon recovered themselves & Norman McLeod said, "Look the blessed creatures are crying," in his broad Scotch.'

Mrs. Kingsley, whose sense of the ludicrous was more apt than her husband's to function during solemn occasions, was delighted to tell the family that during the wedding the Archbishop had given 'four names of the Princess at a time to the Prince (or rather four, then two) to repeat, thinking he might not have known the Princess long enough to say all her six names off at a breath'.

After the wedding Kingsley wrote to a friend about the young royal couple: 'Stanley's report of their private life at Sandringham is all that one could wish. I always believed that the P. needed only a good wife to keep him strait; & now that he has one, all will go well.'

Kingsley's Cambridge lectures were given during the first term each year, and while he was teaching the Prince, he had to keep all three terms. For the first three years he and his family took a Cambridge house, but when he found the expenses of two establishments too great, he left the family at Eversley and himself went up only twice a year, once for the period of the lectures and once for examinations. While he was in Cambridge, his work at Eversley was taken over by Frederic Stapleton and Septimus Hansard, but he thought that Sir William took advantage of his absence to bully the curates, so he was glad to be able to spend more time in the parish after the Prince's departure from Cambridge.

In the meantime Mr. Maurice had still been having trouble with the high church party over his disavowal of eternal damnation. Kingsley was more quiet than he usually was when 'The Master' was attacked, but his name was none the less still closely associated with Maurice's. In February 1863 Maurice and Dr. Pusey exchanged letters in *The Times* and Maurice once more patiently explained his position in a pamphlet. Less patiently he organized a written protest against Dr. Pusey's treatment of Benjamin Jowett, one of the contributors to the notorious *Essays and Reviews*. When Kingsley read Maurice's letter in *The Times*, he congratulated him:

'You have burst out of the thicket upon poor old Pusey like a "Reem" of Bashan, horning him hip & thigh, tossing him over your back like any buffalo or borellé, & rushing on triumphant through the scrub, not caring to look back for your victim. He will answer, "exili voce", like the witch's ghost out of the earth, or Homer's suitors with a "batlike squeak": but I do not think you need mind a voice from the world below. That letter is quite enough for English commonsense. I hope you will back it up by silent disdain, if he rejoins.

'Puseyism is dead, & knows it: & is therefore, like an evil sprite, venomous & querulous. But remind it that it is a sprite, as you have done, & dead & d——.'

If Pusey was defeated in the exchange of letters, there were other ways in which he could show he was still very much alive. That summer the Prince and Princess of Wales attended the Oxford Commemoration, and according to custom His Royal Highness sent in a list of those whom he would like the University to honour with the degree of D.C.L. The Prince suggested Kingsley's name, and there were many Oxford men who supported him, including Arthur Stanley and Max Müller, but Pusey, as head of the high church party and as Professor of Hebrew, rallied the opposition, taking the ground that Kingsley's works were dangerous, particularly *Hypatia*, which he said was calculated to encourage young men in profligacy and false doctrine, and unfit to be read by 'our wives and sisters'. The vote would probably have gone through Convocation in Kingsley's favour, but Pusey threatened to make a disturbance in the Sheldonian during the ceremony if Kingsley appeared for a degree. Kingsley was disappointed but withdrew his name, writing Hughes that he thought 'the occurrence one of which to be justly proud. . . . The Council, & Stanley, behaved excellently well, & not at all cowardly. They would have fought the thing through if old P. had not declared his intention to cry Non Placet in the theatre, & have a fracas before the Prince's face, & that had to be avoided at all risks.'

The personal embarrassment to Kingsley was somewhat eased by the knowledge that he was supported by two journals which were not particularly friendly to him on other occasions. On 8th June 1863, *The Times* reprinted, presumably with approval, a paragraph from the *Spectator*:

'Dr. Pusey has found another opportunity for gratifying his rabid theological tastes. . . . [Kingsley's] name has . . . been withdrawn, on account of the determined opposition offered in the Hebdomadal Board by Dr. Pusey, Dr. Mansel, and others of the bigoted section. Their ground for opposition was, it is said, the heretical and immoral character of Mr. Kingsley's works, more especially of *Hypatia*—a work which, though it necessarily describes the external aspect of a slowly rotting society, is in tone and object the highest of all Mr. Kingsley's writings. Did the Hebdomadal Board make their selections as members of the council of the Index?'

The next year his friends at Oxford offered to propose his name again, but Kingsley said with dignity that the degree was an honour that must be given, not fought for. When Bishop Wilberforce invited him in 1866 to preach a Lenten sermon in the University Church, he answered that he could not appear publicly in Oxford without a public retraction or apology 'for that scandalous imputation, which though privately made, was allowed to become notorious through the public Press'. Wilberforce protested that he did not know what was meant, but Kingsley stuck to his guns the rest of his life in spite of his 'great hankering' for an Oxford D.C.L. All the injustice of Pusey's attack was fresh in his mind the next winter when he became involved with Pusey's former associate, Newman.

One of the greatest pleasures of being at Cambridge was that Kingsley had more opportunities for getting to know some of the most influential and exciting men of his day, several of them strange companions for him. Kingsley frequently went with Froude to Fryston, where he met Richard Burton and Swinburne, either of whom would seem to have fitted more easily than Kingsley into that charming temple of pornography presided over by Richard Monckton Milnes, Lord Houghton. Froude liked to tell of a dinner at Fryston where Swinburne stood on a sofa, reciting some of his most passionate verses, 'making himself as wicked as he knew how', and of how Ruskin sailed up to the poet with outstretched arms, exclaiming, 'Exquisite! divine!' Kingsley wrote no criticism of Swinburne and his poetry, but one of Swinburne's biographers tells of the annual dinner of the Royal Literary Fund in 1866, when Kingsley and Swinburne were called on to respond to the toast: Historical and Imaginative Literature. After Swinburne had spoken, Kingsley arose and paid extravagant compliment to the lady poets of the century, who had changed the nature of literature, ending with a strange tribute to his fellow-speaker:

'It is both creditable to the ladies and creditable to literature that the change has taken place. As long as literature was the coarse, fierce, and often vain thing that it was two hundred or one hundred years ago, ladies dared not deal with it. . . . Till Mr. Swinburne arose . . . I was ready to say, Who will write for us such poetry as that of Miss Rossetti, that of Miss Jean Inglelow, or that of that exquisite spirit, lost to earth but not to heaven, Miss Adelaide Procter?'

Kingsley was not a malicious man, so the natural assumption would be that he was strangely ignorant of the younger poet's works, were it not that in 1868 he told Sir Charles Bunbury 'that Swinburne's volume of objectionable poems shows true poetic genius, and the most abominable of them all has the highest poetic merit'. In the absence of any clear indication of what he intended, one can only suppose that his audience at the Royal Literary Fund dinner was as puzzled by the strange and inappropriate tribute as readers are a century later.

Even better than the chance to meet literary men at Fryston was Kingsley's becoming a close friend of Sir Charles Bunbury of Barton Hall, Suffolk. He and Mrs. Kingsley frequently stayed there together, and when he had to come up to Cambridge alone for lectures and examinations, he would spend as many weekends there as possible, frequently with military or scientific men as the other guests, for the Bunburys were connected with both the Napier family and the Lyells. In the house there was a superb series of Reynolds family portraits which Kingsley loved, and there was a good scientific museum and arboretum. There he first met Joseph Hooker and Sir Charles Lyell, and through them got to know Huxley and Darwin. In 1862 he stayed with Lord Ashburton at the Grange and talked over Darwin's *Origin of Species* with the Duke of Argyll and Bishop Wilberforce; one would like to have a record of the comments of 'Soapy Sam' Wilberforce, who had recently been publicly and humiliatingly defeated by Huxley in debate over the book. That summer the Kingsleys spent a month's vacation with the Duke of Argyll and Lord John Manners in Scotland.

In the neighbourhood of Eversley Kingsley was much at home in such great houses as Strathfieldsaye, where the Duke of Wellington ('that old noodle') collected strange animals the Kingsley children loved seeing. The Duke's menagerie included brown llamas, a pet ostrich, a black alpaca, and an elephant, in special shoes to protect the lawn, which drew the mowing-machine.

One of the houses where Kingsley most liked going was Heckfield Place, belonging to Lord Eversley, former Speaker of the House of Commons, a genial white-haired gentleman of the old school, tall, broad, and courtly. After his wife's death her place as hostess was taken by Lord Eversley's pleasantly eccentric daughter; Miss Shaw-Lefevre used to sleep through her own dinner parties, but as if to make up for that lapse, she entertained charmingly at other times, occasionally having a table set up on the roof of the house, where she served tea in zinc cups to startled guests who popped through a trap door preceded by a bewigged footman. For some time Miss Shaw-Lefevre did not use the railroads, but when she reluctantly accepted them, she used to have her brougham fastened on a flat truck to ride up to London in the only way befitting a gentlewoman.

Another less colourful neighbour was John Walter, chief owner of *The Times*, whom Kingsley frequently visited at Bear Wood, although his calls seem to have made little difference in the attacks the newspaper made on him.

Mrs. Kingsley says that her husband's 'second home' was in Eversley at Fir Grove, the home of the distinguished judge, the Right Hon. Thomas Erskine, and his family. The Erskines moved to Eversley in 1852, and in the twelve years before the death of the judge, Kingsley had his financial help in parish charities and the benefit of his 'sound and manful shrewdness'. After his death Kingsley wrote Erskine's son: 'I have learned more from your father of the actual practical business of life than I ever learnt of any man.'

After the embarrassment of the Oxford episode, Kingsley had some comfort in becoming a Fellow of the Geological Society, and tried to convince himself that F.G.S. was as satisfying a combination of letters as D.C.L. He wrote Bunbury, humbly asking to be proposed for membership in the Society: 'To belong to it has been an old ambition of mine: but I feel how little I know, & how unworthy to mix with the really great men who belong to it. . . . But I long to get in; & have pride enough to wish to be proposed by worthy men. I may say, that unless I could be proposed & seconded by two such men as you & Sir Charles Lyell, I would not come forward at all.'

The whole subject of evolution was one which Kingsley was stimulated to think of by his friendship with Lyell and Bunbury, and by Huxley and Darwin, with whom he exchanged a number of letters on the problem. Occasionally he was worried by the puzzle which beset so many other Victorians: if Darwin's hypothesis was correct, did not that mean that survival (and perhaps creation) must be random rather than designed? The scientists were in a curious position, for 'they find that now they have got rid of an interfering God—a master-magician, as I call him—they have to choose between the absolute empire of accident, & a living, immanent, ever working God'. In an attempt to solve the problem, he dabbled for a time with grafting on to Darwinism the idea that the physical was a direct and absolute manifestation of the spirit, 'that souls secrete their bodies, as snails do shells'. His scientific friends soon killed his suggestion, but in the meantime, it had prompted his most charming, probably his most successful book, *The Water-Babies*.

Mrs. Kingsley's version of the writing of the book is that her husband was reminded at the breakfast table one spring morning in 1862 that *The Heroes* was dedicated to Rose, Maurice, and Mary, but Grenville had no book of his own. Without a word

Kingsley went to his study, locked the door, and in half an hour returned with the first chapter of the story, written off without a correction. It is obvious that he had already been mulling it over for some time, for the rest of the book was written nearly as easily and rapidly, so that most of the copy went directly to the printer without revision. It appeared serially in *Macmillan's Magazine* in 1862–3 and then was published by Macmillan, dedicated 'To my youngest son, Grenville Arthur, and to all other good little boys'.

Like many good books for children, *The Water-Babies* has increasing meaning as the reader matures, but the additional connotations do not detract from the original impression. That is to say, the book can be read simply as the delightful adventures of a small chimney sweep who escapes a cruel master and learns to live in the pale green world of stream and sea. Children who know the geography of Eversley take an extra dimension of pleasure from the references to the frogs on the Great-A, the otters on Cordery's Moor, and the Garth Hunt in Eversley Wood. A more adult reader will see in the story a parable of spiritual regeneration; those who know the scientific quarrels of the Victorians can spot Kingsley's version of the positions of Huxley, Owen, and Bishop Wilberforce. One psychiatrist has even used the story as evidence of Kingsley's desire to return to the womb. All these subsidiary aspects of the book and others are undoubtedly there, but they merely enrich the texture of the story of little Tom. For the first time Kingsley allowed his doctrinaire beliefs to be dominated by his imagination, made his ideas implicit in action, and used his poetic talents in narrative and characterization rather than only in set-pieces of description. The result, if only a minor masterpiece, is probably Kingsley's most satisfactory work.

Although he wrote *The Water-Babies* so easily that it seemed mere recreation, by the end of 1863 Kingsley was increasingly tired in body and spirit from the work of preparing his Cambridge lectures and from the constant criticism they evoked. His health was in poor shape, as Mrs. Kingsley tells us, for the controversy with Newman which broke forth early in 1864.

CHAPTER XIII

'What, Then, Does Dr. Newman Mean?'

To paraphrase Voltaire on a more elevated subject, if Newman and Kingsley had not existed, it would have been necessary to invent them. To many Englishmen in the early 1860 s Newman stood for all that was fascinating, elegant, perverse, and spurious in Roman Catholicism. The very subtlety and strength of his mind only made him more suspect, but few of his contemporaries can have been aware that behind the façade of intellect lay wells of emotion far deeper, more complicated, and ultimately more productive of action than his conscious mind. Kingsley, unsubtly outspoken, trumpeting a blatant Protestantism, with a deeply ingrained suspicion of Newman, might have been created for the specific purpose of coming into conflict with him. To say which of them was right is merely to restate their quarrel; what is more important is the pity of the spectacle they created, and only the heartless could feel anything but pity at the public demonstration of the least admirable traits of two good and talented men, neither of whom ever recognized fully all the issues at stake.

For years, in print and out, Kingsley, confident that he was the mouthpiece of his countrymen, had been blasting everything that Newman stood for. It was probably not deliberately, certainly not maliciously, that he mentioned Newman in a review of Froude's *History of England*, vols. VII and VIII, in the January 1864 issue of *Macmillan's Magazine*.

In writing of the 'deep demoralization' brought on in Europe by the dogma that truth and falsehood, morality and immorality depended solely on the Pope's 'setting his seal to a bit of parchment', Kingsley mentioned in passing:

'Truth, for its own sake, had never been a virtue with the Roman clergy. Father Newman informs us that it need not, and on the whole ought not to be; that cunning is the weapon which Heaven has given to the saints wherewith to withstand the brute male force of the wicked world which marries and is given in marriage.'

What Kingsley dimly remembered was a sermon called 'Wisdom and Innocence' which Newman had published in 1843, before his submission to the Roman Catholic Church. Kingsley was obviously giving his general impression of the sermon, but what Newman had preached was quite the reverse. In describing the weapons with which the Christian Church defends itself, prayer, holiness, and innocence, he had said that to the world of physical strength these weapons were so incomprehensible that it must believe that the Church conquered by craft and hypocrisy. 'The words "craft" and "hypocrisy", are but the version of "wisdom" and "harmlessness", in the language of the world.' Newman's prose, even his sermons, is not for quick skimming, and Kingsley may simply have misunderstood; more probably, hating 'priestcraft' as he did, he made a ready identification of himself with 'the world'. Less patently but more profoundly indicative of the way in which his mind was working is the final part of the passage from the review: '. . . which Heaven has given to the saints wherewith to withstand the brute male force of the wicked world which marries and is given in marriage.' Neither masculinity nor matrimony is mentioned by Newman; they are the invention of Kingsley's memory. The worlds of conscious thought which separated the two men are obvious; here Kingsley suggests the equally impassable psychological barrier which must always keep them from understanding one another.

In writing of the Oxford Movement, Sir Geoffrey Faber has penetrated understandingly into the half-world of unrecognized sexual abnormality, faintly redolent of incense, in which New-

J. H. Newman, c. 1863

man and his circle lived. Newman not only believed in celibacy for the priesthood, both Anglican and Roman Catholic, but mourned as lost his close friends who took the mistaken step of matrimony. Feeling no attraction to women himself, he could not understand those who did. For marriage he substituted passionate friendships, innocent of overt manifestations but no less perfervid for their lack of physical release. In that pre-Freudian climate there were surely few who recognized the significance of the somewhat high-pitched relationships; it is probable that Newman had little such awareness himself, and there is no reason to think that Kingsley had any. But without consciously giving abnormality a label, Kingsley felt something vaguely unhealthy about Newman, aside from his doctrinal position, and it becomes apparent in his remarks on 'brute male force' and 'marriage'.

For Kingsley 'effeminate', which he so frequently used in describing Roman Catholicism, had an old-fashioned meaning which included self-indulgence and lack of public spirit, as well as the modern significance of the word. When he applied it to Newman, however, the term may have had a more specifically sexual connotation. Both Sir Geoffrey and Professor A. D. Culler have pointed out the peculiarly feminine qualities which his friends and admirers ascribed to Newman, all the way from Matthew Arnold's famous description of his graceful apparition gliding through the gloom of St. Mary's to Henry Scott Holland's saying that he looked 'delicate as an old lady, washed in milk'. Aubrey de Vere noted his resemblance to 'a very great lady'. W. G. Ward had an extraordinary dream in which he sat at dinner next a veiled woman of great conversational brilliance; at last Ward told her in admiration that he had never been so charmed since his talks at Oxford with John Henry Newman, at which the lady drew aside her veil and said: 'I am John Henry Newman.'

Kingsley himself had written in 1851 of Roman and Anglo-Catholics: 'So far from siding with Dr. —— he is, in my eyes, one of the most harmful men now in England; and **** in spite of his holiness and purity, is not the man to whom I would intrust anyone I love.' If Mrs. Kingsley's blanks and asterisks in her printed version of the letter do not conceal Newman's name, he is at least included in what Kingsley went on to say: 'In him, and in all that school, there is an element of foppery—even in dress and manner; a fastidious, maundering die-away effeminacy, which is mistaken for purity and refinement; and I confess myself unable to cope with it, so alluring is it to the minds of an effeminate and luxurious aristocracy.'

The connection of religion and sexual feeling in Kingsley is manifest in a letter written to a country clergyman:

' "Go to the blessed Virgin," said a Romish priest, to a lady whom I love well [Mrs. Anthony Froude]. "She, you know, is a woman, and can understand all a woman's feelings."

'Ah! thought I, if your head had once rested on a lover's bosom, and your heart known the mighty stay of a man's affection, you would have learnt to go now in your sore need, not to the mother, but to the Son—not to the indulgent virgin, but to the strong *man*, Christ Jesus—stern because loving—who does not shrink from punishing, and yet does it as a man would do it, "*mighty* to save".' In the same letter he told his correspondent: 'I have been through that terrible question of "Celibacy versus Marriage" once already in my life. And from what I have felt about it in myself, and seen others feel, I am convinced that it is the cardinal point.'

Kingsley never met Newman, although they had many friends in common. Sir William Cope, for example, was intimate with Newman, and in 1859 we find Kingsley writing him in polite and guarded tones to thank him for some of Newman's works which Sir William had pressed him to read; Froude, of course, knew Newman, and his brother had been one of the inner group at Oxford. There is no documentary proof of how much Newman and Kingsley knew of each other's personality, but the probability is overwhelming that each had a fairly detailed knowledge of how the other struck his friends. Kingsley's correspondence shows that he read most of what Newman wrote, and it is highly unlikely that Newman was unaware of the passing references to him which Kingsley made in his various writings. We have seen how constantly irritated Kingsley was at Newman's advocacy of celibacy, and his own pronouncements in favour of virility must have seemed uncouthly animal to his maidenly opponent. The Froude review was the occasion for the clash between uxoriousness and misogamy, although these terms were never clearly stated after Kingsley's remarks in *Macmillan's*.

Layer after layer of belief and personality show how fundamentally opposite the two men were: Catholic and Protestant; Roman and English (one is tempted to write 'Teuton'); traditionalist and modern; humanist and scientist; even Oxford and Cambridge, with all those terms conveyed in the 1860s; subtlety and bluffness; misogamy and uxoriousness: it is difficult to find any point of reference on which they were not opposed, and on which their terms of battle might not have been declared. It has seemed necessary to dwell on their sexual differences because it is at such deep-seated, less articulate levels of the personality that one must look for an explanation of the deadly enmity which characterized their controversy, enmity which is not fully explained by the overt grounds on which they contested.

Late in December 1863 Newman received a copy of *Macmillan's* from an anonymous sender who had marked the offending passage in Kingsley's review. In quiet protest he wrote to Macmillan, denying that he sought either reparation or even an answer to his letter: 'I do but wish to draw the attention of yourselves, as gentlemen, to a grave and gratuitous slander, with which I feel confident you will be sorry to find associated a name so eminent as yours.' Newman's remark was particularly unfortunate because Kingsley had been holding aloof for some years from writing for *Macmillan's*, and he had refused to associate himself with its founding, on the grounds that he had had enough of party periodicals. *Macmillan's* was mildly Protestant in sympathy, but otherwise it was of no particular party, and Kingsley had finally relented so far as to print *The Water-Babies* there before its publication as a book; the review of Froude, however, was his first non-fictional contribution. When Kingsley saw the letter he decided to write Newman 'as kindly as he can', Alexander Macmillan told Maurice. 'Old passages about Froude and others have left a bitter flavour in his thoughts and feelings about the great pervert.'

The letter Kingsley sent was more condescending than kind: 'That my words were just, I believed from many passages of your writings; but the document to which I expressly referred was one of your Sermons on "Subjects of the Day", No. XX., in the volume published in 1844, and entitled "Wisdom and Innocence".

'It was in consequence of that Sermon, that I finally shook off the strong influence which your writings exerted on me; and for much of which I still owe you a deep debt of gratitude.

'I am most happy to hear from you that I mistook (as I understand from your letter) your meaning; and I shall be most happy, on your showing me that I have wronged you, to retract my accusation as publicly as I have made it.'

One of the more curious aspects of the exchange of letters was that it was Newman who first brought up the idea of gentlemanlike conduct on which Kingsley was to base his case, and that Kingsley first used the *de haut en bas* manner which was to characterize Newman's attitude.

Kingsley's review had been clearly signed with the initials C.K., and we are told that his name was listed on the cover of the magazine, so there is a rather disingenuous note in Newman's answer to Kingsley, telling him that 'no person whatever, whom I had ever seen or heard of, had occurred to me as the author of the statement in question. When I received your letter, taking upon yourself the authorship, I was amazed.' The day after writing Kingsley, Newman wrote to 'X.Y.' ('a gentleman who interposed between Mr. Kingsley and Dr. Newman') and reiterated his protestation of ignorance:

'No one, whose name I had ever heard, crossed my mind as the writer in their Magazine: and, had any one said that it was Mr. Kingsley, I should have laughed in his face. Certainly, I saw the initials at the end; but, you must recollect, I live out of the world; and, I must own, if Messrs. Macmillan will not think the confession rude, that as far as I remember, I never before saw even the outside of their Magazine.' Newman was in many aspects unworldly, but one can scarcely help feeling that his double protestation must be unflattering either to his candour or to his intelligence.

Although Newman had originally said that he wanted no public apology, he was unsatisfied with Kingsley's account of his intentions. On January 14th Kingsley wrote once more:

'If you fancy that I have attacked you because you were, as you please to term it, "down", you do me a great injustice . . .

'The course which you demand of me, is the only course fit for a gentleman; and, as the tone of your letters (even more than their language) make me feel, to my very deep pleasure, that my opinion of the meaning of your words was a mistaken one, I shall send at once to Macmillan's Magazine the few lines which I inclose.

'You say, that you will consider my letters as public. You have every right to do so.'

The letter he proposed sending to *Macmillan's* was either naïve in the extreme or a more deviously worded attack on Newman than one would expect of Kingsley. The final part of it was particularly ambiguous:

'Dr. Newman has, by letter, expressed in the strongest terms, his denial of the meaning which I have put upon his words.

'No man knows the use of words better than Dr. Newman; no man, therefore, has a better right to define what he does, or does not, mean by them.

'It only remains, therefore, for me to express my hearty regret at having so seriously mistaken him; and my hearty pleasure at finding him on the side of Truth, in this, or any other, matter.'

Kingsley seems to have been surprised when Newman wrote, still calmly, indicating the ambivalence of the phrases and pointing out what the average reader would take them to mean. Kingsley thought that Newman was guilty of saying one thing and implying another; his own letter shows that he was capable of the same kind of writing.

Once more Kingsley answered, agreeing to change his public apology, with the hope of putting an end to the correspondence, sure that he had done all that honour demanded;

'I do not think it probable that the good sense and honesty of the British Public will misinterpret my apology, in the way in which you expect.

'Two passages in it, which I put in in good faith and good feeling, may, however, be open to such a bad use, and I have written to Messrs. Macmillan to omit them. . . .

'. . . it seems to me, that, by referring publicly to the Sermon, on which my allegations are founded, I have given, not only you, but every one an opportunity of judging of their injustice. Having done this, and having frankly accepted your assertion that I was mistaken, I have done as much as one English gentleman can expect from another.'

After revising his apology, Kingsley sent it off to *Macmillan's*, where it duly appeared in the February issue:

'In your last number I made certain allegations against the teaching of Dr. John Henry Newman, which I thought were justified by a Sermon of his, entitled "Wisdom and Innocence" (Sermon 20 of "Sermons bearing on Subjects of the Day"). Dr. Newman has by letter expressed, in the strongest terms, his denial of the meaning which I have put upon his words. It only remains, therefore, for me to express my hearty regret at having so seriously mistaken him.'

The apology may lack something in fervour, but for a public who had seen only Kingsley's review and none of the correspondence, it must have seemed reasonable, dignified, and wholly adequate. Macmillan told Maurice: 'Kingsley has written what seems to me a very nice letter to the Magazine.' To Kingsley he wrote: 'I don't think Newman has any sort of right to "ask for more" than you now give him. I have forwarded your letter to him and retain a copy. I really think he must be content with what you have said. Whether the bogies behind are, is another question.'

The whole affair would probably have stopped there had Newman not decided to publish the exchange of letters in a pamphlet: *Mr. Kingsley and Dr. Newman: A Correspondence on the Question Whether Dr. Newman Teaches that Truth is No Virtue?* In it he included an excerpt from the review, ten letters by himself and Kingsley, and a final section called 'Reflections on the Above'. Until now Newman's tone had been unimpassioned, and Kingsley, as we have seen, had gradually softened his attitude. In his 'Reflections' Newman suddenly launched into the sort of sarcasm at which he had no master. The section is short, but it stands as the culmination of the little pamphlet, and is obviously the reason for its publication. Newman had said that Kingsley had misrepresented his words; here, much more successfully and more deliberately, he uses the very method of which he complained:

'I interpose: "You are taking a most extraordinary liberty with my name. If I have said this, tell me when and where."

'Mr. Kingsley replies: "You said it, Reverend Sir, in a Sermon which you preached, when a Protestant, as Vicar of St. Mary's, and published in 1844; and I could read you a very salutary lecture on the effects which that Sermon had at the time on my own opinion of you."

'I make answer: "Oh . . . *Not*, it seems, as a Priest speaking of Priests;—but let us have the passage."

'Mr. Kingsley relaxes: "Do you know, I like your *tone*. From your *tone* I rejoice, greatly rejoice, to be able to believe that you did not mean what you said."

'I rejoin: "*Mean* it! I maintain I never *said* it, whether as a Protestant or as a Catholic."

'Mr. Kingsley replies: "I waive that point." '

Newman's motives for publishing the correspondence are obscure, since he had told Macmillan that he wanted no public retraction. Wilfred Ward, the apologist for the *Apologia*, inadvertently gives a most unattractive account of the way in which Newman seized on Kingsley's remarks as an opportunity to get attention and to justify himself before the English public. Newman's affairs had not prospered in the two decades since he had left the Anglican Church, and in 1864 he was living in obscurity in Birmingham, suspected of unorthodoxy by many in his own Church and thought by many Anglicans to have led a life of deceit before going over to Rome:

'. . . the encounter, though it presented great difficulties, offered, as I have said, a great opportunity. Kingsley's popularity and notoriety would advertise a combat with him, and make it notorious; thus it meant an excellent chance of gaining the attention of the world at large. Moreover Newman, if he defended the Catholic priesthood with conspicuous success, was sure to win, as their champion, quite a new position among his co-religionists.'

The last time Newman had had much sympathy in England was in 1852 when he was sued for libel by the renegade priest Achilli; on that occasion Newman's enormous bill for costs had been paid by a popular subscription of both Catholics and Protestants as a protest against the personal immorality of Achilli and the intolerance of Roman Catholicism which he was fomenting. In 1862 Newman had had a heady success over the *Globe*, which published a report that he was considering returning to the Anglican Church; his letter of denial was a masterpiece of sarcasm about the English Church. And in early 1863 he had worsted Maurice by a letter to *The Times* showing that Maurice was wrong in his comments about Tract 90. But Kingsley was a bigger and more popular fish than Maurice. Whether or not Ward is right in saying that Newman was lying in wait for the proper opportunity to put his case before the public, it is true that hitherto he had been the injured party meeting false accusation with mildness; with the appearance of *Mr. Kingsley and Dr. Newman* he changed from the defensive to the offensive.

On the publication of the pamphlet Newman received support from an unexpected quarter: Richard Holt Hutton, editor of the *Spectator*. Hutton, who admired both Kingsley and Maurice, rightly feared that Newman might not get a fair hearing from a prejudiced British public: 'Mr. Kingsley, in the ordinary steeplechase fashion in which he chooses not so much to think as to *splash up* thought, dregs and all,—often very healthy and sometimes very noble, but always very loose thought,—in one's face, had made a random charge against Father Newman in *Macmillan's Magazine*.'

What has obscured judgment in this controversy is the natural feeling of observers that if one man was wrong, the other must be right. Hutton's judgment against Kingsley is correct, but it is partial. Another reader, Lady Franklin, wrote that Newman's 'Reflections' gave her 'a more unfavourable impression of Dr. Newman than before, for the more apology Mr. Kingsley makes for his original rash utterance, the more does the other taunt & press upon him & ends with a low comic paraphrase of the correspondence in a colloquial style, utterly unworthy of a priest & a gentleman'. To an unprejudiced observer both statements seem true.

As Newman probably expected, Kingsley was stung into unwise reply. Froude urged him on, but Alexander Macmillan counselled moderation and told Kingsley that if he felt he must reply, the pages of the magazine were the proper place for his answer to appear. Instead Kingsley published a pamphlet, *What, Then, Does Dr. Newman Mean?* It was a disastrous failure; having already accepted Newman's explanation of the meaning of 'Wisdom and Innocence', he could only drag up other writings of Newman and appeal to the lowest anti-Papist prejudices of his readers by showing that no man could be honest who believed in such things. Tract 90, monks, nuns, miracles, stigmata, the continued virginity of Christ's mother, and, of course, celibacy: all are held up for ridicule. 'I am answering Newman now,' Kingsley wrote while working on the pamphlet, 'and though of course I give up the charge of conscious dishonesty, I trust to make him and his admirers sorry that they did not leave me alone. I have a score of more than twenty years to pay, and this is an instalment of it.'

When the writing was finished, Kingsley told Macmillan: 'Froude highly approves of the pamphlet, & thinks that N. won't answer. It has made me quite ill with anxiety.' Macmillan was less sanguine about his success than was Froude: 'The old saying attributed to Talleyrand that the use of words is to conceal thought might be extended in certain cases to intellects which would thus be described as having the power of perplexing the truth,' he wrote Froude. 'In this art Newman is a master, and thank God C.K. is not even a learner.'

Newman realized that the attack had shifted from the charge

of disregard for literal truth to a question of the honesty of his whole life. His consideration of what to do was brief:

'My perplexity did not last half an hour. I recognized what I had to do, though I shrank from both the task and the exposure which it would entail. I must, I said, give the true key to my whole life; I must show what I am, that it may be seen what I am not, and that the phantom may be extinguished which gibbers instead of me. I wish to be known as a living man, and not as a scarecrow which is dressed up in my clothes. . . . I will indeed answer his charges and criticisms on me one by one, lest any one should say that they are unanswerable, but such a work shall not be the scope nor the substance of my reply.'

The result, of course, was one of the greatest books of the nineteenth century, the *Apologia pro Vita Sua*. But it was not the *Apologia* which most modern readers know. Newman wrote in a state of near collapse and published weekly pamphlets, which were then gathered together and republished as a book. The first two pamphlets were called 'Mr. Kingsley's Method of Disputation' and 'True Mode of Meeting Mr. Kingsley'; these two sections and the concluding 'Answer in Detail', which deals in 'Thirty-Nine Blots' with Kingsley's error of statement, were written in the same sarcastic tone which had characterized the closing section of *Mr. Kingsley and Dr. Newman*. Beginning in 1865 these sections were withdrawn from editions of the *Apologia*, either because Newman felt that he had already humiliated Kingsley sufficiently or because he thought that those sections fitted uneasily with the gravely moving history of his religious opinions which is the modern text of the *Apologia*.

Ward suggests that the reason Newman left out the most sarcastic sections when republishing was that he had never felt any real anger with Kingsley, and had merely simulated it for rhetorical effect. Newman wrote Sir William Cope at Kingsley's death: 'I never from the first have felt any anger towards him. As I said in the first pages of my "Apologia", it is very difficult to be angry with a man one has never seen. A casual reader would think my language denoted anger,—but it did not. I have ever found from experience that no one would believe me in earnest if I spoke calmly. . . . Rightly or wrongly, this was the reason why I felt it would not do to be tame and not to show indignation at Mr. Kingsley's charges . . . much less could I feel any resentment against him when he was accidentally the instrument, in the good Providence of God, by whom I had an opportunity given me, which otherwise I should not have had, of vindicating my character and conduct in my "Apologia".' It is difficult—at least for this writer—to feel much sympathy either with Newman's assumed anger or with his calm assurance that Heaven, intervening directly to refurbish his reputation, provided Kingsley as a victim.

Seven years before, Kingsley had been involved in a minor altercation with a Wesleyan critic, to whom he wrote in words which strikingly foreshadow his position in the Newman affair: 'I have spoken my mind very solemnly, and neither, as you fancy, in heat or haste; and you have spoken yours calmly and courteously in return. I fear that we shall not alter each other's opinions much, so leave the matter in God's hands. I shall be quite silent on any charges which you may bring against me. My business is attack, and not defence. If I cannot make myself understood the first time of speaking, I am not likely to do it by any subsequent word-splitting explanations.'

Wisely, he did not attempt a reply to the *Apologia*. While it was appearing weekly, he was in France and Spain, where he had gone with Froude, who was planning work on manuscripts in Madrid. 'All my friends say, go, but I must not be the least burden to you,' he told Froude in accepting the invitation. 'Remember that I can amuse myself in any hedge, with plants and insects and a cigar, and that you may leave me anywhere, any long, certain that I shall be busy and happy.'

Kingsley and Froude arrived in Paris 'with several men we knew, among others Captain Blackett. The splendour of this city is beyond all I could have conceived, and the beautiful neatness and completeness of everything delight my eyes. Verily these French are a civilised people.' In the morning they went 'to the Madeleine, where a grand ceremony was going on, consisting of a high priest brushing people with a handkerchief, as far as I could see'. From there they went 'to Notre Dame, where old women were adoring the Sacrament in a "tombeau" dressed up with cloth and darkness, two argand burners throwing light on it above, and over it a fold of white drapery exactly in the form of the sacrificial vitta on the Greek vases, from which it is probably unconsciously derived'.

From Paris they went to the Spanish border, where Froude left Kingsley, to travel on to Madrid. Kingsley's letters home catch the atmosphere of spring in a southern climate, telling of almond trees in pink and crimson clouds of blossom, low houses roofed with purple-ribbed tiles, boys on stilts tending miniature cows, little yellow oxen hardly bigger than donkeys wearing 'brown holland pinafores on their backs', and horses with foxes' brushes nodding between their ears to keep off the flies. But for all his delight at the beauty of France, he could never avoid thinking of it in terms of England: Biarritz was 'just a cross between Bude and Scarborough', and Pau 'a mixture of Bath and Edinburgh'. Because he was still far from well, he lived quietly, drinking his *café-au-lait* before bathing in the morning, lounging on the rocks until luncheon, 'smoking penny Government cigars, which are very good; then *table d'hôte* at six'. The length of his walks, abbreviated though they were by illness, astonished the French, for 'the Mossoos can't walk, you see, and think it an awful thing'.

He was constantly irritated by signs purporting to be English ('why can they never spell English words?'), but he liked the people immensely for making France such 'a go-a-head place': 'I am quite in love with these Frenchmen. They are so charmingly civil and agreeable. You can talk to any and all classes as equals. But, alas! I have fallen among English at the *table d'hôte*.'

Because he had the inevitable digestive trouble at Pau ('the water is horrible, I suppose from the great age of the town'), Kingsley did not follow Froude into Spain, but wandered through the country north of the Pyrenees and on the Mediterranean coast, everywhere finding Protestant sermons in Roman stones. In Narbonne he visited the 'real dungeons of the Inquisition, and saw real chains and torture rings, and breathed more freely when we came up into the air, and the guide pointed to the Pyrenees and said "*Il n'y a point de démons là*".' He came by 'Beziers, where the Inquisitor cried, "Kill them all, God will know His own," and they shut them into the Madeleine and killed them all—Catholics as well as Albigenses.' At Avignon he visited the Popes' palace: 'We are still here under the shadow of that terrible fortress which the Holy Fathers of mankind erected to show men their idea of paternity. . . . Men asked for bread, and they gave a stone, most literally.' At Toulouse he saw a church in which there 'are 7 altars round the back of the apse, to some 15 saints & martyrs whose bodies are (or are not) there. Among others the Body of St. *George*! (who never existed) & of St. Susanna of Babylon—in Daniel's time! ! ! . . . [and] one of the stones with which St. Stephen was stoned! ! ! ! ! !'

As he prepared to leave for England he wrote Fanny: 'I cannot say that I have become more tolerant of the *cafards*, who set up on every high place their goddess-virgin. But I have learnt to love these French people, and to feel that we have much to learn from them, just as they have from us.' To Frederic Stapleton he wrote on the same subject: 'When I get back, I will tell you further volumes as to what I have seen of the Mari-idolatry of France. I could not have conceived such things possible in the 19th. century. But I have seen enough to enable me to give Newman such a revanche as will make him wince, if any English common sense is left in him, which I doubt.'

Wearing a beard ('If I am laughed at, I shall shave it off') and with his pockets bulging with Basque shoes worked in red and purple worsted for Mary and Rose, and a scarlet Basque cap for Grenville, Kingsley returned to England 'better, but not well, and unable to take any mental exertion'. When he heard of Newman's *Apologia*, he wrote Macmillan: 'I shall not read him yet till I have recovered my temper about Priests—which is not improved by the abominable idolatory which I have seen in France.' Most of the impartial journals recognized at once the excellence of the *Apologia*, and on the strength of it Newman's reputation rose, just as he had expected, both in Roman Catholic circles and in England in general.

Kingsley's ultimatum on seeing the *Apologia* was sent to Macmillan:

'I have determined to take no notice whatever of Dr. Newman's apology.

'1. I have nothing to retract, apologize for, explain. Deliberately, after 20 years of thought, I struck as hard as I could. Deliberately I shall strike again, if it so pleases me, though not one literary man in England approved. I know too well of what I am talking.

'2. I cannot trust—I can only smile at—the autobiography of a man who (beginning with Newman's light, learning, & genius,) ends in believing that he believes in the Infallibility of the Church, & in the Immaculate Conception. If I am to bandy words, it must be with sane persons.

'3. I cannot be weak enough, to put myself a second time, by any fresh act of courtesy, into the power of one who, like a treacherous ape, lifts to you meek & suppliant eyes, till he thinks he has you within his reach, & then springs, gibbering & biting, at your face. Newman's conduct in this line has so much disgusted Catholics themselves, that I have no wish to remove their just condemnation of his doings.'

After the initial rawness healed, Kingsley could speak in a kindly fashion of Newman. In 1868, when he read 'The Dream of Gerontius', he wrote Sir William: 'How poor my words are in expressing in prose what Dr. N. has exprest in poetry, I am well aware. But I am thankful to any man, who under any parabolic, or even questionably true forms, will teach that to a generation which is losing more and more the sense of reverence.' At Kingsley's death Newman, who had earlier called him 'a furious foolish fellow', told Sir William that he had said a Mass for Kingsley's soul as soon as he heard of his death; that he still misunderstood Kingsley is clear from his statement that he rejoiced to find him 'as it seemed to me, in his views generally nearing the Catholic view of things'.

It is customary to say that Kingsley provoked a work far greater than any of his own, that he was the grain of sand whose useful irritation produced a pearl. The statement is meaningful only if one looks solely at the final form of the book and forgets the controversy which led to its inception. *The Times*, the *Saturday Review*, the *Quarterly Review*, and others joined the *Spectator* in praising the work, and one is apt to be fooled into thinking that most Englishmen looked dispassionately at it and seriously weighed it as an answer to Kingsley. Perhaps the fairest statement of what the average Englishman thought was that of the *Athenaeum* of 26th March 1864, which found Newman deliberately provocative and Kingsley silly:

'Except that it makes yet another controversy of the season, a subject for club-gossip, and a dinner-table tattle . . . this discussion can have no particular result. It is famous sport; the world is amused, the athletes get admired, and there is an end. Of all the diversions of our dining and dancing season, that of a personal conflict is ever the most eagerly enjoyed. . . . And how briskly we gather round a brace of reverend gentlemen, when the prize for which they contend is which of the two shall be considered as the father of lies!'

As usual, *Punch* observed the whole proceedings with amusement and noted on May 7th: 'PROFESSOR KINGSLEY's last Collection of Lectures is entitled *The Roman and the Teuton*. His next book, with some general remarks on DR. NEWMAN, will probably be *The Roman and the Tutor*.' A month later, on the occasion of the visit of the Prince and Princess of Wales to Cambridge, *Punch* suggested as part of the entertainment that the 'Professor of Modern History will discourse on Muscularity, finishing up with a set-to with MR. JACKSON, Professor of the Noble Art'.

Most observers of the controversy were interested only in judging the contestants on points; how little most of them cared about the issues at stake was indicated by Richard Monckton Milnes, who wrote at the news of Kingsley's death: 'How preferable was Newman's gentlemanlike falsehood to his strepitose fidgety truth.' The quarrel brought notoriety to both men by exposing the muddled thinking of one and the arrogant clarity of the other's mind, and it resulted in the greatest autobiography of the century, but if the issue involved was Truth, one can only wonder how much it was served by either Newman or Kingsley.

CHAPTER XIV

The Englishman's Burden

In the summer of 1865 Emma, the young Queen of the Sandwich Islands, came to England on a visit to Lady Franklin. The widowed Queen, who had recently lost her young son, came to help ensure the success of an Anglican mission to her own people. The Queen's court was somewhat informal because she was surrounded with 'Yankees', and Lady Franklin occasionally wished she would behave more circumspectly in England; unless she was supervised, the Queen was apt to close a letter simply with 'Yours, Emma'. The royal visitor was tall, slim, and rather good looking, with fine dark eyes, a low voice, and skin which Jane Franklin described as 'a sort of chesnut colour'. In the autumn while visiting Ely, Kingsley met Queen Emma, and a few days later he wrote Lady Franklin to ask if the Queen would like to stop at Eversley on her return from a stay with Tennyson. Perhaps aware that she had wanted her son to attend either Eton or Rugby, he suggested that from Eversley she could visit Wellington College: 'Mr. Kingsley regards it as perhaps the best public school in the world & says that *our* Queen would be much interested in Queen Emma's visiting the college as its connexion with the Prince Consort whose creation it was even to its last details gives her a deep affection for the place.' If possible, the Kingsleys wanted the Queen to remain overnight with them; 'as Queen's Chaplain, Professor at Cambridge &c. he is emboldened to offer her such plain hospitality as Mrs. Kingsley & he can give her & he thinks it may not be uninteresting to H.M. to see the ménage of a plain country clergyman.' Mrs. Kingsley was determined that the hospitality, though simple, would be as far from plain as she could make it; she arranged luncheon with the Bensons at Wellington, flowers from all the neighbouring gardens, pine-apples from Lord Eversley's conservatory to make the Queen feel at home, and then wrote Jane Franklin (who thought she had been snubbed a bit by Mrs. Kingsley on a previous occasion) to ask about etiquette in entertaining the Queen. Lady Franklin assured her that Queen Emma would prefer simple hospitality and liked to have a rest in the afternoon. 'Mrs. K. adds that it is hoped some one will suggest to H.M. to ask for half a holiday for the boys which will immediately be granted & which will enable them to set up a good cricket match in her honor.' Although the invitation included Lady Franklin and her niece, it was so worded that they realized it would be more convenient if they returned to London. The house was jammed sufficiently in any case, for Emma brought with her an aide-de-camp, a six-foot lady-in-waiting, Mrs. Hoapili, and two servants. The correspondence on 'the Wellington college affair' became so large that Lady Franklin feared she would be buried under it.

All went well. After the tour of Wellington Queen Emma went into the hall to see the boys eating and won their hearts by tasting their pudding. When she remembered to ask for the half holiday, 'Ponsonby, then head of the school, called for three cheers for Queen Emma; and as they resounded through the dining hall at the granting of her request, she was startled almost to terror, for it was the first time in her life that she had heard the cheers of English public school boys.' She slopped through the mud to see her first cricket game and gallantly, if uncom-prehendingly, examined bats and balls and punched pads. At Eversley the domestic staff coped with the influx of visitors, and the Queen's long hours in bed permitted Mrs. Kingsley to lend a hand to the overworked servants. Since Lady Franklin and her niece were not remaining overnight, all the children were allowed to stay at home and meet the Queen. Rose Kingsley asked the lady-in-waiting to write in her book of 'Likes and

Dislikes', but she could not quite rise to the literary questions. On more concrete questions she fared better: her favourite hero was Kamehameha I, who helped civilize and Christianize his kingdom, her favourite food was 'poi and fish', and her favourite flower the 'lehua'.

Lady Franklin, who had not been overly pleased either by Mrs. Kingsley's frequent letters or by her half-hearted invitation, wrote in her journal on October 12th:

'Mrs. Kingsley also favors me with another letter today, feeling she says, as if she must express something of what is in her heart as to my visit & Queen Emma's. "We do thank you so for coming to us, even for that short hour." And as to Queen Emma's visit, it was quite perfect; & but for its shortness & the thought of her deep sorrows, it would have been one of the most unmixed pleasures they ever enjoyed in their lives—she is so deeply interesting & touching writes Mrs. K.—so young, so dignified & yet so simple, so sorrowful & yet at times so bright & sparkling—she is something quite new & most attractive. We shall always love her & the thought of her will be a new interest in one's life. At the chapel the boys sang with all their hearts, and Queen Emma has since written to the boys herself. She got a little nap in driving from Eversley to the college, went early to bed & slept all night, coming down next morning at 10 o'clock to prayers & breakfast. Mr. Murray [the Under-Secretary who was in charge of Queen Emma's arrangements in London] & his wife came to breakfast . . . at 2 o'clock they saw her into the train at Wokingham with tears in their hearts & eyes lest they shd not see her face to face again. Their people all along the road were at their cottage doors with bows & curtseys & uncovered heads & she took kindly notice of them all. . . . Mrs. K. apologises for her long letter by saying her heart was bubbling up & she felt she must open it to some one who knew & loved Queen Emma.'

Writing to Alexander Macmillan about 'one of the most interesting visits of our life', Mrs. Kingsley said that the Queen 'told me that she & the late King (her delightful husband) used to take especial delight in reading *The Waterbabies* to their little

Prince a boy of 4 since dead! The King delighted in all Mr. Kingsley's books, & I have promised Queen Emma a copy of each of his *Novels & Poems*. Would you order me a set *plainly* & not expensively bound in calf, to present to H.M. who is one of the most charming women I ever met, so delightful, so simple—so sad & yet so bright at moments & full of intelligence.'

Certainly some of Kingsley's delight with Queen Emma came from his deeply felt veneration for royalty which remained with him to the end of his life; when supporting the erection of the Albert Memorial, he said that it was 'good to have in a land great beacons of that kind, which attract the attention, and impress the imagination of the most brutal and careless'. But Queen Emma's colour must have been a stumbling block for him; perhaps he could forgive her for it since she, like the beautiful quadroon of *Two Years Ago*, had a strain of white blood in her veins. His contempt for the coloured races combined with his distrust of Americans to produce his attitude during the American Civil War. In 1862 he wrote to Sir Charles Bunbury about the 'American Question':

'I have thought of nothing else for sometime; for I cannot see how I can be professor of past Modern History without the most careful study of the history which is enacting itself around me. But I can come to no conclusion save that to which all England seems to have come—that war will be a gain to us, that the rapacity & insolence of these men must be sternly checked; that they must be taught that there are not only laws, but courtesies, to be observed between all nations who pretend to a voice in the parliament of the world. . . . So strongly do I feel the importance of this crisis that I mean to give as my public lectures next October term, the History of the United States.'

Lincoln, Kingsley thought, was a 'poor cute honest fellow', risen from splitting rails to a post he was unfit to fill and responsible for a proclamation so detestable and such a violation of the Constitution and his own oaths, that almost nothing but secession remained possible. All that such a proclamation could do otherwise would be to stir up the slaves to rebellion; 'then a dozen gentlemen will ride in, against 500 negroes, shoot, & hang till they are tired; & the little sparks of rebellion will be crushed out—and the condition of the slave worsened for 50 years'.

When he came to read up for his lectures, Kingsley told Hughes 'that the Northerns had exaggerated the case against the South infamously'. All the same, he thought the war 'a blessing for the whole world breaking up an insolent & aggressive republic of rogues, & a blessing to the poor niggers, because the South once seceded, will be amenable to the public opinion of England; & also will, from very fear, be forced to treat its niggers better'. For the first time Kingsley found himself violently opposed to Hughes on an ethical matter, and to his annoyance Ludlow, with whom he was accustomed to disagree, was in perfect unanimity with Hughes. Even Mr. Maurice, who was basically not interested in politics, finally swung around to supporting the North because of its attitude to slavery. For the rest of his life Kingsley seems to have felt that the Negro was really incapable of self-government, and though he called slavery an abomination, he frequently seemed to think that it was the most expedient way of dealing with an inferior race. 'The negro', he wrote Hughes, 'is quite devoid of that self-government, either personal or municipal which is the only training for political self government; & the want of which has wrecked free institutions in France & Spain—& till now, again & again in Italy. But the contact with, or rather intermingling with, free white settlers from the Northern states may teach them, what the Romance nations of Europe have not taught themselves. . . . A system of feudalism, gradually dying out & leaving the negro quite free, would be, to judge from history, the most prudent & practical method.' Later, in the Eyre controversy and during his own visit to the West Indies, he was to reiterate his contempt for the Negro. Some of his feeling sprang from the loss of his own family income when slavery was abolished by the British. When asked for a subscription to help the freed slaves, he refused: 'The negro has had all I ever possessed; for emancipation ruined me. . . . I am no slave-holder at heart. But I have paid my share of the great bill, in Barbados & Demerara, with a vengeance: & don't see myself called on to pay other men's!'

He liked little about America and despaired of its future: 'they have exterminated their southern hereditary aristocracy, and their northern hereditary aristocracy, the Puritan gentlemen of old families have retired in disgust from public life'. Although little could be expected of such a country, he none the less recognized its importance, and he was one of the most ardent supporters of the proposal to establish an 'American Lectureship, to be founded by a Mr. Yates Thompson, of Liverpool, and supplied by the authorities of Harvard College, United States'. After all, Harvard represented the 'northern hereditary aristocracy', and it was important for young Englishmen to know of a rapidly growing country: 'If in the second century before the Christian era the Romans had offered to send a lecturer to Athens, that he might tell Greek gentlemen of what manner of men this new Italian power was composed, what were their laws and customs, their intentions, and their notion of their own duty and destiny —would Athens have been wise or foolish in accepting the offer?'

The conservative wing in Cambridge, who were afraid 'to pander to that which is perhaps the worst vice inherent in the North-American character, namely, SELF-CONCEIT', rallied from near Cambridge all the antiquated parsons who would support them, and the vote was taken in a Senate House crowded with clergymen imported for the occasion and recognizable by their rustic appearance, ancient and shiny silk gowns, elaborate white ties and shabby hats instead of college caps. The roundup succeeded, and the lectureship was defeated, although, as Leslie Stephen wrote James Russell Lowell: 'Every intelligent man in the place voted for the professorship, including even Kingsley, who was very energetic about it, though he has been unsound upon America generally.'

Kingsley's feelings about the coloured races came out again in 1866 in the case of Edward John Eyre, governor of Jamaica. Eyre, who had been a well-known explorer in Australia, came into unpleasant prominence in October 1865, when a group of natives rioted and killed some twenty Europeans. In an attempt to quell the riot, Eyre had over six hundred natives killed or executed within a month, including a coloured leader named

Gordon. When the news of his actions reached England, there was sufficient protest against his handling of the riot to cause a royal commission to inquire into his actions; they found that Eyre had acted with commendable promptness in stopping the riot, but with unnecessary vigour and disregard of individual rights. In July 1866 the 'Jamaica Committee' was formed with the intent of having Eyre prosecuted for murder. The foremost members of the committee were John Stuart Mill, Huxley, Herbert Spencer, Goldwin Smith, and Tom Hughes. Two months later an equally strong committee was formed for the defence of Eyre, headed by the curiously assorted trio of Carlyle, Tennyson, and Ruskin. Both Charles and Henry Kingsley supported the defence committee, and Ludlow naturally worked for the Jamaica Committee. Feelings between the two committees were bitter (Carlyle called his opponents a 'knot of nigger philanthropists') but their quarrel was indecisive. The Eyre case dragged on until 1872, when he was vindicated in his actions, although the intervening years of controversy had successfully prevented his ever holding public office again.

Eyre's affairs slowly tailed off, but the two committees at least produced inadvertently one definite result, the rupture of Kingsley's last close friendship with a man of his own age and station. Hughes said years later that he did not feel competent to write about Kingsley's life because he 'saw so very little of him after "Governor Eyre" and the American Civil War divided us so sharply'.

For years, Kingsley's relations with Ludlow had been deteriorating, but this was the end at last. When, as a tired old man who had survived his friends, Ludlow was sorting his papers, he wrote of his relations with Kingsley:

'I continued corresponding with him till the time of the Jamaica Committee, tho' not with the same fulness as before, as I had to crush a plan which he proposed to me, after the stoppage of the Journal of Association, for setting up a new party, & I do not think he liked this. Again, as time went on, I found that he no longer cared to receive from me criticisms on his writings, unless purely eulogistic. I was surprised, after his enthusiastic abolitionism at the time of Fremont's candidature, at the guarded terms in which he acknowledged my book on the "History of the United States, from Independence to Secession", & at his never saying anything more to me about it. Then, when the Jamaica massacres took place, & T. Hughes & myself joined the Jamaica Committee, I was amazed to hear that without saying a word to either of us, he had himself joined the antagonistic organization, the Eyre Defence Fund. I then wrote to him to say that our paths now ran so divergent that it was useless to correspond any longer. I was probably too hasty in doing so. A little later, I heard he had become an avowed pro-Southerner in the American Civil War.

'From that time we neither corresponded nor met each other until Mr. Maurice's funeral, when we met, I am glad to say, on perfectly friendly terms.'

It would be too much to suggest that Kingsley was lonely, for he had all the acquaintances and casual friends that a man could ask; he remained nearly as close as ever to Maurice; and, as always, the centre of his existence was his family. It is difficult at this distance to see why Maurice had so many enemies, for he hated controversy, he was deeply loved by all who knew him well, and it becomes increasingly clear that he was one of the great theologians of the century. But for all his ability, he had never held a suitable position. At last, in 1866, using his professorial influence as one of the electors, Kingsley managed to get Maurice elected Knightsbridge Professor of Casuistry, Moral Theology, and Moral Philosophy at Cambridge. Some of Maurice's enemies hinted that the first part of the title of the chair was only too fitting, but Kingsley was delighted at seeing his beloved Master rewarded at last. He attended Maurice's lectures, and as often as possible he spent the evening with Maurice, frequently bringing with him promising undergraduates. Occasionally the young men were put off by the shyly awkward Maurice, and there are several contemporary accounts of how Kingsley worked desperately to get their attention away from Maurice until the older man could feel easy with them and exert his own peculiar charm.

Cambridge was also made pleasanter for Kingsley by the presence of his son Maurice at Trinity Hall. True, he was in constant academic difficulty, but Kingsley loved having part of his family with him. In other respects Cambridge became less and less happy for Kingsley, for he was working too hard, often spending three-quarters of the year preparing the twelve lectures he gave during a single term, and there was no time for the other writing he wanted to do.

His last novel, *Hereward the Wake*, '*Last of the English*', first appeared serially in 1865 in *Good Words*, and was then published in book form by Macmillan.

Both then and ever since, there has been considerable difference of critical opinion over *Hereward*, varying between the belief that it is his best work and the more generally accepted view that it lacks the vitality of his earlier books. Certainly it smells of the lamp, and the reader frequently tires of the footnotes and tables which Kingsley inserted to show that he was inventing nothing but only taking the story from the old chronicles. The book was not so successfully financially as its predecessors had been, and one can only imagine that the average reader must have tired of skipping over the linguistic derivations which are liberally scattered through the story, interrupting it for what is of interest to only a very few—and those probably not readers of Kingsley. As always he had trouble finding the proper tone for archaic conversation. His strong sense of locale is once more responsible for some of the best parts of the book, as he describes the Fens, Crowland Abbey, the West Country, and, less successfully, Flanders. For a change, there is only the single strand of story, the adventures of Hereward.

It would be too much to expect Kingsley to write of monks and abbeys without betraying his strong Protestant dislike of such things, but in general his prejudices are subordinated to the plot, rather than dominating it. One of the best reviews of the novel was written in the *Nation* early in 1866 by a young American named Henry James, who was just cutting his critical teeth:

'For his leading points, Mr. Kingsley abides by his chroniclers, who, on their own side, abide by tradition. Tradition had made

MODERN HISTORY.

of Hereward's adventures a most picturesque and romantic story; and they have assuredly lost none of their qualities in Mr. Kingsley's hands. . . .

'It is the absence of the old attempt at philosophy and at the writing of history which makes the chief merit of "Hereward" as compared with the author's other tales. . . . An important requisite for an historian is to know how to handle ideas, an accomplishment which Mr. Kingsley lacks, as any one may see by turning to his lectures on history, and especially to the inaugural lecture, in which he exhibits his views on the philosophy of history. But in the work before us, as we have said, he has adhered to his chroniclers, and as there is a world of difference between a chronicler and an historian, he has not been tempted to express many opinions.'

Hereward was the last novel Kingsley completed, but he made at least two other attempts to write in that form. He projected a New Forest story to be called *Darling, the History of a Wise Woman*, and though he wrote Macmillan in May 1866 that 'the New Forest novel is hatching slowly but well, I think', nothing more came of it. It was presumably of this novel that he wrote Macmillan in July 1867: 'I fear I *must* wait, at least. I am not sure that it would be good if written now. I am sure that the course of reading on which I am now will help to make it far better, if it is ever written, by carrying on my idea of mixing my heroine up, in after life, in French political intrigue, & shew how the simple country girl has more wisdom from above, than all the diplomats ever get from *below*. Let it seethe & simmer. But don't ask me to write it yet.'

At the beginning of 1868 he suggested to Macmillan 'the plan of a novel, or Romance. The autobiography of a poor English Scholar from about 1490—& going on to about 1530–40 who should see the outburst of the Reformation, know Erasmus, Rabelais, &c, be at the Sack of Rome in 1526—at Marguerite of Navarre's court at Pau, & generally about the world. I have sketched the man, & much of the scenery & incident, in my head: & I can't help feeling that people might like it. The man would be a simple miller's son out of my own parish, & come back to end his days here.' A few days later Mrs. Kingsley wrote: '*He is so overdone* that I quite shrink from the Novel. I believe it will just finish him! & I am *very* uneasy.' Kingsley and Macmillan accepted her advice, and no more novels ever came from the Rector's pen.

In the spring of 1867 Kingsley undertook a new sort of literary work for which he was singularly ill-suited: the editorship of *Fraser's Magazine*. During the few months he substituted for Froude, who was doing historical research in Spain, he tried to change the character of the magazine: 'I want to make it gradually a vehicle for advanced natural science, and have written to several leading men in that sense.' When Sir Charles Bunbury agreed to contribute, Kingsley wrote: 'I have had hopeful answers from others & trust I shall be able to raise Frasers again in the scientific world.' During this period he corresponded frequently about education with Huxley, with whom he agreed on the necessity of practical, scientific training for young men. 'I sometimes dream', he said in a lecture on 'The Theology of the Future' in 1871, 'of a day when it will be considered necessary that every candidate for ordination should be required to have passed creditably in at least one branch of physical science, if it be only to teach him the method of sound scientific thought.'

But while he was writing Huxley about education in science, his own teaching of history was coming under severe attack. Ever since he had taken the chair at Cambridge, his old enemy, the *Saturday Review*, had been sniping at him. One of the most prolific writers in that magazine was the historian E. A. Freeman, who naturally resented Kingsley's professorship, since he had made several abortive attempts himself to get a chair of history. In 1864, in a review of *The Roman and the Teuton*, the *Saturday* took aim at Kingsley:

'Of all the strange appointments ever made, that which turned Mr. Kingsley into a Professor of History seemed at the time to be the very strangest. . . . Other Professors, whether competent or incompetent, had at least some outward and visible connexion with the subjects which they undertook to teach. . . .

But the appointment of Mr. Kingsley seemed a mere inexplicable freak. There was apparently no more reason why he should be made a Professor of History than why he should be set to command the Channel Fleet. . . . The thing seemed a joke. . . .

'. . . Mr. Kingsley once could, and still can by an effort, write good sense and good English, but there are pages on pages of these Lectures which are simply rant and nonsense—history, in short, brought down to the lowest level of the sensation novelist. . . .

'. . . Mr. Kingsley is a clever man, a warm-hearted man, and an honest man; but of all men living he is the least qualified to undertake the work of an historian or an historical Professor. He confesses that his Lectures "are not, in the popular sense, history at all", and it is beyond our power to find out any more esoteric or recondite sense in which they deserve the name.'

For several years the choleric Mr. Freeman kept up his fire at Kingsley. 'Have you ever heard of the *Saturday Review*?' Alexander Macmillan asked a correspondent; '. . . if by a chance you have come occasionally on that obscure print, and seen in it any article abusing the *Times*, J. A. Froude, or Charles Kingsley, the chances are Freeman wrote it.' Although Macmillan thought Freeman the most able historian in England, 'I will take an even wager that he can abuse anyone who differs from him or who commits what he thinks a historical blunder, more intensely than anyone I know.'

In October 1867 the *Saturday* was gratuitously insulting in reviewing Gregory Smith's *Faith and Philosophy*: 'One thing amuses us greatly in these smaller essays—namely, the tone which Mr. Smith assumes toward Mr. Kingsley. He evidently looks upon him quite seriously.'

Although he disagreed with it in most other matters, Freeman found *The Times* an ally against Kingsley. In a review of his *Three Lectures on the Ancien Regime* in November 1867, Kingsley was treated nearly as unkindly by that newspaper as ever he had been by the *Saturday Review*:

'We cannot say that it will silence the calumnies of the uncharitable persons who have insinuated that the appointment of

Mr. Kingsley to the chair of Professor of Modern History at Cambridge was a sign that the University despised the subject, or knew little about it. . . . Mr. Kingsley has repeatedly shown that he cannot grasp the whole of a subject, examine it thoroughly in all its bearings, and form a judicial estimate of it; his opinions are sometimes hasty and crude; his manner vehement, illogical, and discursive; and these defects, we regret to say, are not absent from the present volume.'

For a time it seemed almost fashionable to make fun of Kingsley's historical acumen, ignoring the fact that first-rate historians like Froude, who knew Kingsley's limitations as a scholar, thought of him as an excellent teacher and lecturer. Some sense of the personal way in which he approached history, ready to bend it to his own uses, is indicated by his answer to a correspondent who wrote in 1866 pointing out a factual error in *Westward Ho!* Kingsley said that he had quoted the statement from a printed source: 'Heaven knows if it be *true*; for what is true in history?'

Although it was not written until three years later, a malicious and witty little jingle by William Stubbs reflects the popular opinion in 1867, not only of Kingsley but also of Froude, who became Rector of St. Andrew's:

Froude informs the Scottish youth
That parsons do not care for truth.
The Reverend Canon Kingsley cries,
History is a pack of lies.

What cause for judgments so malign?
A brief reflexion solves the mystery—
Froude believes Kingsley a divine,
And Kingsley goes to Froude for History.

Although Kingsley seemed arrogant enough to those who knew him but little, he was thin-skinned and lacking in confidence. The constant barbs were hard for him to take, and in real anxiety he offered to resign for the good of the University. 'I feel more & more my own unfitness for the post,' he wrote

Maurice. 'My memory grows worse & worse, & I am only fit for a preacher or poetaster: not for a student of facts (moral & historical at least).' The climate of Cambridge was troublesome, too: 'I cannot live in that relaxing air, & the malaria of the river acts as poison on my insides.'

Before resigning, he agreed to take the advice of his friends. Fanny wrote Mr. Maurice her view of the situation: 'Charles you see is quite ready to wait till he sees you & the Vice Chancellor [W. H. Thompson, Master of Trinity College] & he has written him a most kind letter. I have *long* wished him to give up the Professorship, simply because it is too much for his brain! The responsibility & the work which are so heavy now, would not weigh upon him so, if he had nothing else to do—but the *Parish work* & the *writing* besides, is too much for any man of his organization—& if I had not felt he wd. so like to be at Cambridge while our dear boy Maurice was there, I shd. have persuaded him to give it up 3 years ago, & *so I think* would Sir James Clark—But I quite agree with you that this is a most unfortunate moment—& I wd. not yield to that insolent Times for the world! Especially as *I* believe the article to have been written by a certain Mr. *Woodham* a Times writer, who was trying for the Professorship when *Charles got it*, & he has never forgiven him, getting the post he coveted himself. I feel with you that if people are to succumb to this Tyranny of the Press, it will end by swallowing up all free action & all free speech—so I am glad to have this move delayed, though I long to have Charles relieved from the fearful responsibility of his Cambridge work. It is a great & noble work & I believe him to be so *morally* fitted for it, independent of all intellectual power—but he could not give up his Parish work—& the wretched necessity of writing for the *Children's* sake—combined together are too much for him—& will kill him, unless he is relieved from a great deal of it by the Queen's giving him a Canonry which I am sure she will do *when she can*.

'We are so hampered too just now by having his Mother living with us, & the difficulty it is to leave her & go to Cambridge *together*—also by his idea that Cambridge disagrees with me. It is true that I *have* been very ill there but that would not dissuade me from going, in order to be with him.'

Maurice and Thompson counselled Kingsley not to resign for another year or two. In the meantime he waited for preferment from the Queen, but when it was not forthcoming after nearly two years, he gave up his chair. He wrote to Thompson on 1st April 1869: 'I have obtained leave from the Queen to resign it at the end of the academic year, and have told Mr. Gladstone as much, and had a very kind reply from him.' Dr. Thompson showed how quickly public opinion could change; when he attended the inaugural lecture of Kingsley's successor, J. R. Seeley, whose powers he underestimated, Thompson sat disdainfully through the lecture and as he left said with an air of waspish innocence: 'Dear, dear, who would have thought that we should so soon have been regretting poor Kingsley!'

Once he had actually resigned his professorial chair, Kingsley had to wait only four months for ecclesiastical preferment. Mrs. Kingsley wrote her good news to Miss Bulteel:

'The Queen has most kindly given him the vacant canonry at Chester which lapsed to the crown by the Elevation of Dr. Moberly to Salisbury. It is *not* a rich Canonry, being £500 a year, but it enables us to remain at Eversley, & to have a nice change once a year for 3 months without giving dear Charles very heavy work. The Dean (Dr. Howson) is an old friend of his, & a very energetic man who is trying to make the Cathedral do a real work, & has services in the Nave every Sunday; at which he & the resident Canon preach Every Sunday, & the Bishop once a Month. There is a very good furnished house, which the 4 Canons inhabit by *turns*, which does not *sound comfortable*, but it will save us the great outlay of furnishing, which would have absorbed a year's income, so we are well-satisfied & very thankful—& feel that we can go on in our own quiet way—& not alter our mode of life at all, in a nice old fashioned town like Chester, which is *Everything to Me*. It will indeed be a blessed rest, after the heavy work & responsibility of the Professorship, which Charles gave up in June.'

During the months before his installation at Chester, Kingsley turned to the parish with his full attention for the first time in many years. He and Fanny were able to have more fun together, too. They went to London for a meeting, which Fanny could not resist attending because she knew that she would come into the room on the arm of John Stuart Mill. In the neighbourhood of Eversley there were more parties than usual, although they attended few of the 'Innumerable Croquets' because Mrs. Kingsley could not 'stand the incessant racket'. In the autumn Eversley was immensely gay, with the arrival of 'a flying column of 2500 men—500 horses artillery baggage &c encamping in Bramshill Park' for three days. 'It was the prettiest sight I ever saw', said Mrs. Kingsley, '& we all had the Scarlet fever for the 3 days they were there—even our old *Nurse* took *the Complaint*, & was up in the Camp all day with the rest of the Parish!'

A canon's stall was as high as Kingsley's ambition reached, he told Raikes Currie: 'You were never more right than when you said that I should not like to be a Bishop. I have been too much behind the scenes in bishops' palaces, their intrigue, vulgarity, toadyism, & pretensions: and for my childrens' sake, far more than my own, I should dread being a bishop. And even a Deanery I shrink from: because it would take me away from home. The home to which I was ordained, where I was married; & which I intend shall be my last home: for go where I will in this hard working world, I shall take care to get my sleep in Eversley churchyard.'

In November he went to Chester for his formal installation, and on 2nd December 1869, he fulfilled the dream of a lifetime when he and Rose embarked at Southampton for the West Indies.

CHAPTER XV

Eminently Victorian

For forty years Kingsley had been dreaming of visiting the lush landscapes of the West Indies and South America. His second-hand knowledge of the tropics was already enormous, and out of it he had written careful set-pieces for *Westward Ho!* and had created the curious jungle nightmare sequences of *Alton Locke*.

In a peculiarly vivid way he felt a sense of identity with the places where his forebears had lived, and to visit the West Indies was to return to the land where his mother had spent her youth. The mystical kinship he felt with the West Country and which he was to experience in Chester was paralleled in the New World: 'Tell my mother that the old fig-tree at Harmony Hall, of which she dreamt, is standing still, and that we are going to visit a planter in Trinidad, who began in Barbadoes with Douglas, who managed Clapham for her father. So do things come round.'

His letters home show the dilemma of the amateur scientist, so overcome by the riches in sight and so aware of the shortness of time that he hardly knows where to look first. 'I soon found that, where the flora was endless, & all new, I must give up every other source of information & interest, if I intended to collect all I saw, & so only picked certain things which struck me—& too often lost them again.'

From Trinidad, at the end of January, he wrote his wife about the bewildering complexity of the New World: 'I have seen enough already to last me my life. I keep saying, "I cannot *not* have been in the tropics." And as I ride, I jog myself, and say, You stupid fellow, wake up. Do you see that? and that? Do you know where you are? and my other self answers, Don't bother. I have seen so much, I can't take in any more, and I don't care about it all. So I am in a state of intellectual repletion, indigestion, and shall take full twelve months to assimilate and arrange the mass of new impressions.'

His long letters to the family are carefully and fully written, for he intended revising them for publication after going back to England. The effect is frequently curiously studied:

'It must suffice if you find in this letter a sketch or two—not worthy to be called a study—of particular spots, which seem typical, beginning with my bath-room window as the scene which first proved to me that we were verily in the tropics.

'To begin with the weeds on the path, like, and yet unlike, all at home—then the rattle of the bamboo, the clashing of the huge leaves of the young fan-palms, the flower-fence, the guinea-grass, the sand-box, the hibiscus, with its scarlet flowers—a long list; but for the climax, the groo groo palms, a sight never to be forgotten—to have once seen palms breaking through, and as it were defying the soft rounded forms of the broad-leaved vegetation by the stern force of their simple lines; the immovable pillar-stem, looking the more immovable beneath the toss, the lash, and flicker of the long leaves, as they awake out of their sunlit sleep, and rage impotently for a while before the mountain gusts, to fall to sleep again. Like a Greek statue in a luxurious drawing-room, sharpcut, cold, virginal, showing, by the mere grandeur of form, the voluptuousness of mere colour, however rich and harmonious; so stands the palm tree, to be worshipped rather than to be loved.'

The constant travel from one island to another seemed to keep Kingsley in good health. 'I assure you I am very careful,' he wrote Fanny. 'I had to lie off a mangrove swamp in burning sun, very tired, after having ridden four hours, and been shoved over the mud in a canoe among the calling crabs, by three niggers, and I did not feel it the least, though the mud stank, and the wind was off shore, because before I got into the canoe, I took a good dose of quinine, which I always carry.' Trying out some 'wonderful angostura bitters', which he reported were tonic not alcoholic, he found the effect magical, and he proposed bringing some home to fight ague and low fever.

The records Kingsley kept of plants and animals are detailed and accurate, although many of them were new to him, but too often his anecdotes of the Negroes and the Chinese fail to demonstrate more than routine observation. To his mother he admitted: 'I am afraid I don't like the negroes, specially the women; but I delight in the coolies, who are graceful and well-mannered, and will be the saving of the poor West Indies, I verily believe.' The most vivid sections of his writing about the inhabitants are those in which he tells of native magic and the 'obeah-man', showing how they parallel demonism in the ancient world.

Kingsley and Rose spent seven weeks in the West Indies, and returned to Eversley at the end of February. Their stay was deliberately short, for they wanted to demonstrate that a round trip of less than three months was entirely practicable. On their return Kingsley was pleased to see that the Customs men at Southampton refused to look at the luggage; a few hours later they were safe in Eversley with a kinkajou and a parrot to add to the Rectory menagerie.

Shortly after he arrived back in England, Kingsley told Macmillan that he was polishing his letters from the West Indies for the readers of *Good Words*. 'Here I am home, thank God, safe, & better than I have felt for 7 years; & Rose quite well. The whole trip has been a great success, for which I cannot be thankful enough to God. I have made many new friends, collected, & made notes of, a vast number of facts, & have more coming home to me; & I think I can write something worth reading. Meanwhile I have many curious facts—& deductions, about which I shall consult you. They are not fit for Good Words, & perhaps not for publication at all. I want also to talk with you about the plan of the book. It will be much enlarged (I hope) & altered from these Good Words letters—& I long for illustrations, if it be possible. I tried to get photos: but the photographer was such a lazy dog I could get nothing done.'

The 'Letters from the Tropics' in *Good Words* were expanded into a two-decker travel book, *At Last: A Christmas in the West Indies*, dedicated to Sir Arthur Gordon, governor of Trinidad, with whom Kingsley and Rose had spent Christmas. Mrs. Kingsley tells us that it was written with an ease and pleasure which he had not felt since *Two Years Ago*, and to his surprise it sold well. He told Macmillan: 'I began to fear that I should never again write a saleable book.'

On 1st May 1870 Kingsley went into residence at Chester for his first three-month period. The beautiful old city with history reflected in its unspoiled architecture recalled to him his own ancestral connection with Chester, so that he felt 'that he was coming home, for although he was landless, his ancestors had not been. . . . He was glad to come to a county where many of his kin had lived, and where he had many friends, and he had no higher ambition than to live and die Canon of Chester. . . . He did not wish to thrust himself forward, to originate anything grand, or be in anybody's way; but if they could find him reasonable work, as he was a rather overworked man, he would be happy to do it, without any regard to creed, politics, or rank in any way whatsoever'.

Mrs. Kingsley was glad to see that he was equally happy with his ecclesiastical duties: 'My husband likes his Cathedral Services. Especially daily the 8 o'clock AM & the 5 PM. He feels his soul at anchor at those two hours day by day—& he can take refuge in the Chapter room & Library (which are one) when we are likely to be invaded in the Residence. There he is safe from Every one except parties of *Americans*—whose first act when disembarking at Liverpool is to come over to Chester & see the *oldest* thing they can—i.e., a Cathedral—& then the Old Verger who unfortunately is a great Hero worshipper invariably tells them who the Canon in Residence is, & asks if they wd. not like to see *him too*! They are all paraded into the Chapter room too suddenly for Mr. Kingsley to make his Exit.'

Like many others who had disliked Kingsley's writings, Dean Howson learned to be fond of his new Canon. They had met before, and Howson had been touched at Kingsley's kindness to him when he lectured at Cambridge, but when he heard of the new appointment, he was fearful: 'There seemed to me an incongruity . . . between the author of "Alton Locke" and cathedral life.' To Howson's surprise Kingsley was conscientious about his cathedral duties, reverent in public worship, and his sermons drew large congregations, which came at first to see what manner of man a Christian Socialist canon could be, and grew constantly throughout his residence. What Howson liked most was Kingsley's respect for official position, for he had clearly expected arrogance: 'That he was far my superior in ability and knowledge made no difference. I happened to be Dean, and he happened to be Canon; and this was quite enough.'

Realizing that a residence of three months each year made it difficult to undertake projects which demanded continuous supervision, Kingsley concentrated on building up scientific studies in Chester. For years he had been corresponding with Huxley about the need for well-grounded studies in the new sciences for nineteenth-century Englishmen, and this was his chance to carry his theories into practice. All the energy which had previously gone into literature and history was now directed into his classes. He began with a class on botany in the city library, expecting to have at most sixteen to twenty young shopmen and clerks, but the classes grew so quickly that he had to move into a larger hall, and he agreed to give a field lecture each week as he walked into the countryside with his students. Once the group was so large that a Chester man who met them thought they must be a dissenting congregation walking to the opening of a new chapel in the country. Within a year the class had become the nucleus of the Chester Natural History Society.

During his second year at Chester his lectures were on 'The Soil of the Field', 'The Pebbles in the Street', 'The Stones in the Wall', 'The Coal in the Fire', 'The Lime in the Mortar', and 'The Slates on the Roof', which he later gathered together to publish as *Town Geology*, dedicated to his Chester class. The excursions became larger and went farther afield, so that special trains had to be provided. Mrs. Kingsley tells us that Kingsley and his daughters, he with geological hammer in hand and botany box slung over his shoulder, would meet from sixty to a hundred enthusiasts for these journeys. 'Those were bright afternoons, all classes mingling together . . . all travelling in second-class carriages together without distinction of rank or position, to return at the end of the long summer evening to their old city, refreshed and inspirited,—with nosegays of wild flowers, geological specimens, and happy thoughts of God's earth and of their fellow creatures.'

The three years he spent at Chester were among the happiest of Kingsley's life. Mrs. Kingsley was in better health than usual and his children were growing up. To be sure, Maurice had been something of a disappointment, for he could not settle down to a decision on his future: both the Indian Civil Service and engineering were possibilities, as were natural history and painting, but none of them kept his interest. After leaving Cambridge without a degree he studied at the Royal Agricultural College at Cirencester, and from there he went to South America to seek his fortune in raising sheep and cattle. After a year he came back to England, where Mrs. Kingsley had hoped for him to take over £2,000 of her own money, since two of her trustees had agreed: '. . . after I had written to him to tell him of it & that he Must come home at once, to sign papers, my 3d. Trustee (who I am afraid I shd. like to poison or drown or something dreadful) says he won't let me touch a farthing of my money.' During most of his father's residence at Chester, Maurice was in North America, surveying in New Mexico, exploring in Mexico, and prospecting in the Rocky Mountains. He was still without permanent employment by 1874, but his parents remained hopeful that he would eventually get the position he deserved, since he was a sincere Christian and all the travellers who came back from the New World were agreed on his charm.

Rose, on her return from the West Indies, volunteered to go to Germany with her cousin, Mary Grenfell, to nurse during the Franco-Prussian War. Her father's letter of recommendation shows how completely she had absorbed his ideals:

'My eldest daughter wishes to know if—& how—she can be of use in the hospitals for the wounded on the Rhine, & especially at Bingen. She has, at the Chester Infirmary, thoroughly qualified herself for a hospital-nurse, & has received a certificate to that effect. The Lady-Matron under whom she was trained— a woman of great talent & experience, assures me that there is nothing connected with hospital work, & the care of wounds especially, which she cannot do with her own hands; & that she is capable of organizing & commanding a staff of nurses. As my daughter, I need not say that she has been brought up in a thorough understanding of practical matters relating to cleanliness, ventilation, & sanitary matters in general. She possesses, I am bound to say, a very remarkable power of attacking, commanding, & using those with whom she has to do. She is perfectly free from vanity, envy, superstition, & all those little vices & weaknesses which make so many lady-nurses troublesome. . . . She (& I) object to her belonging to any Protestant sisterhood, or engaging herself to "obedience" to any Englishwoman, or English society of ladies. But she is most ready to give hearty obedience to any medical man—a class for whom she has learned thorough respect.'

There is no record that Rose Kingsley ever nursed in Germany, and in 1871 she went to America again, this time to visit Maurice in the Rocky Mountains. Her journals of the trip were converted into a book, *South by West*, which she published anonymously with a preface by her father.

Mary Kingsley, whose talents were as various as her father's, studied at the Slade School and showed considerable ability as a painter, but so far she had not demonstrated the literary flair which was to make her a popular novelist later in her life. And though William Harrison had been her father's curate since 1868, there was as yet no hint of the romance which was to culminate in their marriage in 1876.

Grenville was even less qualified than his brother for academic work; he seems to have been overly indulged by his mother and profoundly disinclined to his studies. As a boy he emulated Maurice's ambition to be a civil engineer, but as his mother once said in gentle reproach: 'He knows a great deal about Engineering already, but not much about civility.' He attended Winton

House, the school kept by his father's old friend, C. A. Johns, then had six months of home tuition by a tutor from Germany to prepare him for Harrow, where he stayed a little over a year, and at the age of sixteen his education was finished.

There is no hint of reproof in Kingsley's correspondence for the rather poor showing made by his two sons, and there is no reason to think that he ever recognized it. Instead, he was always full of hope for the future. When Grenville was ill, his father wrote Mrs. Kingsley: 'If ever you see that prognathous, drooping look, about the outside of G's upper lips (which he has had more than once since he was born) he should have idleness & food & fresh air at once, & nothing else. As for fear—there is none. He will make a huge man, & a clever one.'

By now Kingsley had nearly everything he had been seeking for more than thirty years: fame, clerical advancement, moderate financial security, and literary reputation. Macmillan was willing to print almost anything he wrote, and when nothing new was forthcoming, he could reprint reviews and essays from periodicals or assemble some of the sermons he had preached. His enthusiasm for science was well known, so that in 1872 he was invited to be President of the Midland Institute in Birmingham, and even his old enemy *The Times* reviewed his presidential inaugural lecture with approval. His views were received with respect, whether they were his pro-German reflections on the Franco-Prussian War, his endorsement of Huxley's theories of scientific education, or his wavering support of John Stuart Mill and woman suffrage.

Outwardly, all was well. But the old fires were banked. So long as he was alive Charles Kingsley could not be without curiosity about mankind and nature, but by now his opinions were beginning to stiffen, and he was no longer tempted into the speculative excesses of his youth. The public voice that sounded from Eversley and Chester no longer was distinguishable from the utterances of the intellectual establishment. For a quarter-century he had been an irritant to England, and it was only as he dwindled into slow respectability that England discovered that she had become attached to that irritation, and on the whole preferred being pricked to being agreed with. Once Kingsley had been the inspiration for a generation of young men who wanted to be both Christian and rebel; in the last five years of his life he was the comfort of the middle-aged and orthodox.

This kind of hardening of the spiritual and intellectual arteries is the normal fate of man, but less to be expected in Kingsley than in others, and certainly not at the early age of fifty. Although his eyes still flashed, his hair was white, his digestion ruined, and his appearance so altered that friends who saw him after a gap of a few years were appalled at the advance of old age. All around him his intimates were dying—but they were of another, an older generation. Mr. Maurice died in 1872 and Kingsley's mother the following year. When he heard of the death of Norman McLeod, Kingsley could not keep from saying: 'Ah, he is an instance of a man who has worn his brain away, and he is gone as I am surely going.'

By the end of 1872 Kingsley needed rest from Eversley. 'I write to tell you, with most sincere regret,' he notified Sir William Cope, 'that I have been forced to obtain from the Bishop a year's leave of absence from this beloved & charming, but unwholesome, place.

'Mrs. & Miss Kingsley become seriously unwell whenever they return hither, & recover again as soon as they go into more bracing air. And I, who have fought against the malaria of the place as long as I could: am not as strong as I was; & my doctors advise for me, as for Mrs. & Miss Kingsley, rest & change of air for some time.' Because Grenville was to begin school there early in 1873, Harrow was chosen as the Kingsleys' resting place until time to go to Chester for the early summer.

Since coming to Chester, Kingsley had had several chances at other clerical advancements. The Deanery at Rochester was reputedly offered to him, and in 1872 he reluctantly declined becoming Dean of Winchester, torn between the need of more money for his children and the knowledge that the responsibility would be bad for both his health and Fanny's. Instead, he hoped for the next vacant stall at Windsor, which would be as rewarding financially as Winchester without an equally heavy burden of work. In March 1873 Gladstone wrote with an offer he could hardly refuse: 'I have to propose to you, with the sanction of her Majesty, that in lieu of your canonry at Chester, you should accept the vacant stall in Westminster Abbey. I am sorry to injure the people of Chester; but I must sincerely hope your voice will be heard within the Abbey, and in your own right.'

Kingsley would have been happy for himself to stay in Chester the rest of his life, and in his three terms of residence there he had so endeared himself to the local people that knots of them are said to have gathered around the Cathedral in sorrow when the news of his impending removal arrived. But the stipend of Westminster was £1,000, exactly twice what he received at Chester, and he felt that it would be unfair to his family to turn it down. To Mrs. Kingsley's intense relief, it meant that he could now stop the writing which she hated so because she was afraid it would kill him. 'Had I been an old bachelor', he wrote, 'I would never have left Chester. Meanwhile I had sooner be Canon of Westminster than either dean or bishop. But I look back longingly to Chester. . . . My eyes fill with tears when I think of it.'

His old friend, Dean Stanley, welcomed him to Westminster, where he kept residence in September and November. The regret at leaving Chester was soon forgotten in the pleasure of being a member of the chapter of England's most august church. 'It was', he said, 'like coming suddenly into a large inheritance of unknown treasures.' The congregations in the autumn were chiefly of middle and working class men: 'If I find I can get the ear of that congregation, it will be a work to live for, for the rest of my life. What more can a man want?' His medical advisers had recommended a sea voyage before beginning at Westminster, but he felt capable of continuing for a year before taking his much-needed rest because his surroundings at the Abbey gave him renewed strength. The house in the Cloisters was charming, 'the mere feeling of room in it is most pleasant, and the beauty outside under this delicious gleamy weather, quite lifts my poor heart a-while'.

The feeling of strength was illusory, and during the latter part of 1873 he stayed as much as possible at Harrow, going back to Eversley only on such important occasions as the Bishop's first confirmation there. Usually on these flying visits he stayed with Sir William Cope, and the two men found that as they mellowed with age their mutual irritations vanished, and they would sit talking in the library at Bramshill until the early hours of the morning.

By this time Kingsley was a social lion, and many books of reminiscences of this period give us glimpses of Kingsley at the more interesting dinner tables of London. Shirley Brooks, editor of *Punch*, noted in his diary on 25th March 1873: 'To Crowdy's to d. to meet, first time, Canon Kingsley; very delightful—very like Gladstone. His stammer not much at dinner, but in the evening when he naturally sought to speak more eagerly, it was marked. Says he had made himself a voice—speaks from his lower depths, and holds his upper lip tightly down, working with the under one—so does the Bishop of Winchester. . . . I was going about 11 but as he could not go to his train [to Harrow] till near 12, he told me "not, on the first meeting, to lower myself in his opinion by keeping good hours". So I stayed, and smoked more. He is always smoking a pipe, he says.'

Years later W. P. Frith wrote that of all the people he had met at Brooks's dinner table, two of the most lively were Charles Kingsley and Mark Twain, who 'were there the same evening I think—the former with the drawback of a slight stutter, delighting us with his bright talk; and the latter with his quaint humour'.

Another impression of Kingsley as a dinner companion was that of Mary Gladstone, who met him for the first time at Windsor: 'I was very lucky, having for my neighbours the Dean of Windsor and Mr. Kingsley, with which I was delighted for love of one and curiosity about the other. . . . There were very few general topics, and my conversation with Mr. K was very interesting. Music, Morris, Coleridge, the West Indies, his own novels. . . . After talking to Mr. Kingsley for some time, [the Queen] came and said Goodbye, and off we trotted to join the Household.'

CHAPTER XVI

New Worlds

On 29th January 1874, Kingsley and Rose sailed west once more, this time for North America, on the White Star Line's new high-speed *Oceanic*. The vessel was under the command of Captain Kiddle, 'a very handsome imaginative Norfolk man'. Kingsley and Rose had large staterooms, and there was a 'delicious warm bath, handsome saloon, & every luxury'. The return trip cost them $140 each, but for that large sum they had great comfort, and they could count on a voyage lasting less than two weeks. They were seen off by Mary Kingsley and Dean Howson, who arrived from Chester, and as the obvious celebrity of the ship, Kingsley was introduced to the owner of the shipping line, who had also come to Liverpool for the sailing.

Both Kingsley and his daughter thrived on facing into a stiff wind, and they surprised their fellow travellers by being on deck at every possible moment. Kingsley made friends with the captain and the other passengers, and became particularly close to General J. T. Wilder of Chattanooga, who was returning to Tennessee and was interested in what he heard of Maurice Kingsley, for he thought he might find him work on the railways which he was promoting.

The avowed purpose of the trip was rest, but Kingsley was incapable of such a thing, and he had brought with him five lectures, for he was to speak under the auspices of the Scottish-born lyceum entrepreneur, James Redpath. Since he intended to travel over most of the United States and part of Canada in less than six months, there was little danger of his speaking so often in one place that he would need more than five talks. The one which he intended to use most was a rather highly coloured account of Westminster Abbey which he thought would appeal to American audiences hungry for descriptions of the Old World. His next favourite lecture was on 'The First Discovery of America', which gave him a chance to talk about the Norse explorers whom he loved. The other talks were on the Athenian theatre, 'Cyrus, Servant of the Lord', and 'Ancient Civilisation'. All the lectures were delicately calculated to be delivered by a clergyman, touched with piety but avoiding dispute on theology. 'I have been advised to give, not a course, but a few single & disconnected lectures,' he wrote an American correspondent. 'They are written with a view of increasing the cordiality between our two countries. I should wish it also to be known—that I am not going to repay American courtesy by writing a book about the States. I go there as a guest & a learner, not as a critic, & there is no fear of any "American Notes" from my pen.' He may have intended no book, but a letter from his wife to Macmillan after his return home in the summer of 1874 tells us that he was then working on 'some papers for Good Words on America & California which he promised Mr. Isbister before he left England last year'. In any case his death came so suddenly after his return from America that Kingsley never had the chance to publish anything about his travels there.

Rose Kingsley acted as his secretary during the trip, dealing with the lecture bureau, travel arrangements, and the invitations that poured in from Americans.

When the *Oceanic* arrived, members of the Lotos Club came on board and took the Kingsleys and their baggage through Customs without having it looked at. The Kingsleys stayed first at Staten Island with George William Curtis, who wrote for *Harper's Weekly* and 'might be mistaken for a very handsome cultivated Oxford or Cambridge man'. The air was like champagne and the 'days already an hour longer than in England, & a blazing hot sun & blue sky. It is a glorious country, & I don't wonder at the people being proud of it'. The trees, like the people, he found 'all English *with a difference*. I have met with none but pleasant clever wellbred people as yet, afloat or ashore'. Curtis, one of Redpath's veteran lecturers, gave Kingsley helpful hints on his tour, and there seemed 'little difficulty in making $500–$1000 a week, if God gives me health & luck'.

From Staten Island he went to New York to speak to the Lotos Club at a gala dinner where the guests included Bret Harte and Chauncey Depew. After speaking he was escorted to the nearby Century Association, where the welcoming deputation was led by William Cullen Bryant. The next day he paid his devoirs to the best-known of American preachers, Henry Ward Beecher, brother of Mrs. Stowe. His first public appearance in America was before the Essex Institute in Salem, speaking on Westminster Abbey; the *Boston Daily Globe* noticed that his delivery was 'very peculiar, being a strange combination of slow and rapid utterances, monotone and nervous exclamation. Frequently, whole sentences have a peculiar intoning, which is attributed by those who should know, to his cathedral experience'.

From Cambridge Kingsley wrote home of being in 'a little haven of rest, where I arrived last night, & Longfellow came to dinner, & we dine with him tonight—& yesterday in Boston dear old Whittier called on me, & we had a most loving & like-minded talk: & this morning I have spent chiefly with Asa Gray, & his plants—so that we are in good company'. New England generally was 'the saddest country. All brown grass, ice polished rocks, cedar scrub, low swampy shores—an iron land, which only Iron people could have settled in.'

The lecture at New York was a greater success than Redpath expected: 'I draw not the mob, but the educated, & R confesses that none of *his* men ever had such "high toned" audiences before. Moreover, they are finding out that I can *speak*, which no Englishman of late has been able to do; & I was expected to mumble & hesitate like the rest.' That there was room for divergence of opinion about Kingsley's speaking ability is indicated by the review of the lecture in the *New York Daily Tribune*, 28th February:

'Canon Kingsley's presence is not what one looks for in a public speaker; he looks only a shy gentleman, embarrassed at finding himself famous, and only half at home behind the slim music-stand that he wishes were a lectern. While the Rev. Mr. Potter is introducing him, he shrinks, covered with confusion, blushes in his arm-chair, and when the time comes, rolls himself off his cushion, seizes his manuscripts as a sheet anchor, fumbles off his last kid glove, straightens himself up, and launches out with a voice that sounds like the wail of miserable sinners in his own Abbey service. For an hour and a half this mournful cry keeps on, with scarcely a change of note, with hardly a dying fall, and with such wide-mouthed rolling vowels and outlandish accent that many a time what he is saying might as well be Greek for all that can be made of it. There is but one gesture—the right elbow supported by the left hand, and the right hand or its forefinger waving like a pennon, appealing, threatening, emphasizing, doing all the work of two hands and answering the awkward angularity of the body's swaying back and forth.'

In Philadelphia nearly 4,000 people crowded the Opera House; every seat was occupied, and the aisles and steps filled with listeners who stood through the entire lecture. President Grant invited him to a dinner-party in Washington, he was asked by the Speaker of the House of Representatives to open the session with prayer, and he was shown around the Smithsonian Institution by Joseph Henry, but he was beginning to be a bit homesick, dreaming of his family every night; 'my dreams are more pleasant, now I sleep with my window open, to counteract the hideous heat of these hot-air-pipes'.

When he returned to Boston at the end of March he had already made $2,744. The people, he wrote, were 'fine generous kindly wholesome folk, all classes of them, as I ever want to see, & if they had not this horrid twang—women much more than men—they would be delightful. But our host and hostess here (the Fields) have none'. He was staying with the inveterately pro-English James Fields, head of Ticknor and Fields, who had published many of Kingsley's books in America. His wife Annie, one of the most energetic hostesses in Boston, noted in her journal that Kingsley reminded her 'in his nervous unrest somewhat of Dickens, but a fuller man, or more conversant with English Literature, especially of the Early Ballads we have never known'.

Kingsley told the Fields that he thought their countrywomen very ugly because they failed to use their lips sufficiently: 'They are often pretty enough until they begin to talk and then it is not only impossible to understand them but they lose all flexibility of the mouth and lips and pick the words out instead of playing with them and singing them.' He was annoyed, too, at the way Americans asked him about his writings. 'We never talk shop in England,' he said, 'but here unfortunately everybody attacks me about my books. The other day in P[hiladelphi]a I saw a man coming forward and making ready to say, "Aren't you the man who wrote——?" So I thought I would be beforehand with him and said, "I'm the fellow who wrote 'O Mary, go and call the cattle home'. I know what you're going to ask me and I save you the trouble—good afternoon" and I turned and went off.'

Most of the American writers he liked immediately: Mark Twain and Bryant he had admired for years, Whittier was an 'old saint', and Longfellow 'charming'. Only Holmes seemed provincial and conceited. Mrs. Fields observed with pleasure that Kingsley's bearing with Longfellow was 'so modest and appreciative. He always bowed to Longfellow as his master—and when he once differed with him in opinion over the poetry of Collins, he bowed low and said—"My master, I must still think it very beautiful."'

Whittier later asked a friend in his Quaker fashion: 'Did thee meet Kingsley? I like him hugely; he is a manly man.' After Kingsley's death Whittier wrote Mrs. Kingsley: 'It impressed me strongly to find the world-known author ignoring his literary fame, unobservant of the strange city whose streets he was treading for the first time, and engaged only with "thoughts that wander through eternity". . . . I was conscious in his presence of the bracing atmosphere of a noble nature.'

Another American author who had formed a less pleasant impression of Kingsley some years before was Hawthorne, who had been told by an English companion that Kingsley was a dangerous man with a radical defect in his moral nature. Hawthorne's informant continued by calling him 'a sensualist (not, as far as I understood, that he practically sins in that way) in his disposition; in support of which view, he said that Kingsley had made drawings such as no pure man could have made, or could allow himself to show or look at'.

There were stops in New Haven with the Canon's 'namesake and distant kinsman, Dr. William Kingsley, of Yale College' and with Mark Twain at Hartford. Then over the border to Montreal, where Kingsley called on Ashton Oxenden, 'who is very cordial for a bishop'. In Quebec the Bishop was 'a good fellow, a Hampshire man, & a fisherman'. When they reached Ottawa for Holy Week, Kingsley and Rose stayed with the Governor-General, the Earl of Dufferin. On April 9th Kingsley wrote home of being 'safe & sound having run 500 miles in 30 hrs to Baltimore, from the delightful Dufferins, who want us to come back again'. President Grant invited them to another dinner party, 'so we shall have seen quasi-royalty, British & Yankee both in one week'. In Washington the advertising for the lecture called him 'Sir Canon Kingsley, LL.D., of London'.

With spring beginning, the Kingsleys were anxious to go to the western United States; their route took them to Ithaca and Cornell University, to Niagara Falls, Toronto, Detroit (where Kingsley tried unsuccessfully to get rid of a cold he had caught at Niagara), 'across the huge rushing muddy ditch, the Mississippi', to St. Louis, where they stopped for a week. Kingsley was ill again, this time from the sudden hot weather; he was weak but intent on continuing the westward journey and so neglected caring for his cold.

At Omaha Kingsley looked across the river to '*Council Bluffs! ! !* 30 years ago the palavering ground of trappers & Indians (now all gone)—& to that very spot—which I had known of from a boy, & all about it, I meant to go—*if I had not met you*—as soon as I took my degree, & throw myself into the wild life, to sink or swim escaping from a civilization which only tempted me, & maddened me with the envy of a poor man!' On May

14th eleven Americans and five English 'quite filled, but did not crowd, the magnificent Pullman car' provided by Cyrus Field and J. A. C. Gray, who were hosts to the party on the trip west. The first stop was Salt Lake City, where Kingsley preached in a crowded church. Of Brigham Young's offer of the tabernacle to accommodate a larger audience, Kingsley 'took no notice whatever, a course strongly approved by the excellent Bishop', since Kingsley and Field had been reported by some of the Salt Lake papers to have gone to Provo 'to pay court to Brigham Young'. At the time there was great interest in Mormonism; in Boston, Kingsley's successor at Tremont Temple had been Mrs. Ann Eliza Young, nineteenth wife of 'the tyrant', who told her audiences 'A Woman's Story of Polygamy'. After he had seen Mormonism at home, Kingsley rejoiced in English morality: 'Thank God we at least know what love & purity mean. I am afraid that others besides Mormons are forgetting that in the E. States: & that Mormonism is not very horrible in the eye of many educated & strong minded women there.'

By private Pullman and then by special train the party continued through Reno to Carson City, Virginia City, and Sacramento before embarking on the high spot of the journey for Kingsley and Rose, a long trip through the 'Yo Semite & Big Trees'. Most of their days in the Yosemite Valley were spent on horseback, and Kingsley forgot his ill health, saying he felt like a boy again. On Whit Sunday he preached in the little parlour at Black's Hotel. A long ride through the Sequoias was made comfortable with a roaring fire in a deserted shanty and picnic lunch with 'excellent beer' eaten on 'a bed of fragrant hemlock twigs'.

From Yosemite the party went to San Francisco for ten days, while Kingsley visited the environs of the city and gave a few lectures. His hopes of making a large sum of money from lecturing had already been disappointed, for he had overestimated both his fees and the ability of Americans to sit in stuffy halls when spring was breaking. The relative scarcity of engagements in the west was not completely unwelcome to Kingsley, for he still suffered from his bad cold, and he found that he was bored with repeating the same lecture. As he had expected, the talk on Westminster Abbey was the most popular, and he had given it so many times that as early as his second visit to Boston he said that he sometimes felt like stopping in the middle and telling the audience to collect their money at the door and leave quietly without making him finish the lecture. And though 'these dirty greenbacks', as he referred to his earnings, came in slowly, he found that his expenses were not heavy. The luxurious trip west had cost him nothing, and nearly everywhere he stayed he was not allowed to pay anything by his hosts.

At Berkeley Kingsley talked to the entire College and said that he was 'forcibly impressed with the singular coincidence that the site of the University bore the name of the man who, next to Plato, had taught him the most instructive lessons in philosophy'. With great tact Kingsley 'talked of the future rather than of the present'. He was beginning to lose his enthusiasm for America, and though he admired the energy of its inhabitants he could not help wishing heartily that he was 'safe home; for there is no place like England—& all the superior Americans say so themselves'.

Americans were all right in their place, but Kingsley now had one of them in his immediate family, since Maurice had married Marie Yorke at the legation in Mexico City while his father was in Canada, and already there had been trouble with her family. Some years later Mrs. Kingsley wrote of Maurice that since he was 'a strong conservative, the institutions of America social and political are naturally repugnant to him though he has made many friends there'. It was with a sense of relief that Kingsley was able to inform his wife that there was no longer any danger of Rose's repeating her brother's mistake by becoming involved with the dashing young Captain Howard Schuyler, whom she had met on her earlier trip to America. Schuyler, by 1874 the chief engineer of the North Pacific Coast railway in San Francisco, had been a great Indian fighter and had had a distinguished career in the Civil War. In San Francisco Kingsley wrote home that 'Howard Schuyler is going to be *married*—so that bugbear is gone, *thank God ! !*' In the meantime Mary's romance was going well, and she and William Harrison had become engaged, to her father's satisfaction. 'Your letter about Mary,' he wrote Mrs. Kingsley, '& what I have heard of hers to Rose, have made me very happy.'

In San Francisco Kingsley's furious activity of the past few weeks caught up with him, and the cold he had been nursing ever since Niagara broke forth once more in the sea fog, so that the doctors had to order him to leave the city. On June 10th the party turned east, and after a difficult journey of four days reached Denver, where the unpredictable George Kingsley providentially turned up to diagnose his brother's illness as pleurisy and send him off to the English comforts of Dr. Bell's ranch at Manitou, near Colorado Springs:

'Here we are, my darling, in perfect peace at last after the running & raging of the last 3 weeks—& safe back over those horrid deserts, in a lovely glen, with red rocks, running & tinkling burn, whispering cotton wood, & all that is delicious—with Pike & his snow seemingly *in* the back garden, but 8,000 feet over our heads. Oh it is a delicious place—& the more so, because we get excellent English food—the American is to me more & more disgusting—hear no more the Everlasting yang-twang of the Natives. . . .'

They remained at Manitou through June, enjoying the party of Englishmen who gathered there, including the Honourable Dudley Fortescue, his nephew Lord Ebrington, and Mr. and Mrs. Henry Cadogan Rothery.

After a week at the ranch of Cholmondeley Thornton, the Kingsleys went for another week to Glen Eyrie, the remarkable house of General William Palmer. The General, who believed a man's house to be literally his castle, built an ancient fortress in the early 1870s, complete with turrets and towers and other bastions against savage raids, and constructed of weathered stones which gave it a look of great age. The roof of tiles brought from an ancient English church replaced an earlier one which Palmer thought looked insufficiently old. For all his antiquarian interests, the General's sympathies did not extend to chimneys, so he had a tunnel dug into the mountain to carry off the smoke of his medieval fireplaces. With an understatement not habitual to him, Kingsley noted simply: 'This is a wonderful spot.'

From Glen Eyrie Kingsley wrote on July 14th: 'I cannot believe that I may see you within 21 days. I never longed so for you & home—& count the hours till I can cross the great valley —on this side of which God has been so good to me: But oh for the first rise of the Eastern hills, to make me sure that the Mississippi is not still between me & beloved Eversley. I am *so* glad you like Westminster. Yes, we shall rest our weary old bones there for awhile, before kind Death comes—& perhaps see a bevy of grandchildren round us there—Ah please God *that*. . . . I look forward to a blessed quiet Autumn, if God so will—having had—if not a rest—yet a change of scene—which will last me my whole life, & has taught me many things—especially, to thank God that I am an Englishman, & not an—well, it is not the fault of the dear generous people, but of their ancestors & ours.'

Kingsley returned to England tired, aged, and in no better health than when he left; it is difficult to believe that he did not know the seriousness of his continued physical debility. For years he had been running out of energy at intervals, but there had been more serious warnings as well. From the time he was seventeen, when he had a congestion of his left lung, he knew that he had a large adhesion of the pleura and lung, and though he felt twinges in heavy fog, he was inclined to believe that it had done him no harm. In 1865 he told Hughes that he was recovering from an ulcerated bowel which had been worrying him for fifteen months. That his recovery from the lung adhesion was not complete is indicated by the attack of pleurisy he suffered in San Francisco, and his letters to his wife from the United States suggest that he was not completely rid of the second complaint. On his return he worked unceasingly in his parish in the sultry August weather caring for the sick, forgetting that he was ill himself. In September, when he went to Westminster, he had 'a severe attack of congestion of the liver', so that he was unable to preach on his first Sunday of residence

Kingsley and Mrs. Kingsley outside the study window of Eversley Rectory

(Copyright *Country Life*)

and had drastically to limit the number of his sermons for the rest of his stay.

For a time he seemed to be on the mend, but he was given a severe setback early in October when Mrs. Kingsley had a bad attack of angina pectoris. He had nursed her out of immediate danger by the beginning of November, but by then he was so emaciated that one of his friends who heard him preach at the Abbey was shocked to discover him an old man with bent back and shrunken figure.

Kingsley claimed that he often knew long before the actual event when one of his friends was going to die; after Mansfield's death he had written: 'There was a great mist just beyond him, & he was fading away into it, dim & large. Then I knew that he would die, & denied it to myself: but it was true.' To a comforting friend after Mr. Maurice's death, he claimed to have 'seen death in his face for, I may almost say, two years past'. Without necessarily believing in his extra-sensory powers, one may wonder whether Kingsley did not feel the approach of his own death. Certainly, during the last six months of his life he became a calmer, easier man than he had ever been, and the change was noted by those around him. The ruptures in old friendships were repaired, and he took on the autumnal gentleness of a man whose essential business with life was finished.

At the end of November, the day after his last service in the Abbey, he went to a lecture by Dr. Caird, where his old enthusiasm asserted itself, so that he could hardly restrain himself from shouting, 'Bravo', several times during the talk. As he left the Abbey after the lecture he walked across the damp cloister and caught a fresh cold, but he made light of it. On December 3rd he made his last journey to Eversley, happy at taking Mrs. Kingsley home. When they arrived at Eversley she had a relapse and he was told that there was no hope for her. 'My own death-warrant was signed', he said, 'with those words.' When his Fanny asked if it were cowardly to shrink from leaving her husband and children, he exclaimed: 'Cowardly! Don't you think I would rather some one put a pistol to my head than lie on that bed there waiting?' He administered Holy Communion to Mrs.

Kingsley and read aloud all their favourite poetry: Wordsworth's 'Intimations of Immortality', Milton's 'Ode to Time', passages from Shakespeare, and Arnold's 'Buried Life'. Gently he assured her that her wish for funereal simplicity would be observed, and constantly he nursed her, to the neglect of his own health.

Some years before, Kingsley had quarrelled with his old friend Mr. Stapleton over a neighbourhood scandal, and the two had not spoken since. 'Mrs. Kingsley was prayed for today and Mr. Heynes told me she was alarmingly ill,' Stapleton wrote in his diary on December 6th. 'I determined to go & see him after Church. I felt very acutely the state of things with one with whom I had so long been on very friendly terms. He was at the door when I arrived. I was painfully affected. He took my hand in both his and said, "I am very grateful to you for this great, great kindness in coming to me at this moment." I said, "I remember nothing but your kindness to me when I was in such similar affliction." . . . I confess I was much agitated and I said, "But do say how she is." He replied, "Oh she may die at any moment." I said, "May God grant that she may recover."' Six days later Kingsley called with William Harrison on Mr. Stapleton: 'It seemed to be a great comfort to him to be in my house on friendly terms.'

On December 28th it was clear that Kingsley was suffering from pneumonia, and he took to his bed at last, promising his wife to 'fight for life'. That night he wrote the first of a series of notes which he and Mrs. Kingsley exchanged from their respective bedrooms. On December 30th he wrote her: 'I am somehow past fretting—almost past feeling. I love you, & you love me, & that is enough for time & Eternity. But I am well aware that I must stay where I am, & you know that if I dared come I would.' At last the pain of being separated was too great, and careless of the fact that his recovery was said to depend on his keeping in a constant temperature, he raced through the cold to her room and sat beside her holding her hand, saying: 'This is heaven, don't speak.' Then his coughing started once more, and he had to return to his room. He and his wife never saw each other again.

He was kept under sedation as his condition grew worse, and in his dreams he would return to the West Indies, the Rocky Mountains, and California, and when he woke he would talk of them to his nurse and tell her of Maurice's travels and adventures in America.

The local medical man, Mr. Heynes, called for Dr. Hawkesley from London, who said he had never seen 'a more splendid fight for life' and seemed sure of Kingsley's recovery. Finally, on January 20th, the Prince of Wales, whose little sons had sent Kingsley letters and drawings during his illness, sent his own doctor, Sir William Gull, to look at the Canon. After Sir William's departure Kingsley suffered a haemorrhage and knew that he could not live much longer. He asked Rose: 'Does Fanny know of this last accident?' 'Yes,' Rose replied, 'she knows everything.' The answer made him think that Mrs. Kingsley was dead, and for the last two days of his life he sent her no more messages, sure that 'the dream of his life was fulfilled of their dying together'.

Early in the morning of January 23rd he was heard repeating the Burial Service, and when he was finished he turned on his side and spoke no more before his quiet death at midday.

'You will perhaps choose Eversley,' Dean Stanley telegraphed to the family, 'but the Abbey is open to the Canon and the Poet.' Mrs. Kingsley, who survived her husband sixteen years, had no hesitation about what he would have wished. Five days after his death he was buried in the plot in Eversley churchyard which they had chosen together years before. The bells of Westminster Abbey and Chester Cathedral tolled at the hour of his funeral to mark the passing of a national figure; the humbler tolling at Eversley Church mourned a faithful parish priest and a happy husband and father, the two aspects of his many-faceted life by which Charles Kingsley would have wanted most to be remembered.

Selected List of Printed Authorities

The primary source for printed material is Mrs. Kingsley's two-volume biography, *Charles Kingsley: His Letters and Memories of His Life*, first published by Henry S. King and Co., in December 1876 (although the date printed on the title page is 1877). The copyright passed within a few months to C. Kegan Paul and Co., and eventually was acquired by Kingsley's own publishers, Macmillan and Co. Since its initial publication, the book has passed through at least thirty-one editions or reprintings, many of which contain additional material.

Kingsley's own writings were so numerous that it would be burdensome to list them here. The interested reader is referred to Mrs. Margaret Farrand Thorp's excellent bibliography, published in 1937 as an appendix to *Charles Kingsley, 1819–1875*.

The following list of books and articles includes only those which I have used directly, and ignores the standard reference volumes and the scores of books one must necessarily read for background material. Unless otherwise indicated, the place of publication of the books is London.

Abbott, Claude Colleer, ed.: *The Correspondence of Gerard Manley Hopkins and Richard Watson Dixon*. (Oxford University Press, 1935.)

—— *Further Letters of Gerard Manley Hopkins*. (Oxford University Press, 2nd ed., 1956.)

Able, A. H.: *George Meredith and Thomas Love Peacock: A Study in Literary Influence*. (University of Pennsylvania, Philadelphia, 1933.)

Adrian, Arthur A.: 'Charles Kingsley Visits Boston', *Huntington Library Quarterly*, November 1956, pp. 94–7.

Baldwin, Stanley E.: *Charles Kingsley*. (Cornell University Press, Ithaca, 1934.)

Benson, Arthur Christopher: *The Life of Edward White Benson, Sometime Archbishop of Canterbury*, 2 vols. (Macmillan & Co., 1899.)

Brown, W. Henry: *Charles Kingsley: The Work and Influence of Parson Lot*. (The Co-Operative Union Ltd., Manchester, 1924.)

Cartwright, Julia, ed.: *The Journals of Lady Knightley of Fawsley*. (John Murray, 1915.)

Chew, Samuel C.: *Swinburne*. (John Murray, 1931.)

Cottingham, C. Elizabeth: *A Little History of Eversley Collected from Various Sources*. (Henry T. Morley, Reading, n.d.)

[Davenport, Reginald C.]: *A Brief Account of the Kingsley Family*, by An Outside Member. (Privately printed, 1911.)

De Vane, William C.: 'The Virgin and the Dragon', *The Yale Review*, September 1947, pp. 33–46.

Dexter, Walter, ed.: *The Nonesuch Dickens: The Letters of Charles Dickens*, 3 vols. (Nonesuch Press, 1938.)

Ellis, S. M.: *George Meredith*. (Grant Richards, 2nd ed., 1920.)

—— *Henry Kingsley, 1830–1876: Towards a Vindication*. (Grant Richards, 1931.)

Faber, Geoffrey: *Oxford Apostles: A Character Study of the Oxford Movement*. (Faber and Faber, 1933.)

Fields, Annie, ed.: *Life and Letters of Harriet Beecher Stowe*. (Sampson Low, Marston & Co., 1898.)

Frith, W. P.: *My Autobiography and Reminiscences*, 3 vols. (Richard Bentley, 1887–8.)

[Gosse, Edmund]: *Father and Son*. (William Heinemann, 1907.)

Gosse, Edmund: *The Life of Philip Henry Gosse, F.R.S.* (Kegan Paul, Trench, Trübner & Co., 1890.)

Graves, Charles L.: *Life and Letters of Alexander Macmillan*. (Macmillan & Co., 1910.)

Green, Roger Lancelyn, ed.: *The Diaries of Lewis Carroll*, 2 vols. (Cassell & Co., 1953.)

Greg, W. R.: *Literary and Social Judgments*. (N. Trübner & Co., 2nd ed., 1869.)

Gribble, Francis: *The Romance of the Men of Devon*. (Mills & Boon, 1912.)

Haight, Gordon S., ed.: *The George Eliot Letters*, 7 vols. (Oxford University Press and Yale University Press, New Haven, 1954–6.)

Hawthorne, Nathaniel: *The English Notebooks*, ed. Randall Stewart. (Modern Language Association of America, New York, 1941.)

[Hughes, Thomas]: 'Charles Kingsley', *Macmillan's Magazine*, March 1877, pp. 337–42.

Hughes, Thomas: *Memoir of Daniel Macmillan*. (Macmillan & Co., 1882.)

Hutton, William Holden: *William Stubbs, Bishop of Oxford*. (Archibald Constable, 1906.)

Jagow, Kurt, ed.: *Letters of the Prince Consort, 1831–1861*. (John Murray, 1938.)

Kendall, Guy: *Charles Kingsley and His Ideas*. (Hutchinson & Co., 1947.)

Kingsley, Charles: *Alton Locke, Tailor and Poet. An Autobiography*. With a Prefatory Memoir by Thomas Hughes. (Macmillan & Co., 1876.)

[Kingsley, Frances E., ed.]: *Charles Kingsley: His Letters and Memories of His Life*. Edited by His Wife, 2 vols. (Henry S. King & Co., 1877.)

Kingsley, George Henry: *Notes on Sport and Travel*, with a Memoir by His Daughter Mary H. Kingsley. (Macmillan & Co., 1900.)

Layard, G. S.: *A Great 'Punch' Editor: Being the Life, Letters, and Diaries of Shirley Brooks*. (Sir Isaac Pitman & Sons, 1907.)

Lee, Sidney: *King Edward VII: A Biography*, 2 vols. (Macmillan & Co., 1925–7.)

Lowry, Howard F., ed.: *Letters of Matthew Arnold to Arthur Hugh Clough*. (Oxford University Press, 1932.)

Ludlow, John Malcolm: 'Some of the Christian Socialists of 1848 and the Following Years. I', *Economic Review*, October 1893, pp. 486–500.

—— "Some of the Christian Socialists of 1848 and the Following Years. II', *Economic Review*, January 1894, pp. 24–42.

—— 'Thomas Hughes and Septimus Hansard', *Economic Review*, July 1896, pp. 297–316.

Lyell, Mrs. Henry, ed.: *The Life of Sir Charles J. F. Bunbury, Bart.*, 2 vols. (John Murray, 1906.)

Lyon, William: *Chronicles of Finchampstead.* (Longmans, Green & Co., 1895.)

Mack, Edward C. and Armytage, W. H. G.: *Thomas Hughes: The Life of the Author of Tom Brown's Schooldays.* (Ernest Benn, 1952.)

Macmillan, George A., ed.: *Letters of Alexander Macmillan.* (Privately printed, Glasgow, 1908.)

The Magdalene Boat Club: A Short History with a List of Crews and Appendices. (Magdalene College Association, Cambridge, 1930.)

Maitland, Frederic William: *The Life and Letters of Leslie Stephen.* (Duckworth & Co., 1906.)

Martin, Robert Bernard, ed.: *Charles Kingsley's American Notes: Letters from a Lecture Tour, 1874.* (Princeton University Library, Princeton, 1958.)

Martin, Theodore: *The Life of His Royal Highness the Prince Consort*, 5 vols. (Smith, Elder & Co., 1875.)

Martineau, Violet: *John Martineau: The Pupil of Kingsley.* (Edward Arnold, 1921.)

Masterman, Lucy, ed.: *Mary Gladstone* (*Mrs. Drew*)*: Her Diaries and Letters.* (Methuen & Co., 1930.)

Maurice, Frederick, ed.: *Life of Frederick Denison Maurice, Chiefly Told in His Own Letters*, 2 vols. (Macmillan & Co., 3rd ed., 1884.)

Newman, John Henry: *Apologia pro Vita Sua*, ed. A. Dwight Culler. (Houghton Mifflin Co., Boston, 1956.)

Norton, Charles Eliot, ed.: *Letters of Thomas Carlyle, 1826–1836.* (Macmillan & Co., 1888.)

Paul, Herbert: *The Life of Froude*. (Sir Isaac Pitman & Sons, 1905.)

Pope-Hennessy, Una: *Canon Charles Kingsley*. (Chatto & Windus, 1948.)

Purnell, Edward Kelly: *Magdalene College*. (F. E. Robinson & Co., 1904.)

Pym, Horace N., ed.: *Memories of Old Friends: Being Extracts from the Journals and Letters of Caroline Fox of Penjerrick, Cornwall, from 1835 to 1871*. (Smith, Elder & Co., 1882.)

Raven, Charles E., *Christian Socialism, 1848–1854*. (Macmillan & Co., 1920.)

Ray, Gordon N., ed.: *The Letters and Private Papers of William Makepeace Thackeray*, 4 vols. (Oxford University Press, 1945.)

Reid, T. Wemyss: *The Life, Letters, and Friendships of Richard Monckton Milnes, First Lord Houghton*, 2 vols. (Cassell & Co., 2nd ed., 1890.)

Sutcliffe, W. Denham: 'The Original of Robinson's Captain Craig', *NewEngland Quarterly*, September 1943, pp. 407–31.

[Tennyson, Hallam]: *Alfred Lord Tennyson: A Memoir by His Son*, 4 vols. (Macmillan & Co., 1898.)

Thorp, Margaret Farrand: *Charles Kingsley, 1819–1875*. (Princeton University Press, Princeton, 1937.)

Tuckwell, W.: *Reminiscences of Oxford*. (Cassell & Co., 1900.)

Tupper, Martin Farquhar: *My Life as an Author*. (Sampson Low, Marston, Searle, and Rivington, 1886.)

Walford, L. B.: *Memories of Victorian London*. (Edward Arnold, 1912.)

Ward, Wilfred: *The Life of John Henry Cardinal Newman*, 2 vols. (Longmans, Green & Co., 1912.)

Ward, Wilfred, ed.: *Newman's Apologia pro Vita Sua: The Two Versions of 1864 and 1865, Preceded by Newman's and Kingsley's Pamphlets*. (Oxford University Press, 1931.)

Watson, Robert A. and Watson, Elizabeth S., ed.: *George Gilfillan: Letters and Journals, with Memoir*. (Hodder & Stoughton, 1892.)

White, William, ed.: *The Journals of Walter White*. (Chapman & Hall, 1898.)

Selected List of Printed Authorities

Wolf, Lucien: *Life of the First Marquess of Ripon*, 2 vols. (John Murray, 1921.)

Woodward, Frances J.: *Portrait of Jane: A Life of Lady Franklin.* (Hodder & Stoughton, 1951.)

Index

Index

Index

Index

Index

Index